✝WELVE BONES

Praise for *Sixteen Souls*

"*Lockwood & Co.* meets *The Taking of Jake Livingstone*
by way of York's most haunted landmarks, *Sixteen
Souls* delivers fun and frights in equal measure.
A fantastically spooky, thrilling adventure"
Kat Ellis, author of *Wicked Little Deeds*

"*Sixteen Souls* is the perfect mix of eerie and heart-warming. With
vivid characters, fierce friendships and flawless twists, this book
immediately pulled me in – I laughed, teared up and could not put
it down. YA fantasy readers and ghost-story lovers, this is for you"
H.M. Long, author of *Hall of Smoke and Temple of No God*

"A captivating take of loss, friendship and love
that had me gripped from first to last. I finished it
with a smile on my lips and a tear in my eye"
Menna van Praag, author of *The Sisters Grimm*

"A gorgeously written debut that had me absolutely
gripped. Rosie Talbot has created a deliciously creepy
world with characters that you'll fall in love with"
Amy McCaw, author of *Mina and the Undead*

"I never have a problem screaming about books I genuinely
love, and I love this book. The author's ability to evoke entire
settings with minimal details is just amazing. The writing
is rich; the characters sharply drawn. Welcome to the world,
Charlie Frith – I can't wait to watch other readers fall in
love with you. The only thing that made me scream louder
than this book was finding out there will be a sequel"
K.D. Edwards, author of *The Tarot Sequence Series*

†WELVE BONES

ROSIE †ALBO†

SCHOLASTIC

Published in the UK by Scholastic, 2023
1 London Bridge, London, SE1 9BG
Scholastic Ireland, 89E Lagan Road, Dublin Industrial Estate,
Glasnevin, Dublin, D11 HP5F

SCHOLASTIC and associated logos are trademarks and/or
registered trademarks of Scholastic Inc.

Text © Rosie Talbot, 2023
Cover illustration © Andrew Davis, 2023

The right of Rosie Talbot to be identified
as the author of this work has been asserted by them under
the Copyright, Designs and Patents Act 1988.

ISBN 978 0702 32533 5

A CIP catalogue record for this book
is available from the British Library.

Printed and bound in Great Britain by
Clays Ltd, Elcograf S.p.A

Paper made from wood grown in sustainable forests
and other controlled sources.

1 3 5 7 9 10 8 6 4 2

www.scholastic.co.uk

For the dead.
Please forgive the living, we're trying our best.

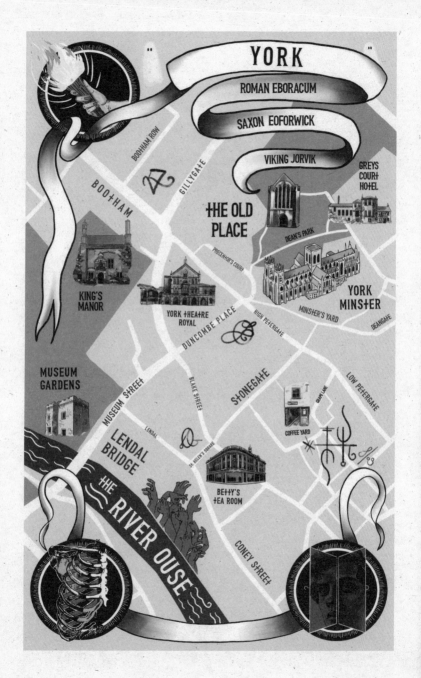

I

THE MOST HAUNTED HOUSE IN ACOMB

They say York is the most haunted city in Europe. Don't I know it.

We live out in the suburbs in a plain bungalow with a scrubby lawn and an ugly porch. It doesn't look like much, but there are currently four ghosts in my not-exactly-huge bedroom. I reckon that's an above average spirit-per-square-metre for any home.

"That the only tie you got, lad?" asks Mr Broomwood. My elderly, very deceased neighbour has taken a break from wandering our cul-de-sac to pop in uninvited and share his opinion on my outfit.

I pick at a pulled thread in the cheap polyester fabric, feeling defensive. "What's wrong with it?"

Broomwood wrinkles his nose and sniffs, crossing his arms over his stripy dressing gown. The dead don't *look* dead, not to me. They seem like the living, plain as day and just as solid.

"It's not very … professional," he says.

Ollie smirks from where he's leaning against my chest of drawers. "That's rich coming from someone spending his afterlife in pyjamas and a dressing gown."

Ghosts appear however they remember themselves and rarely change their appearance. It's kinda hard to do; it takes a lot of self-awareness and Broomwood's always been the kind of bloke to stick his nose into other people's business rather than sort out his own. I reckon he'll be trailing that dressing gown cord for a good few decades yet.

"It's a *date*, not a job interview." Not that I'm experienced at interviews either. I can't even get a part-time job, no matter how many CVs I hand out. Digging my dress shoes from under the bed, I glance about for my shoehorn. Getting stiff leather shoes on my prostheses is a proper faff. "The place Sam's booked is posh. I think it has stars."

In the seven years since I died from meningitis, lost both my legs below the knee, and started seeing ghosts, I never met anyone who was like me. Until Sam.

He changed everything.

Obviously, I didn't stay dead. I've Heather, my first ghost, to thank for that. The doctor who treated me for meningitis gave up her life to bring me back from the dead and make me a seer. She's sitting on my bed, spinning her hospital ID between her fingers, her stethoscope getting wrapped in the lanyard. Dante, our ghost collie dog, is curled up beside her, dozing.

"Literal or metaphorical?" asks Ollie. With his unruly red hair, wide mouth and flat cap, he looks like a regular artful dodger ready to pick my pocket, but he's been dead a century and likes to go to lectures up at the uni. Heather introduced us when I was eleven. I needed a mate my own age who'd understand all the spooky stuff I couldn't tell my living friends. "Metaphorical means—"

"I know what it means, old man." I look down at my outfit. "It's not *that* bad, is it?"

Except the tie is crap and my shirt's too tight over my shoulders.

"Speaking as a mate." Ollie's smile is awkward. "You look like you're going to your exam resits."

"Well, I can't just wear my best trackies." Unclipping one of my prostheses, I turn it upside down, grip it between my knees and wedge the footshell into the dress shoe. When it's in, I clip the prosthesis back on and make a few adjustments with the shoehorn until I'm satisfied it's on right. Now for the other leg.

"I think you look very handsome, Charlie." Heather gives me one of her soft smiles.

Ollie rolls his eyes. "Which is exactly what your mam will say, but that doesn't change the fact you don't look like *you*."

Maybe that's a good thing right now.

"I don't have anything else decent." I wave at the rejected polo shirts and sweatpants strewn about my room.

Our room, I should say. As always, Ollie's current interests take over the walls. Photocopies of Sappho's poetry are pinned to one side of my bedroom, with some of *The Trenchcoat*

3

Brigade Vol. 1 on the other. Spider-Man and Thor figurines clutter the shelf over my desk along with my school textbooks, gathering dust. The desk itself is covered with photocopies of Leonie and Sam's mathemagics notes and my own shaky attempts at drawing glyphs.

If there's one thing I've discovered this summer it's that I'm *not* a natural mathemagician. I'm crap at basic maths, so why I thought throwing in phantasmic theory, magical concordances, osteomagi and whatever the hell necroscopics is, would make it easier, I don't know.

Seeing as afterlives depend on me mastering this stuff, I can't give up.

All my mates have their futures planned. Leonie's set on science at Oxford. Mitch started his chef internship at a fancy restaurant in town. A gallery in London is interested in selling Sam's paintings, if he ever agrees to part with any.

The only thing I'm half decent at is helping the dead. Five months ago, I vowed to keep the souls of York safe from occultists like Caleb Gates who want to trap them and syphon their energy. But I'm no match for that kind of power. Gates threw a table with his *mind*. If I'm going to stop them messing with the local ghosts then I need to be faster, stronger, *better*.

There's only one way I know to do that: possession.

It's not supposed to be possible. Seers are solid flesh-and-bone to the dead, there's no way to walk into our skin without killing us, which is why being around ghosts is so dangerous. If one of them decides to attack me … yeah, it's not fun.

But possession *is* possible, at least, it is for seers who are part of The Hand, the secret organization of seers and ghosts who sent two of their own after Gates. A ghost called Dusan possessed a seer called Jan Liska right in front of us. Yeah, I was bloody and bruised and zip-tied to a table leg at the time, but I know what I saw. They moved as one, faster and stronger than either of them was alone.

They called it "walking the mirrored way", or just "mirroring".

That's the advantage I need to keep my promise to defend the ghosts of York. Problem is, we've no idea *how* mirroring works. No matter how many books on mathemagics I trawl through, I can't find anything about it and I can't ask Sam for help.

Heather scratches between Dante's ears. Snorting awake, the collie rolls over for belly rubs, his tail wagging happily. "Sam's not going to stop liking you because of a tie."

"That's not the point," I say, reminded that I've other reasons to stress tonight. I want Sam to feel proud to be with me. This is his world we're venturing into, with cloth napkins and stuff. It is quite likely he'll be wearing velvet, and a cravat and he'll have a silk pocket square that matches his socks or something. And he'll look *well* fit.

"Your ears are going pink," says Ollie. His grin is wicked.

"Shut up."

Apparently, Sam has "news", something he wants to talk about tonight and I'm on edge. Maybe he wants to break up because there are just too many bad memories here. York's where Gates brutally murdered his dad in front of him. His mum still has that place in Italy and they've not settled on a house here, so maybe Sam's about to tell me he's moving after all and he doesn't want to handle long distance.

It makes sense that he'd want to end it now, before our six-month anniversary … but then why the nice restaurant?

He's not gonna make me dress up all fancy to get dumped, is he?

All right, I'm losing the tie. I didn't have it done up tight but the knot won't undo. My fingers fumble with the polyester silk, pulling the wrong bit and the bloody thing snares, closing on my neck. It's like a noose.

No, no, no.

A hook under my heart, a pulse in my ears and the world rushes closer. Cloying air. Rope on my skin. After falling into a deathloop of a man being hanged I can't stand anything pressing around my throat. I scramble to get the tie off.

"Tuck it back under." Heather hurries forward, hands raised, but she can't help me. Ghosts can touch *me*, but not my clothes. "Yeah, like that, then ease it off."

I can't.

A knock. The door swings open. "You ready to go, lad? It's gone half-past—"

Footsteps. Hands on mine.

"Let me, son."

Dad. His fingers work slowly, but they work. The tie slides off. He places heavy hands on both my shoulders. "All right?"

Unbuttoning the top of my shirt, I nod and breathe. In. Out. In. Out. The anxiety fades to a pattering at the back of my skull.

With my prostheses and shoes on, I'm as tall as Dad. We've the same blocky features, strong jaw and light brown hair. Frith men look like they belong in the boxing ring. Grandpa was the same, but he spent a lifetime bottle-feeding lambs and stomping the Dales. Dad drives a taxi for a living. If there's a fighter in the family it's me, but the battles I face are secret.

"Take your time," he says.

My folks don't know the half of what's happened to me – not about the ghosts, or the multiloop, not about how Sam's dad really died or what Caleb Gates did to us – but they know they almost lost me, again. And it's not like I've ever been good at acting "normal", thanks to the whole seer-of-dead-souls thing.

"I'm all right," I say, trying to sound sure.

"You look good." Dad pats my shoulder. "Sam's a lucky lad, eh? Smitten, if you ask me, and a good thing too because your mam's already half-planned the wedding." A bark of laughter as he catches my wide-eyed expression. "You know her, she's just pleased you've found a good'un. Don't be nervous, eh? Tonight's going to go great."

"I'm not nervous," I say.

"Liar," whispers Ollie.

Dad's smile tightens, worry creeping in at the edges. "Just … keep an eye out, yeah? Don't risk being out late on your own, and call me if you need a lift."

"We'll keep out of trouble."

"Yeah, well, trouble seems to find you anyway." He winces. "I just mean I'll rest easier when they arrest that gang attacking random people. Until then, you need to be sensible, all right? No risks."

I get why he's concerned and maybe I should be scared, but a gang of dickheads is honestly the least of my worries. Usually, the dead give me more trouble than the living. Last week the ghost of a local tradesman surprised me in the public loos and demanded I leave a positive review on his son's Trust-A-Trader profile. He wouldn't take, "Not while I'm having a piss, mate," for an answer. It took the combined effort of Heather, Ollie and George Villiers to get him to leave long enough for me to leg it.

I don't reckon he would've hurt me, but some ghosts will if given the chance.

What am I supposed to tell my old man?

"Yeah, I'd be worried too, Dad, except, on top of dealing with bonkers requests from ghosts, the deathloops, and Hungry Ones who want to eat us, me and Sam have been waiting for The Hand to show up and explain some stuff. No, I don't know why they've not sent someone yet either, and I'm kind of on edge about it, to be honest."

If they do show up, maybe they'll invite us to join their organization and share their secrets so we can mirror with two ghosts and become proper powerful. No angry souls, deathloops or occultists will be able to hurt us ever again.

Ha! Dream on.

I rub my neck. The past few months haven't been easy on me or Sam. Every day with him is different. Sometimes he's the old him, bright and eager, wanting to help troubled ghosts and solve every riddle there is. And then there are the darker days, when the memories of his dad's death swallow him and even getting out of bed is too much.

I can't fix him. He can't fix me. Instead, we take it day by day. That's enough to keep us going.

But what about next summer when he'll be going off to uni and I'll be stuck here still trying to pass my exams with no idea what I want to do with my life? Being at the beck and call of the local ghosts keeps me busy, but it doesn't exactly pay the bills.

One crisis at a time. Sam might be about to break up with me. I've got to get through tonight first.

Do I need a smarter coat? It's October, too cold to go without, but all I've got is my old black puffer.

"Let's go," I say, knowing I'm overthinking.

Dad heads out. "I'll start the car."

I shove an extra pair of compression socks and a screwdriver into my pocket on the way out, just in case I need to add some padding or adjust my prostheses.

"We'll see you in the car." Heather nods, clearly a bit anxious. I swear she's always on edge these days. When I ask, she says there's nothing wrong. It's just *everything* I guess.

I look back. Ollie gives me a thumbs up. Dante yips softly, tail wagging. Even Broomwood is looking a little emotional. With a subtle wave, I turn from my undead family, slap on a smile and brace myself to face my living family.

From the front room I can already hear my twin sisters singing "Charlie and Sam sitting in a tree" at the top of their six-year-old lungs.

2

WEATHERING

A half-hour later I'm standing on the corner where Grape Lane meets Swinegate, cursing into the cold air. Three dead girls in big, hooped dresses gasp at my bad language. I wave an apology as they scamper through the wall of a nearby beauty bar, their giggles echoing around the crossroads.

Seeing ghosts ignore the laws of physics used to worry me loads. I had all these rules so I wouldn't have to face the strange collision of life and afterlife, like asking Heather and Ollie not to walk through walls. It doesn't bother me so much now. Still looks weird, though.

From the front yard of the Slug & Lettuce pub, a bunch of drinkers watch my outburst with awkward interest.

Oh, great, an audience.

That used to bother me too, but I'm getting better at not

giving a shite what people think. Sam always says, "We don't owe anyone normal," and he's right.

In York, time is carved above doors. It hangs in wrought-iron signs and hides in the lichen-speckled bricks of Georgian fronted shops and restaurants. It's a history that comes with plenty of ghosts – soldiers of all eras, citizens of old Jorvik, dust-covered blokes in overalls, wool merchants, railway workers, ladies in fine gowns, gents in capes and ruffs, chocolatiers in smart aprons – an endless procession of afterlives playing out on these streets and in these buildings.

All of them are ghosts I've promised to defend.

I thought occultists bottled souls as trophies, collecting them like a kind of Cabinet of Curiosity. Yeah, it's worse. They catch them to siphon off their phantasmic essence for use in magical theorems (the fancy word for spell), which *kills* the ghost. For good, forever. Occultists don't care that earthbound spirits are conscious, capable of thought and are, you know, *people*. They just see them as energy to be used.

Now, less than a fortnight after it was laid down, the protective ward we painted above the entrance to Coffee Yard has bled to a pale smear, autumn rains washing the plaster almost clean.

Bollocks.

Without working wards, occultists can lay ghost traps and snare any passing soul. I've got to get this fixed.

I squint at the faded mark, as if that's going to help. Ghosts, no problem. Magic? That's different. I can't see spells or theorems without help. My anxiety spikes.

"That's been scrubbed at." Heather puts her hands on her hips. "Might have been the district council cleaning up."

Ollie whistles for Dante, who's sniffing at something up the lane. "For a city with so many ghost tours, you'd think weird occult symbols around the place would only add to the ambiance. You could call the tourism board and pitch the wards as a mystery trail, make them a feature for tourists, like those cat sculptures."

"Maybe you're on to something," I say, taking photos of the faded ward and dropping them into the Team Spectre group chat.

The oldest part of York is packed with the dead. Every corner and crossroads needs a ward to stop anyone laying ghost traps. So far, we've only managed to protect the streets between Low Petergate and Davygate.

A reply from my mate Mitch:

Will swing by after work and take a look.

Like his girlfriend, Leonie, Mitch has a pair of cryptolenses – spelled glasses that allow the wearer to see magic and ghosts. He'll be able to tell if there's active power under the washed-off paint.

If there's not, we're fucked.

Dante gives an excited yip and barrels up the lane. Lanterns in shop windows cut through the evening gloom, highlighting bat-shaped bunting strung up for Halloween. Sam turns the corner, petting a squirming Dante who then bounds to greet

Sam's ghostly escort. Geoff Monroe, a Canadian airman who fell to his death at The Golden Fleece, salutes us and heads off, whistling merrily.

It's not safe for me or Sam to walk the streets alone. Unlike regular folks, ghosts can touch us which means they can hurt us. There was a time I wished I couldn't see the dead – all I wanted was to be "normal". Now, despite the dangers, I couldn't imagine my life without them.

I was so worried by the wards, I forgot to panic about Sam maybe breaking up with me, but now he's here, hands in his pockets, my stomach knots and my chest flitters. He looks relaxed but he can hide a lot of doubt and fear behind that confident swagger. I try to get a read on him, studying the planes of his face and the slight shadows under his eyes. Is he about to end this?

God, I hope not.

My cheeks heat and I wish I had worn better clothes, or clothes that fit me at least.

He's got this fit gentleman-librarian thing going on. Slender, shorter than me by half a head, with a long straight nose, dimpled chin and a white shock of hair among the dark curls at his forehead. Why wear velvet when you can pull off a forest-green blazer that brings out the tawny speckles in your eyes? He has a pocket square – crimson floral – and, yes, it matches his watch strap. That's commitment.

"Hi," he says, flashing that cute side-smile of his. The hopeful fluttering feeling under my sternum swells. Sliding a hand around his waist I pull him close, but not so close that

I crush his right arm or put pressure on his weak shoulder. He leans into me. Elation soaring, I press my lips to his. He smells of cedarwood and tastes of mint.

Maybe it's going to be all right.

"No sling?" I ask, surprised.

"Feeling stronger."

I'm not sure that's a good idea. His right shoulder was badly dislocated when his house collapsed on us back in the spring. The socket is still a bit loose, but it's his decision to make.

"Oh, that *is* bad." Weaving around me, he takes a look at the Grape Lane ward for himself. "Stonegate and Low Petergate are a little faded but nothing like this."

Handing me his silver lighter, he fishes a little baggie of dried herbs from the inside pocket of his coat. He also keeps a palm-sized shallow dish on him for moments like this. I block the breeze for him as he sets fire to a heap of herbs. I forget what's in the mix, but it smells like citrus and peppermint. Smoke trails and catches, wafting over the faded ward on the wall above Coffee Yard.

Along the inside of the little Snickleway there's a flicker of something. I blink, running my hand over the brick as a broken glyph appears. A ghost trap maybe? Mostly invisible and hard to detect, they're designed to spring shut on any ghost that touches them.

Ollie ducks under my arm for a better look. "That's forty years gone."

"When did you become an expert in the deterioration of ghost traps?" I ask.

"I'm not, but I remember the bloke who laid that one and it was forty years ago, at least."

"Well, if there's a problem with our wards then it's not because of that," confirms Sam.

"Do you think we got the ratios wrong then?" I ask, rubbing my face. "Mitch had to ballpark the mistletoe." The ingredients and method to mix the paint and mark the wards are complicated. It took months to get the recipe right, or what we thought was right. "If we have to go back to scratch it's gonna take ages, especially without a proper kitchen to work in. I mean, it's not like I can tell my folks I need to spend three days mixing a pot of homemade paint that looks like clotted blood and stinks like a sewer so I can spend my nights graffitiing the city with occult symbols, and we *need* the wards to work—"

Sam lays a gentle hand on my arm, but I plough on. "I just don't get it; Leonie and Mitch saw them all glow when they were set. Occultists could return to York any day. The wards are our first defence, and I can't even get them to fix—"

"*Charlie*." Sam's got hold of me now, making me face him.

My words dry up. "S-sorry."

"Hey, don't apologize for weird ghost shit. We can only handle what we can handle. I'm worried too."

"I just … thought things would be different," I say. "That we'd have *some* answers."

"Viola's trying her best."

Since Leonie's chance meeting with her at the bookshop, Viola Sampire has filled in plenty of gaps in our knowledge.

Being dead, she can't *use* magic but she can teach it – basic mathemagics, phantomatology, the works. She and Leonie have their heads together most days, working on shields and defensive theorems, trying to unpick the mysteries of magic and find better ways to protect the ghosts of York, and ourselves.

It's slow work.

"I know," I say, not meaning to sound like a prick. Viola's been amazing, even though I'm her worst student. "But The Hand should've *shown* themselves by now."

"I think we're lucky that they haven't." Sam catches my gaze with his and holds it. "When it came down to it, Dusan and Liska were willing to sacrifice every soul in that multiloop to stop Gates. They didn't care about saving them, or us. The Hand are not our friends."

I look away, ears going pink. "I know, I know."

The idea of a Hungry One – ghosts who believe the bullshit rumour that eating seer flesh will bring them back to life – sneaking up on Sam breaks me.

We *need* to mirror. The more I think about it, the more I reckon it's the only way to stay safe. Problem is, the theorems to do it are unique to The Hand, and what we know about them can be listed on five fingers, most of it from Viola who *hates* them.

One: they're a mysterious organization of seers and ghosts who've teamed up to exterminate occultists because they think trapping and bottling the dead to use as batteries for spells is, well, evil.

We're on the same page about that at least.

Two: their leader is called Meryem. When Liska mentioned her, I assumed she was a seer, but she's a soul. A very old, dictatorial ghost according to Viola and not someone we want to mess with.

Three: The Hand are not the answer to my prayers. Yeah, they're the only ones who know how to mirror souls into a symbiotic soul-bond that gives them super powers, but Viola says they'd never share any of that with us unless we join their ranks.

Four: joining them might not be a good idea. They're nomadic soldiers who travel the world fucking up occultists. I get it. Tempting. But it's so easy to break things; I want to learn how to put things back together.

Besides, not all occultists are evil – Rawley was all right, and Viola's nice enough. And I could never *kill* someone, like deliberately. No way.

Five: anyone who tampers with their precious, secretive theorems meets a messy end. I remember Jan Liska, baton in hand facing down Gates, whose body was riddled with lightning, the syphoned essence of trapped souls filling him with unnatural power.

The Hand's secrets are not for occultists to toy with.

The mirrored way is sacred to the death-touched.

Meryem knew you'd try another path.

Jealous of the power that mirroring gives The Hand, Gates tried to push mathemagics to its limit to mimic them. He couldn't actually mirror because he wasn't a seer, so he forced souls into a multiloop and etched a ghost trap into his flesh to bind the ghosts to him.

It worked. He became inhumanly strong, fast and vicious, a living weapon that tore the building down around us. Despite that power, the truly mirrored pair – Liska and Dusan held their own against him.

I want to ask Sam, *Don't you think that's something worth knowing?* but I can't.

Sam doesn't want to know. I get it. Caleb Gates had to torture a lot of ghosts to get what he wanted – Heather and Ollie included. Sam doesn't want to risk being anything like him.

Neither do I. I want to mirror properly, a lifelong bond that both seer and soul choose for themselves. For months, Miri – Sam's hacker friend – has been trawling the dark web for any reference to The Hand. Nothing.

If Meryem's out there, she doesn't give a shit about us. We're on our own.

Sam gives me a supportive smile. "We don't need them, Charlie. We're doing all right."

I'm *not*, though.

He's a talented painter and the heir to a literal fortune, he has options in life. Being a seer is all I've got.

"Seers, I need your help," a sharp call interrupts. We swivel to face a stocky white woman with a strong nose, wearing an oversized plaid shirt and faded jeans, her hair tied into a no-nonsense bun at the nape of her neck. She doesn't look dead, but then again, ghosts rarely do.

"If this is about changing some Wikipedia entry—" I start with a sigh.

"It's not about damned Wikipedia. Numerous remains have been stolen from the study labs at King's Manor and it's been made to look like a cataloguing error." She pauses, maybe to make sure we're paying attention. "I'm Professor Alice Purcell, that was *my* dig. I don't make mistakes, or misplace artefacts."

"You think they've been stolen?" asks Sam.

"I don't think, boy. I *know*." The woman taps her breastbone. "A student has been pilfering the department and I'm not going to let her drag my work through the dirt. I need you to alert my old colleagues, file a police report and put a stop to this immediat— *hey*!"

A pretty, florid-faced bloke in fancy periwinkle blue silks and an impressive wig elbows the archaeologist out of the way. He's definitely deceased. It's a lot easier to tell with the older ghosts, not many folks walk around in antique clothing on the regular.

"Ah, seers, I was hoping to engage you both in a matter of some urgency. My family abode has been long abandoned and fallen into great disrepair; a terrible tragedy, for the drawing room has such a pleasing aspect over the river." Heather steps in, keeping him at arm's length from us, but he keeps going on. "It was dreary before but if you don't remove the deathloop on the first floor ... well, death really will be intolerable."

"Intolerable?" echoes Ollie with a snort. "You look like you're doing fine."

Periwinkle gives him some major side eye. "The loop is *most* distressing, and I am desperate to arrange for new wallpaper."

"We … er, can't get rid of a loop right now." I glance at Sam. He's slid his hands into his pockets, expression flat and still.

Ghosts caught in deathloops aren't like Ollie, who is a free soul and can roam where he likes. And they're not tethered like Heather, who's tied to the hospital by something she refuses to talk about and so can't leave York. Deathloops are bubbles of memory where reality twists around a soul, forcing them to relive their death over and over because the ghost inside either doesn't know they're dead or can't accept it.

They're one of the most dangerous things Sam and I face as seers, but we can do something about them, if we're willing to risk it all. We need to go inside the loops, one by one, and help the soul understand that they're dead. If we can break that cycle, they'll be free. If we fail, we die the same way they did, our bodies taking the punishment.

Inside a loop, Sam keeps me grounded and helps remind me who I am. Without him, I can't help the trapped soul, but entering a loop could trigger his flashbacks.

"Look, we've got lots of requests for help. We'll get to you, but I can't say when," I tell Periwinkle, not wanting to put any pressure on Sam.

We're justified to never walk into another loop again. I mean, we have to *eventually* because I've promised to free all of York's trapped souls. But I need to find a way to do it on my own.

Another thing I'm failing at.

"The missing remains are of historical importance," the archaeologist snaps.

"What use are mouldering bones to anyone?" sniffs Periwinkle.

"You'd be singing a different tune if they were *your* earthly remains."

He glares at her. "I don't see why; I'm not likely to need them again. Surely a rogue deathloop takes priority. Our first-floor rooms are quite unusable."

The autumn clouds have thickened, muffling the city with reflected light. It smells like rain.

"Both of your problems are important," I say. "But as I said, we're busy right now with a lot of folks wanting favours."

And fading wards to fix.

The archaeologist looks at me with a haughty glower. "Am I not good enough to warrant the help you promised all of York's souls?" She sniffs. "If more bones go missing that's on *you*. You'll be responsible."

Her words are a punch to the stomach. She watches the blow land and then vanishes.

"Rude," says Periwinkle.

"Right, that's it, you. Back off!" Ollie shoos him like he's a cat taking a dump in Broomwood's beloved flower beds.

I hate being accused of not caring, especially after we've spent the summer fixing Wikipedia entries, researching ancestors, and even sending the odd, living relative an anonymous note.

"You're going to be late for dinner," Heather warns us.

I'm so stressed. How are we gonna sit with napkins and finery and posh grub and talk about other stuff for a couple of hours? Right now, soul catchers could be roaming York's streets taking advantage of our failure, but Sam wants to talk to me about something and—

"We don't have to go," says Sam.

I look at him, surprised. "But …. you booked already."

"I'll call and cancel." His smile is sad but he's trying to make it reassuring. "You're not feeling it."

I wince; I'd hoped I was doing a better job of hiding my worries.

"And neither am I, honestly." He motions to the wards. "We have to fix this, and fast, so how about Plan B. You, me, room service and a cosy evening of research? See if we can't figure out what's gone wrong."

Heather offers a comforting smile as Ollie chases Dante in circles around the street. "We'll walk you back to the hotel then give the mutt some exercise."

"Yeah, all right," I say, wondering how I can make it up to Sam. "How long before a ghost or three arrive to pester us?"

He hums, thinking. "I'd give it at least an hour."

22

3

GRAYS COURT

Tucked between York Minster and the old city wall, Grays Court is the former home of the cathedral's money men, a place where knights and dignitaries came to stay. Now it's a posh hotel. Sam wanted to rent an Airbnb long-term instead of living here, but his mum insisted on Grays because it has, and I quote, "a deep spiritual resonance that will protect us in our grief".

She's probably on about the mullioned windows, dark wooden panelling in the long gallery, canopied beds, and room service. This place vibrates with the past, air thick with history and the scent of wood wax. It's haunted to match.

The bloke on reception has no idea three ghosts in full livery are trying to read the newspaper over his shoulder. When he closes the article to greet us, they groan in frustration.

Sam orders our usual from room service. I've been here

enough over the summer that the regular staff know me. They've finally stopped going on about how sorry they are that there's no lift. I get it, the hotel is grade one listed, they can only do so much to make the place accessible.

Dante's restless, so Heather and Ollie take him for a walk. We're about to head up to Sam's room when a familiar musical voice floats down the gallery followed by a striking, middle-aged woman with warm tan skin and shining hair. "Ah, Caro!"

"Evening, Mrs Harrow," I say, feeling newly self-conscious about my disastrous shirt. As usual, she's dressed in all black with heeled boots, cobbled streets be damned.

"Please, call me Lucrezia." She kisses my cheek, probably leaving a lipstick mark. "What are you doing back so soon?"

"Complications with the wards," says Sam.

Not gonna lie, it's weird that he's so open with his mum about seeing the dead. I get why he can be: she believes. Even before Sam became a seer, she thought he had special psychic resonance or some shite, so it's not like she's going to accuse him of making it up or hallucinating.

I was jealous of that, until I actually met her. She's either totally smothering him, or she forgets he exists for weeks, too busy organizing pseudo-spiritual retreats for the mega rich.

"Perfetto, now you are free to come with me tonight." Beaming brightly, she tries to steer us towards the door.

"We just ordered food," Sam protests.

"But Charlie must meet Claire—"

He pulls away, wincing. "No, mamma."

"We met on a chakra retreat last year, Charlie. She is gifted with true sight."

I give Sam a questioning look. "Another seer?"

"She's a self-styled medium. A fraud."

"She is not a fraud," Mrs Harrow snaps. "You think yours is the only way to commune with the spirit world?"

"Spirit world?" snorts one of the liveried ghosts. The receptionist is pretending not to eavesdrop. We should probably take this argument somewhere more private than the front lobby of a posh hotel, but Lucrezia doesn't seem to care.

"Come with me, for your father's sake."

A muscle tightens in Sam's jaw. "He's *gone*."

She replies in fast Italian, then takes a deep steadying breath. "Gone but *not* lost. Your father is trapped between planes and needs our help."

Sam's eyes gleam with resentment. I'd like to reach for him but I don't know if that's what he wants.

"That's not how it works," he says.

"And you know everything? At eighteen you know all there is to know about this world and the next. So wise, so mighty." Mrs Harrow shakes her head. "You have a special gift, both of you, but Claire's sight crosses the veil. I have spoken with your father through her—"

Sam swipes at his cheeks as he backs towards the stairs. "Just stop."

The receptionist is full-on staring now, as are the two guests edging around us to check in and the porter carrying their luggage.

Sniffing, Mrs Harrow stands a little taller, addressing me. "I will not abandon my husband to the spectral plane."

The what?

With that, she's out of the door in a cloud of expensive perfume and the swish of silk.

I go after Sam. He's climbing the stairs faster than I can follow in my prostheses. "Hey, wait. Talk to me."

Reaching the first landing, he spins and catches my face in his hands. I'm still on the step below and grip the banister for balance. There are tears in his eyes. His kiss is soft but solid, something I can fall into. It's a kiss that says, *I feel too much right now and I need something to make it stop.*

I kiss him back, putting everything I have into it, wanting this to be the distraction we both need. I can't fix any of this for him. When we walked inside that loop and asked all of the trapped souls to come with us, Mr Harrow refused. Maybe he was too scared, too selfish, or too set in his ways. The hurt in Sam's eyes when his dad failed him, yet again … I'll never forget it. I'd do anything to spare Sam something like that again.

But how can I protect him, or anyone? I'm crap at magic for a start, and what good is working out when my opponent might be amped up with stolen souls and capable of dropping a building on my head?

Gates's wicked grin as he drew in the essence of captured ghosts flashes through my thoughts. I tense.

Sam steps back, looking at me from under long, dark lashes. "Are you … into this?"

26

"Yeah, I'm just worried about you is all." I take his hands. "Your mum—"

With a sigh, he turns on to the landing. "She won't listen to anything she doesn't want to hear."

I follow. "Sounds like Claire Cole is taking advantage."

"She's toured all over the world and there's even talk of a TV show. You know my mother, she laps all that up. I've met her so-called psychic friends before and they're always insufferable."

"You met the medium?"

"I was ambushed with the promise of afternoon tea."

"Lured with cake. Crafty."

"Insidious and downright sneaky. I couldn't get away for an *hour*. She was going on and on about intuition and skill with the dead, which is laughable. Claire's not a seer, that's for sure," Sam snorts. "Of course, mother told her all about what we can do, just like she outed me to everyone in my old life down in Surrey."

Why is he only telling me about this now? It obviously upsets him and I want to be here for him, but I also don't want to pry if he's not ready to talk.

"I used to wish she'd spend time with me instead of travelling Europe," Sam goes on. "But now I'd rather she went back to Italy and left me to it. I just… I worry about her, and Claire Cole's obviously after money."

He's definitely not thinking of leaving then. The knot in my belly relaxes with relief.

"We could warn Claire off," I say.

Sam gives me a half-shrug. "Honestly, I don't care about the money." I try not to goggle when he says shit like that. I can barely pay for my phone.

"I know my father's soul is gone. If any of the ghosts syphoned by Gates come back, it won't be for centuries, but Mother misses him so much and the way he died... There were a lot of things I didn't tell her, about what he did ... his plans."

Sam's gaze dips and he turns away, like he expects me to be angry.

I'm not.

Mr Harrow wasn't a good bloke. He would've killed me if it meant saving his business and he put Sam through hell. But dying the way he did – a bullet to the head right in front of us – was brutal. No other word for it. If Sam wants to spare his mum the worst of it, I get it.

"Do you want to talk about your dad?" I ask. "We haven't really."

"Honestly, no. I'm still too angry at him. I just want to forget."

"All right." I hug Sam close. "Let's drown our sorrows in pasta and research."

When I sit up, the searing pain in my back loosens to a dull ache. I'm in Sam's bed, an open book lodged under my elbow. I check my phone. Shit, gone eleven. I don't remember falling asleep.

Sam's hotel room is ridiculous. The walls are covered in fabric, the bed frame is carved with flowers, and there's a huge TV on the far wall that he never turns on unless I'm over. It's on now, a little pop-up on the screen asking if we're still watching.

In the half-dark I catch a tall shape by the bed and flinch, but it's just his easel. Most of Sam's stuff was lost when his old house collapsed. Since then he's stocked up on art materials and has spent his recovery painting the ghosts of York. The biggest canvas he's done is propped against the wall. As a great patron of the arts, Villiers wanted a couple's portrait with James Reid. Both men stand side by side holding the same glove, which is symbolic apparently. In life, they lived at least a century apart and never would have met. I think it's magical they've found each other in death.

I scan the rest of the room. No ghosts – strange or familiar – lurk in the pooling shadows, so why am I so tense? There's a restless prickle in my bones. Another nightmare?

Sometimes my dreams are filled with the Ragged lad at Bedern, the kid frozen in the snow on The Shambles, the cyclist at Monkgate and the hundreds of other deathloops in York. I reckon I'll dream about them until we can release them from their loops.

That's not what's haunting me tonight. I was caught up in memories of the multiloop. The knife slicing into my back, the stink of the woods, smoke on the air. Sam's lips on mine, pulling me back from the brink of hell.

Periwinkle asked us to clear a deathloop and I said no, the

exact opposite of the promise I made to the ghosts of York. Whoever's trapped in that loop, I want to help them but I don't reckon I'll survive without Sam and there's no way I'm asking him to come with me. Maybe everything's different now that I've been inside a multiloop and lived. Maybe, the next time I walk into a deathloop I'll remember exactly who I am and why I'm there, rather than getting caught up in the trapped ghost's death.

Not likely. I need Sam. It's bloody frustrating.

If I go see to that loop then Heather, or Mitch could come with as back up and pull me out if I can't handle it. Sam won't like that, he'll want to be there too. If it were up to me, he'd never go near another loop again. But it's *not* up to me.

He's curled in bed, little spoon to my big, dark curls crushed into the pillow, breathing deeply. His eyelashes flutter. I fucking love his eyelashes.

Ah, bollocks, he's still wearing his binder.

"Oi," I whisper, gently nudging him.

Groaning, he mumbles something into the pillow and tucks himself up tighter.

"Nah, love, c'mon." I snuggle into the nape of his neck. "My very handsome boyfriend needs to wake up."

He rolls over and looks at me with sleepy eyes. "Why?"

"Because he's fallen asleep in his binder and needs to take it off."

"Ugh." Sam hauls himself up with a huff and pushes the curls off his forehead. "What time is it?"

"Late. I should get home." Books on mathemagics scatter

the duvet. I start to stack them, disappointed we didn't work out what's gone wrong with the wards. According to our notes the wards should be going strong even if the paint is fading. It's the magic that counts, so it might be all right after all.

Sam takes a book from my hands, setting it aside. "Or … you could stay." That cute, trickster smile of his does funny things to my heartbeat. He waggles his brow. "No ghosts."

"Just us," I whisper, realizing it's true. Heather and Ollie aren't back from their walk with Dante yet. We're really alone, which doesn't happen all that often. I want to play it cool, like something hasn't just changed in the last half-second, but it has. "I guess I could stay. I've already taken my legs off for the day."

That gets a laugh. It's true though, once my prostheses are off it's a right faff to put them back on, which I'd have to do to get home. Like, it's actually fine, I'm exaggerating, unless my stumps are proper sore and then I've no choice but to take a break. I'm sitting here shirtless with a fit lad in nothing but his binder and his boxers, curls at odd angles and mischief in his eyes.

I'm not going anywhere.

I shoot Mum a quick text to let her know I'm staying over. It won't be an issue, she just likes to know where I am. Fair enough considering what I've put them through this year.

For a few weeks after me and Sam got together, my folks were proper embarrassing, making us keep the bedroom door open whenever he was over. They finally let it slide when I got a panicked late-night call from his mum. Dad dropped me off at Grays Court at two in the morning and I spent all night with Sam as he cried. That was a hard night but it broke down a lot of walls for both of us.

Last month, Dad tried the whole "don't get your boyfriend pregnant" talk. I don't know who was redder in the face – me probably because Reid and Villiers were in the room waiting for me to move Reid's bishop in the chess game they had going. Of course, they thought the most awkward moment of my life was hilarious.

Me and Sam, we're not there yet. Yeah, eventually we want to do more *stuff*, we've talked about it. But we're both dealing with the fall-out from last spring, mentally and physically. Even though he's been with someone before and I haven't, I think he's more nervous about it than I am, and I'm bloody terrified because he's too important to lose.

Pulling him into my lap, I run my fingers through his hair. The rumble of his voice saying my name sends a heat through my lower belly. I kiss him until we're breathless and panting and all I see is fireworks.

How did I get so lucky?

Something vibrates against my back, making me yelp. My phone. Sam laughs as I groan, then I see who's calling and answer right away. "Hey, mate, thanks for helping out."

"You with Sam?" asks Mitch. He sounds tired.

"Yeah, he's here. Bad news?"

Sam frowns, concerned. I hold up a hand, waiting for Mitch to tell us what's going on. You can't push him; thoughtful and sincere one minute, cracking a joke the next, Mitch is the kind of lad who takes his time and does things his way.

A huff of breath on the line. "I can see the wards clearly enough under the paint. They're glowing, so I reckon they're still active, yeah?"

"Sounds like."

"But there's something else." He pauses. I can hear music in the background, probably from a nearby pub. "I think someone's been messing with our theorem."

My breath catches. Someone else is using magic in York.

"Leonie about?" I ask. She's even better at mathemagical theory than Sam, and we need answers.

"She's getting a lift over now," says Mitch.

"Right, give us ten."

Sam doesn't ask questions, just slides off my lap and starts pulling on his clothes. I grab my liners and ease back into my prostheses, lining up the pins and putting on pressure until each locks into place inside the socket. Pain needles through my stumps, but I don't have my chair so I've no choice. Not that using a wheelchair in central York is a doddle.

On our way out of the room, we almost trip over Ollie and Heather. They've stationed themselves in the corridor, Dante napping at their feet.

"Jeez, where's the fire?" asks Ollie, scrambling up.

Pulling on my puffer, I pat myself down, checking I've got everything. "There's an occultist in York."

4

MAN DOWN

Smelling of hot oil and spun sugar, the tall, slender lad who meets us on the corner where Stonegate and Little Stonegate meet has waves of floppy blonde hair and the kind of smile that has people tripping over themselves for his attention. Even grey skinned and puffy eyed after a long shift, passers-by give Mitch the eye.

Oblivious to the attention, he points at the carved mermaid figurine on the corner where we hid the ward. "How bad do you think it is then?"

Like the ward at Grape Lane, the paint is basically gone leaving a smear of red against the dark green beams.

"Let's see the damage," I say, taking the cryptolenses Mitch offers.

Heather steps aside so a group of blokes out for a night

on the piss don't walk through her. They head off, shoulders hunched against the drizzle.

Wiping drips off the half-moon shaped glasses, I slip them on, dulling the world and making our ward – simple lines like two lit matches, one facing up, one down – gleam. As well as letting regular folks see and hear ghosts, the cryptolenses allow any wearer to see hidden magic.

Someone's messed with the theorem all right. A straight line now crosses the original glyphs, the end of one stem finishing in uneven double lines, the other with a small circle. To the right, is a sort of J or S over a dividing line and a U with dots on top of it. The changes are glowing softly, hard to see, but there.

Turning, I catch sight of Ollie and Heather through the lenses – both washed out and crackling with distortion. If seers look at the dead through cryptolenses it's bloody uncomfortable.

I snatch the glasses off and hand them over. "Sam?"

Slipping them on, he fishes a pocket-sized sketchbook out of his jacket and draws the new glyphs on top of the ward.

I thank Mitch for helping us out.

He shrugs. "It's no bother."

Except it is. When he and Leonie saw me fall into a deathloop a couple of years ago I cut them out of my life rather than tell them about ghosts. I said it was for their safety, but really I was being an insecure prick. Eventually, they found out the truth and we patched things up. My best mate since primary school, me and Mitch just sort of slid back into our old routine. It's the same, but it's different. I got over my crush on him for a start.

Being his mate again is fucking brilliant. I don't want to take advantage.

"Have they all been altered like this?" Sam asks Mitch.

"Yeah, identical."

A happy bark sounds up Little Stonegate. We look around the corner to see a petite Black lass bundled in a warm coat hurrying towards us, Dante leaping about in her wake.

With her curves and curls, round cheeks and big eyes, Leonie's just as magnetic as her boyfriend. I'm impressed she managed to leave Shak's Halloween party without a cloud of hangers-on. She's already wearing her cryptolenses. Unlike Mitch, who only uses his when he needs them, she barely takes hers off. Behind the glasses she's all done up with glitter gems and there are trails of fake ivy threaded through her braids.

"You look swish," says Heather.

"Poison Ivy, right?" asks Ollie.

"Thank you! Everyone just thought I was a tree sprite." Going on tiptoes, Leonie gives Mitch a quick kiss.

"I was gonna go as Harley Quinn," he explains with a shrug. "But I had to work. What do you think, babe?" He motions to the wards. "Are we fucked?"

Leonie looks pained. "Maybe."

"They might have been nullified," suggests Sam.

Heather makes a humming noise. "Why not just erase them?"

"A statement, or a warning." Mitch is worried, and rightly so.

"Maybe they couldn't," I say hopefully. "We're all soul sources for these wards. I mean, all four of us bled into the paint, right, so maybe we're too strong and they couldn't just strip the theorem."

"Too strong?" A cold breeze rustles the fake ivy in Leonie's braids and she shivers. "Charlie, I wish. This" – she peers closer at the ward – "is waaaay above our level."

Pulling out her phone, she consults her notes app, then starts talking about "resonance" and "syphons" and "balancing components".

I bump shoulders with Mitch and whisper, "Do you have a clue what she's on about?"

"Nope," he whispers back, gazing at his girlfriend, a slight smile on his lips. "But isn't she magnificent?"

Yeah, she is.

Logical and methodical, Leonie's a natural at mathemagics. Since she met Viola three months ago, she's been cramming the theory like she's got an exam in it, trying to absorb everything Viola's willing to teach. Even before then, she managed to unpick the components of a ghost trap using only the basic notes she'd saved to the cloud before Caleb Gates destroyed what little information we had at the time.

Like Leonie, Sam's good at all the theorem stuff, though he's taken a step back recently. Me and Mitch have to work hard to pick it up, though Mitch has turned out to be good at the alchemical potion side of things. If it looks like a recipe, he can nail it.

"Shit," says Leonie. "I think whoever did this has actually changed the theorem's expression."

"So they've hijacked it rather than lay a fresh theorem from scratch?" says Sam.

"It's still active," Leonie confirms. "But I've no idea if it's even a ward any more."

Mitch has his arms wrapped tight around himself, like the cold can reach his bones. "They're playing with us."

I list curse words in my head to stop myself from panicking. Someone deliberately sabotaged what mediocre protections we have.

"Can you reverse engineer the modifications, work out what it does now?" Heather asks Sam and Leonie.

Sam shakes his head. "We don't even have the lexicon to understand these changes."

"I'm working tomorrow so I'll run this by Viola first thing," says Leonie. "Hopefully she'll recognize some of the glyphs, or at least what concordance they come from."

As far as I understand, a glyph concordance is like an alphabet. Turns out there are different magical languages. In the same way you can say something in English or in Italian and the overall meaning is the same but the way you say it is different.

"What if catchers did this and they lay traps *tonight*?" I ask. "Are our wards working at all or has all the magic been redirected?"

Leonie pats down her pockets. "There's one way to find out."

"Lay a ghost trap?" asks Mitch.

A wave of music spills from the nearby pub. The streets seem fuller now, more people streaming into the damp even though most places won't be closing for another hour or two.

"If I can't lay a trap then the wards still work. If I can then…" Leonie tails off.

"We're in big trouble," I whisper, grim-faced.

"Anyone have chalk?"

Sam hands her some of the red chalk he uses for sketching.

"That won't leave much of a mark in the wet," I say.

Leonie pulls a pen in a plastic package from her coat, opens it and presses it to her finger. "Doesn't need to, the theorem should still take hold." She clicks the top of the pen and a bead of blood oozes from her fingertip. Ah, not a pen.

"My brother Terry's type one," she says in response to Sam's questioning look. "We have loads of these at home and I got sick of sticking myself with a penknife."

"You sure about this?" Heather asks as Leonie smears her blood on the chalk.

Soul sources and syphons are two of the many things Viola's taught us. Without them, a theorem is just a collection of symbols, numbers and maybe words. To activate it, we have to put part of ourselves into it.

Still, something about this obviously doesn't sit right with Heather. Maybe it's the fact we're laying a ghost trap at all. It feels kind of slimy, but if Leonie manages to do it, she can undo it right away. No souls will get hurt.

"If you turn yourself into a frog we'll get you a nice

terrarium," promises Ollie. "One with a little pond and lots of flies."

Giving him the middle finger, Leonie crouches and starts to draw on the corner flagstone, near the ward.

Mitch, Sam and me fan out, trying to hide what she's doing from passers-by. Some give us curious looks, but no one confronts us. Leonie shapes the first few lines of the trap. The blooded chalk leaves thin streaks through the glow-flecked puddles.

What if The Hand did this?

Why would they mess with our wards? Unless they're testing us or tracking us. No, this is likely an occultist trying to weaken us or confuse us so that they can trap York's ghosts.

Dante backs against me, whining. I glance up and down the street – no cats, ghostly or living, no squirrels, and nothing else that would bother him.

"Oi, what's got into you?" I ask the dog. He's not normally this wound up.

Leonie's hands shake and she slows, gasping with the effort. She presses her free hand to her ribs. "It … hurts. The ward is pushing back—"

Leonie hisses in pain as the chalk crumbles. Mitch flinches, shielding his face. A loud crack. One of the mullioned windows of the nearby shop shatters. In seconds there's a cascade of smashed glass as all of the panes crack, one after the other.

Mitch is beside Leonie. "Babe, your hand."

Her fingers have blistered where she was holding the chalk.

Heather takes a look. "We need to get that under running water."

Leonie recoils. "I'm fine, it's not that bad—"

A scream cuts the night. We all freeze, confused.

"What was that?" asks Mitch, on edge.

Dante suddenly goes charging down Stonegate barking loudly. We don't wait about. Hauling Leonie up, we hurry after him. My prostheses don't have the right flex for running, it risks damage to them and me, plus I'm wearing dress shoes. The best I can manage is a quick stride. Up ahead, the ghost dog darts round the bend towards St Helen's Square.

I shout after him, but he's gone.

Another scream, this time guttural and hollow and filled with pain.

On the corner, a white box van has gone bonnet first into one of the tourist information poles in front of Betty's Tea Rooms. The driver is out of the cab, hurrying back to the intersection of Blake Street, Stonegate and Daveygate and the crumpled shape on the cobbled road.

"I didn't hit him." The driver scrubs at his cheeks, stressed. "I swerved, I swear."

Pushing though the growing crowd – some of them dead, most of them living, I find a man in dark clothes lying on his back, left arm twisted under him, right leg at a messed-up angle. He certainly looks like he's been hit by something.

"Call an ambulance," I tell Sam.

"Leonie's on it."

No electric cables nearby, nothing that looks like it could trip anyone, spark, or catch fire. The bloke doesn't look like he's got a knife or any kind of weapon. I kneel down beside him, ignoring the sharp pain in my stumps.

He's alive but fuck … it's bad. Splintered bone sticks through torn cloth. Mouth gasping, blood on slashed lips, eyes wide and wild with panic. His chest rises and falls as he struggles for breath.

Mitch catches my eye. There's fear there, and a question – what the hell happened to this guy?

"He ran past the church," says a woman on the edge of tears. "Screaming and waving his arms."

Someone mutters about drink or drugs. Yeah, drugs didn't leave him looking like he lost a fight with a truck. Looking up, there's a wall of people around us, useless and staring.

"Give him some space." Sam pitches his voice low so it carries. "Everyone move back."

The onlookers obey but they don't leave. Mitch and Sam turn themselves into a barrier, keeping spectators clear. Leonie's still on the phone. Ollie's asking the ghosts to give us room too. There's a number of them looking on, worried and interested.

Two are ghosts I know well. Young in the face with light stubble, watery eyes and wild curls, James Reid is handsome in a rugged, windswept kind of way. He's the opposite to neat and noble George Villiers, who is all lace and rich cloth and smart grooming. Somehow, they're perfect together. Ushering Ollie over, they talk in hurried whispers.

Dante growls again, low and fearful. I glance past the crowd and the reflected glare of the streetlights to the roof above Betty's. A black silhouette stands against clouds lit by light pollution. It's like someone has cut the shape out of the sky. Slender, its edges blur into the night. The bloke at my feet groans. When I look up again, the shape is gone but the prickle in the air lingers, ash on the wind catching in my lungs. What was that?

Something isn't right, but I've no time to think on it because I need to try and save a man's life.

"Help's coming." I try to sound calm and in control. "Don't move." It's a daft thing to say because his limbs are shattered. His gaze flits wildly, like he's searching for something. Blood pools in the cracks between the cobbles. Where is it coming from? His head? His chest?

Everywhere.

I need to find and stop the bleeding, but that means nothing if he can't breathe. He might have internal damage, broken ribs for sure.

He's trying to talk.

"An ambulance is on its way," I promise him, glancing back at Leonie who says, "Five minutes, tops. Just, hold on."

"Soph—" His voice is weak and mangled, like he's drowning. What's he trying to say? "Sophi—"

"Sophie?" I ask.

He tries to nod.

"Is anyone here called Sophie?" I bellow. "Does anyone know this guy?"

No one comes forward.

He coughs, spraying blood droplets. There are cuts on his lips, his tongue is a gory lump in his mouth. I need to put him in the recovery position, clear his throat and maintain his airway, but rolling him means a broken rib could puncture his lung. That ambulance will never get here in time. He's dying and I don't know what to do.

"Heather, help me."

She's beside me in an instant, firing instructions. I let myself sink into her voice, feeling my panic fade to a steady strength I know will see me through.

A flurry of dark velvet as Villiers crouches on my other side, hissing as he sees the extent of the man's injuries. "James and I witnessed the attack."

"Who did this to him?" I ask, keeping my voice low.

Villiers takes a deep breath. "I fear, Master Frith, that it was not a person at all."

5

SHADOWS

This late, our cul-de-sac is quiet. Most living folks are tucked up in bed sleeping or doom scrolling on TikTok. Pulling in, Dad turns off the engine. I sit in the silence and listen to the thundering in my brain, trying to forget the feel of broken bone under my fingers as Ollie slips out of the side door to do his usual perimeter check of the house, taking Dante with him. Heather's gone to the hospital to find out what she can about the victim. We need every scrap of information we can get if we're going to find what did this.

What. Not who.

After the ambulance left in a wail of flashing lights the police took our statements. It started raining but not hard enough to wash away the blood pooled between the cobbles. I reckon they think this is the work of that gang, but we know better.

Villiers and Reid were chatting to some other ghosts

outside Betty's Tea Rooms about the upcoming Old Souls council election and saw what happened. As the victim came up Daveygate in a hurry, a fiend of swirling shadows leapt from the top of the church on to him. It was dark and there was a press of people around the screaming man, so Villiers doesn't know how he sustained the damage he did, only that it was over within seconds and whatever the shadow was, it wasn't … human. At least not any more.

This isn't happening. I'm not ready. An occultist I understand, but this? I think back to the dark silhouette I saw cut against the skyline – humanoid in shape, but not a person. Too big, too slender, like its limbs had been stretched and then shrouded in shadows. I only had a glimpse, but I know I didn't imagine it.

My palms are still slick with sweat. I wipe them on my trousers, trying not to shake.

We've faced occult magic made of shadows before.

Caleb Gates.

The Shadow Man.

He's dead but, in our world, dead doesn't mean gone.

If he comes back, it will be as a ghost, an angry one. In life, he hated Sam's family. In death, I reckon he'd go after him.

Fuck.

Did Sam get back to the hotel OK? I wish I'd gone with him but the police called Dad to come get me. I've got to make sure Sam's safe.

I'm barely through our bungalow door, blood down my clothes, but Mum doesn't care. She hugs me like she's not seen me for an age, then holds me at arm's length to inspect me, chin wrinkling in concern.

I hate to make her worry. "I'm all right."

For once, there are no dead people in my bedroom. Mum's piled all of my rejected date clothes on my bed – how was that only a few hours ago? I video-call Sam as soon as I get the door shut and let out a long, relieved breath when he answers.

"You again?" He's lying in the half-dark, turned on his side. "If you're obsessed with me, just say so."

"You know it." Propping my phone on my bedside table, I take off my prostheses. "Home safe?"

"Home, yes. Safe? I'm not sure. How do your legs feel?"

I chuck my sweaty compression socks towards the laundry basket and miss, taking out the chess game set up on my dresser. Bollocks. Villiers and Reid will be pissed.

"Sore, but I'll survive." I massage my right stump to ease some of the ache. My skin is patched red, the flesh throbbing. I definitely wore my prostheses for too long today.

I strip off my bloody shirt and trousers, fishing some trackies from the nearby pile of clothes. I really want a shower but I'm sitting on my bed, then lying, my phone propped on the pillow beside me.

Me and Sam are quiet a while, just staring at each other, then I clear my throat. "What if … what if it's *him* come back?"

Sam's lips thin. He doesn't need to ask who I mean. When he looks off camera, I feel something shift in the way he holds himself, like he's slipped on invisible armour. His eyes flick back to mine and there's steel behind his gaze. "Gates can't bring his consciousness back together so soon. He dissolved."

Six souls linking hands. Glass and tile searing the air, sailing at me and Sam. The walls cracking. Gates laughing, the power of stolen ghosts riddling him like lightning, as that laugh turns into a bellow of fury, a blinding flash and then...

Along with Liska and Dusan, our friends and allies tore his soul apart molecule by molecule, expending their essence and dissolving themselves along with him.

"He wasn't used up in the way a bottled soul syphoned into a theorem is used up," I say. "Which means Gates is still out there, spread thin over the city. One day, he *will* come back—"

Sam swallows. "It usually takes centuries."

"Before he died, he became something no one has seen before." My eyes sting. "If anyone can find a way, it's him."

If he's found a way to return then we've got to watch our backs. All that anger and resentment, all that greed mixed with magic and the essence of stolen souls. Fuck. Who knows what he'd become, maybe the weapon he wanted to create. There's no way we're prepared. I wouldn't even know where to start.

"Charlie, ghosts can't do that without help."

"But the shadows—"

"I'm sure Gates wasn't the only one to use magic designed to obscure and confuse. They're not uncommon theorems. Whatever the shadow entity is, it's probably something mathemagics conjured up, not a dead soul."

"Yeah," I say. He's right, but my gut says this is something spectral. "W-what if it *is* Caleb Gates?" I ask, struggling to keep my voice even.

Sam's jaw tightens. "Then we stop him. Again."

His eyes blaze with determined anger and I know that, even if he's scared shitless, he'll do what he thinks is right.

I almost say, "I love you," but stop myself. I don't know why I'm holding out. I guess I don't want to scare him, or pressure him into saying it back before he's ready, or really means it. To be honest, I still can't believe he wants to be with me.

I'm in love with him.

Shit, yeah, that's … terrifying but it's the good kind of scary, much sweeter to think about than the bad kind of scary – which is everything else right now.

We've only known each other six months. I'm just seventeen, he's eighteen. Our parents and friends say we're a nice couple, but at the end of the day they probably reckon we'll part ways when Sam goes to uni and I'm stuck here, still trying to get some basic GCSEs. Most couples would and it's not like me and Sam have loads in common. We were kind of just thrown together by all of this ghost stuff.

On the dark days I worry that the dead are all that's really holding us together. Without the weird part of our lives, we wouldn't have met. We're both going through similar stuff but what if, one day, that's not enough? I'm not good enough for him. He's a billionaire's son. Talented, handsome, clever. I'm flunking out of school, no direction, no idea of who I really am other than being a seer. That's it. That's my whole life. And I'm not even very good at it.

The only thing I know that I want – to be mirrored – he *doesn't* want. If I go after that to protect him, myself and others, then I risk losing him forever.

I'm overthinking again. Sam chose to stay in York because he likes who he is here, with me. Pick two lads to pair up and it wouldn't be us. Somehow, for whatever reason, it works, at least right now.

Let's take it one day at a time.

"Stay until I fall asleep?" I ask, afraid of nightmares but not wanting to say that out loud because it sounds childish.

"Of course." Sam snuggles back into the pillow. "You want me to keep talking?"

"Yeah, please."

He chats about nothing and everything and his voice – deeper than it was a couple of weeks ago – blends with the sound of Ollie arguing with ghost children on the other side of my door and Dante's whine as he pads over, jumps on to the bed and curls against me.

Maybe I imagine it, but just before I fall asleep I hear Sam say, "I love you." In my dream, I'm brave enough to say it back.

6

GRAVE IDEAS

I wake to a weight on my chest and find I'm nose to nose with a flour-covered face that shouts, "Boo!" as soon as I open my eyes.

I gasp and sit up. Cackling, Lorna, the eldest twin by a half-hour, slides off my bed.

"We made you blue pancakes," she says. Her dungarees are dusted white and there is a smear of food colouring on her cheek.

Leaning on the bed, Poppy thrusts a plate at me. "I put glitter in them so you can poop sparkles."

My head is groggy. Light streams through my half-drawn curtains. Broomwood is pacing in the front garden. How long was I out?

"Charlie," Poppy whines. "Pancakes."

I look at the lumpy blue mess on the plate. "Er, yeah … thanks, they look great."

I need a brew and a proper fry-up but nothing's going to get me out of trying the pancakes. Hundreds and thousands grind between my teeth but I tell the girls they're delicious. Ollie sticks his head through the door, sees my face and laughs.

"Heather about?" I ask him.

"Who's there?" asks Lorna.

"Ollie," says Poppy with terrifying confidence.

The girls aren't seers like me, they didn't die and come back to life. But, somehow, they can sense when spirits are around and they can feel their strong emotions – happiness, joy, fear, sadness. Me and Sam call people like them sensitives.

"Heather's back at the hospital," says Ollie.

Reaching for a jumper, I pull it on. There's a chill to the air. Dad keeps the heating low because the rates are going up. "Back? Did she come by?"

"You were sleeping."

Heather taught me how to survive as a seer, introduced me to Ollie, made me feel safe and less alone. What I didn't know until a few months ago was that she was the exhausted, overworked doctor who'd misdiagnosed my early meningococcal septicaemia as a flu.

I died the same day she did. Me from the infection. Her from a stab wound inflicted in the car park by a stranger. She always told me her colleagues couldn't save her, but that was a lie. She could have lived. I should've died. But she chose to take my place, and I woke up a seer. She made me what I am.

She also lied about it for years. For a while, I was very

angry about that. Then I got over myself and forgave her because she *died* for me. Since then, she's saved me more times than I can count, and my life isn't worse than it was before, or better, it's just different. If I couldn't see ghosts I'd lose the only part of who I am that means anything.

Where Heather goes every night is a mystery and no one knows who she spends time with when she's not with us. If I ask about her past, her family, or what her life was like before she died, she changes the subject.

Maybe it still hurts too much.

"No news, then?" I ask Ollie.

He shakes his head. I take that as a sign to get up and transfer into my chair – sleek frame, no push handles, low back rest. As keen as I am to get some answers about last night, I want to be clean. Hauling my aching body into the shower, I wash my hair twice.

Under the water, my nightmares threaten to seep back in. I can't help thinking about the attack. When Heather tried to help the victim her hands went right through his broken body, which means if the shadowy figure is a ghost, then it somehow killed a living person who isn't a seer. That makes no sense. The dead can't hurt the living unless they're seers. It's, like, a fundamental rule of the afterlife.

Either I'm wrong, or this is something new.

Sometimes dealing with the dead is like trying to find my way around my house in the dark, except someone's moved all of the furniture. I think I know the rules and then something changes with no warning.

I shake my head, trying to disperse the worry. I should think about something happier. Sam. Did he really say he loved me last night?

For a second, I'm just grinning, heart pounding, cheeks flushed with warmth. I probably dreamed it, probably. But what if I didn't?

I get dressed in my bathroom. When you're as haunted as I am, you have to set boundaries. This is the one place everyone leaves me alone.

The group chat was active while I was showering; Sam's dealing with some house hunting stuff today, probably his mum dragging him round more viewings. Leonie's working at the bookshop, meaning she's meeting Viola. Hopefully, we'll know what the changes to the wards mean soon.

When I wheel into the kitchen there's a note from Dad to say he got called into work early because someone's gone down sick and Mum's over at Aunt Chrissie's. I'm babysitting for the day. Not ideal, but at least I'll be busy.

Seeing as I'm not wearing them today, Poppy wants to paint the toenails on my prostheses.

"Fine, but not red, it stains."

She settles on baby blue. It could be worse. My socket covers are still decorated with sparkles and a yellow smiley face in permanent marker from the last time my sisters got hold of them.

Late morning, I hear Villiers and Broomwood arguing on the front lawn so I head out to see what the fuss is about. Mrs Tulliver, the old landlady from The Snickleway Inn stands with her tabby cat, Seamus, draped over her shoulders, watching with Ollie.

Villiers puffs his chest. "I was, as you know, the favourite of *three* kings with as much experience of court life as the art of war—"

Reid places a gentle hand on his arm. "Do we expect to go to war, dearest?"

"I've got decades of neighbourhood watch experience," Broomwood jumps in. "And they'll be wanting young blood, not toffs like the last bunch of pompous numpties. I hear you've a bad history of taking advantage of us lesser folk."

Villiers steps up to him, straightening his shoulders. "In assisting Master Frith and Master Harrow I am atoning for the sins of centuries past."

"By 'sins' do you mean illegal land appropriation in Ireland? Don't think those scars have healed—"

Ah, the council election squabble. Again.

"Popcorn?" Ollie asks, elbowing me.

"You know you could *both* be voted in, right?" I call.

There used to be seven ghosts on the Old Souls Council until Gates got them. Instead of an inflexible group of dictatorial bullies, the ghosts of York have agreed on voting in a smaller replacement council of four souls to serve for ten years, with no re-election within the century. All deceased residents of York are eligible to run, and all get a vote.

"Ah, Master Frith!" Villiers turns his back on Broomwood, who strides off muttering, cheeks crimson. Hiding a smile, Mrs Tulliver trails after him.

"James hath something he wishes to discuss," says Villiers.

"I don't know if tis of any import," says Reid. "But the man who was attacked was being haunted by a woman in a white summer gown. In the ruckus, I saw not to where she vanished, only that she was behind him when he fell and afterwards she was nowhere to be seen. Perchance she is this Sophie?"

"He's not a seer," I say. "Heather couldn't touch him." I assumed she was his wife or girlfriend or something, not a ghost.

Villiers taps his foot, impatient. "No matter, mayhap in his fear he spoke the name of his lost beloved."

"Or she was haunting him for fun," suggests Ollie. "There's not much to do when you're dead. Keeping track of the living is one pastime."

I thank Reid for telling me about the ghost anyway. It might be important when we have more of the puzzle pieces.

"Now, art thou prepared for today's instruction, Master Frith?" Villiers asks me.

With everything going on, I'd forgotten we had a lesson. I'm a long way from learning how to mirror, so as soon as my back healed enough for me to work out again, I convinced Villiers to teach me sword fighting. Not that pretty display stuff: the real down and dirty cut-off-your-opponent's-head-in-three-moves stuff, but even that, he says, has to start with a firm foundation of the "true art".

We head out to the garages at the end of our cul-de-sac. It's private up there; the ground is level and there's plenty of space to move. The girls are happy to come along, collecting leaves and making up games. Reid and Ollie keep an eye on them for me. Because my legs are sore I'm sticking to my chair today.

"Let us modify the last strike sequence you learned," says Villiers, handing me his rapier. So long as I stay within ten or so metres of him, I can use it. Beyond that, it fades and reappears back in the scabbard on his belt.

To ghosts and seers, this is a deadly weapon – I've been at the wrong end of this blade before. The hilt feels solid in my hand. I can smell the steel but, to most living people and the material world, it isn't here. I can't cut them with it but dangerous ghosts who want to attack me had better watch out.

We go through the sequence, adapting the moves. Unlike in the wheelchair fencing I've seen on TV, I need to move my chair about. The trick is to train my left side as much as my right so that I can swap which hand I use to push the wheels and which I use for the sword.

I don't always make the switch smoothly. It's hard work and the only pause I get is when Villiers stops me to correct my grip, or demonstrate technique. This would be simpler if seers could manifest stuff from phantasmic essence too. Knowing my luck, I wouldn't get something useful like a sword.

For those souls that have them, manifested items are essentially an extension of themselves. Heather's stethoscope, Reid's bagpipes, Villiers' rapier – they're all things that defined them in life as much as death.

What defines me?

Wish I knew.

The workout is hard and takes all my concentration, exactly what I need to stop my fears slipping back in. They still creep in at the edges. Every sudden noise or loud movement flares my anxiety. I'll start to spiral and I don't have time for that.

Keep busy and don't over think.

"Does thou wish to continue?" asks Villiers. "Or should we retire for the day?"

Adjusting my grip on the hilt, I shake out my arms. I'm about to say that I want to keep going, but then I spot a familiar figure watching from the end of the garages.

One of the ghosts from last night, Professor Alice Purcell. There're smears of dried dirt on her jeans, her plaid shirt is well worn and there's mud on her trainers. I wonder if all academics dress that casual, or if she remembers herself in the clothes she wore to digs because that's where she felt happiest.

"I know who took the bones," she says. "All you need to do is send an email."

I get that she's upset, but compared to murder, it's not exactly top priority. Still, I've nothing else to do right now and it obviously matters to her.

"Who was it?" I ask.

"An MA student in funerary archaeology." The professor wrings her hands. "She's taken at least three ribs, a clavicle, finger bones and part of a femur, mostly Roman remains."

Villiers wrinkles his nose. "And your ex-colleagues think tis a mere administrative error?"

The professor blows out her cheeks. "She's clever, hacking records to hide her trail, never taking too much from one box.

A direct accusation of theft will at least mean an investigation. All of the stolen bones have identification numbers so they can be tracked. I want them found and restored to the archives."

"What's the student's name?" I ask.

"Sadie Sudarma." The Professor shakes her head again. "What a waste of talent. I really have no idea why she'd do something like this. We're taught to treat human remains with respect and dignity. Promise me you'll email."

I turn towards home. "Let's do it right now."

Heather gets back from the hospital in the afternoon. The twins have settled in the living room, watching cartoons. Needing to keep busy, I pick up toys so it's easier for me to move my chair around, and then wash up from our late lunch.

Broomwood's popped back over for a natter, pointedly ignoring Villiers, who is at the other end of the kitchen table battling for victory over the chessboard with Reid. Broomwood wants to know about the attack in town last night. Ollie abandons reading a book about necromancers in space to fill him in.

When Heather finally ghosts in, I take one look at her face and I know.

"He died, didn't he?"

Her nod is slow and sad. "His injuries were extensive."

It's moments like this I'm reminded she's a doctor. I wonder how often she had to break bad news to families when she was working.

"Poor JD," says Ollie.

"We don't know his name, do we?" asks Broomwood, confused.

"It short for John Doe."

"That's an Americanism," says Heather.

Ollie throws up his arms. "Well, we can't just call him 'that bloke', can we?"

"Knight to C2," says Reid.

Removing my marigolds, I roll around the table to move the piece for him. The black knight takes the white.

Reid grins. "Check."

Villiers leans in. "Well played, my beloved, but I shalt vanquish thee, just as I shall crush those who run against me for the council."

Broomwood mimes a yawn.

"No ID on him, then?" I ask Heather.

"None." She looks more tired than usual, which isn't easy when you're dead. Ghosts look the same most of the time, no matter what, and they don't technically need to sleep. She must be proper emotionally rundown if it's showing. "They've no clue who he is or what happened to him."

"King to C2," says Villiers. I move his piece, taking the black knight.

Heather turns away and starts fiddling with her lanyard. Yeah, something's definitely bothering her, but I bet she won't talk to me about it. I pop the kettle on and get some coffee out of the cupboard. I hate the stuff, but she loves it. She can't drink it, but I'm hoping the smell will make her feel better.

"Reid saw a ghost lass in white following JD before he was attacked," I say, trying out the nickname. Ollie gives me a thumbs up. "Might be the Sophie he was asking for, but even if she's not, she might still be able to ID him." I spoon coffee into a filter. "If we get a name we can ask Miri to unearth his digital life. Maybe there's a clue as to why he was targeted, and that might help us figure out what or who he was targeted by."

Realizing what I've just said, I pause, cursing myself for being so daft. What am I like? I'm a *seer*. Just because he's dead, doesn't mean he can't answer our questions. "Heather, where's his soul?"

"He didn't stay."

Ollie wrinkles his nose. "Really?"

I'm surprised too. We don't know why some of the dead stick around and others don't, but many of the ones who do met a sudden or violent death. I'd say JD kinda raised the bar on messed-up ways to die. "You sure he's not haunting the hospital?"

"I'm sure. I was there when he passed." Heather's staring at the salt and pepper shakers on the table, unblinking. "There was a flicker of his soul and then ... gone, nothing."

For someone who sees ghosts, I haven't had much experience with the actual dying part. I've only seen one person die: Mr Harrow. His spirit rose from his body turning into a ghost as we see them, plain as day and solid-looking.

"Was it like he dissolved?" I ask, reaching for the freshly boiled kettle. That happens if a soul is exhausted, or has

61

been fed on by another ghost. Their phantasmic essence disintegrates and stretches out over a huge area. Sometimes it's years before they find the strength to pull their consciousness together again.

Heather makes a face. "No, more like there wasn't anything of him *to* dissolve. It didn't feel natural."

Villiers looks up from the chess game. "Art thou suggesting the shadow fiend destroyed his immortal soul?"

Heather seems at a loss. "I honestly don't know what I saw, only that it wasn't usual."

Closing the dishwasher, I pull a chair out for her and set the coffee down. "Do we think the shadow thing could be a new type of ghost who doesn't play by the rules we know? The way Caleb Gates died last spring, taking the Old Souls and Sam's dad with him—"

"You think the Shadow Man's back?" asks Ollie.

Sam doesn't, but I'm not so sure. Jan Liska's words to Gates play through my thoughts, clagging my mind and thickening my throat. *Do this and you will become monstrous.* Yeah, that shadow entity was monstrous all right, and terrifying.

"I'm saying that whatever attacked JD might be—" I swallow. *My fault.* I can't say it out loud, but it echoes through the kitchen anyway. My cheeks burn with shame.

"Lad, I was there." Broomwood pats my arm. "You and Sam risked yourselves to fix a wrong and to save what souls you could."

Heather has her palms around her coffee, trying to feel the warmth as she inhales the scent. "I'm not saying this thing isn't Gates, or maybe a new kind of ghost we haven't seen before, but let's rule out mathemagical interference first."

"Fine." I drop a message to the Team Spectre group chat. Leonie replies right away.

"They didn't see any active theorems at the scene," I say, still reading my screen. "There's no sign of Viola at the bookshop but Leonie's going to get started on deciphering the glyphs. We need to find this Sophie lass, ask her what she knows."

It doesn't matter if it's an occultist or a ghost, it's on us to find this thing and stop it.

"I'll go look for her, lad." Broomwood gives Villiers a side glance. "What with my years of dedication to the neighbourhood watch, I'm observant and clever. Not much gets past me." He taps his nose.

Villiers pretends not to hear him. Reid hides his smile.

"If there's nothing at the scene, maybe there's evidence of mathemagics on JD's corpse," says Ollie.

He has a point. We all know what that means. I can tell from Heather's expression that she hates the idea. Still, she doesn't argue as I call Sam.

He answers on the third ring.

"New date idea," I say, cheerful. "It's a bit out there, but how do you feel about breaking into a mortuary?"

There's a laugh in Sam's voice as he replies. "I thought you'd never ask."

7

ON THE SLAB

A nurse glances at us as we exit the hospital's main lift.

"They're missing ID," says Ollie.

"Nicking someone else's is too risky." With her gently wrinkled shirt, high-waisted slacks and stethoscope, Heather fits right in here. Her job was her whole life. 'Course, no one else can see or hear her, so that doesn't exactly help us. "Just keep moving."

Dressed in stolen porters' uniforms, me and Mitch pick up our pace. The beeping of distant machinery blends with the squeak of our shoes on the floor and the clattering of the mortuary trolley between us. I keep my eyes on the generic framed artwork, breathing in the bitter tang of antiseptic.

"Almost there," I mumble, for Sam and Leonie's benefit. They're lying corpse-still, and top to tail, hidden under the trolley's cover.

The mortuary is on the ground floor past the pharmacy and before Neuroscience and Sleep Services. The reception area is broad and well lit. Everything smells freshly scrubbed. Hurrying past the empty office to our left, we check there's no one about. We've timed it so that everyone should be at lunch.

When I asked Mitch about missing a shift at the restaurant he near enough bit my head off. I just don't want all this stuff to get in the way of him becoming a world class chef. Ghosts are my whole world, but they don't have to be his. He has a choice.

Parking the trolley in a nook where there are other unused trolleys I unzip the cover and help Leonie and Sam out. We leave our regular clothes underneath. Hopefully no one will try and tidy the cover away in the next fifteen minutes.

"The fridge room is this way." Heather leads us past some more doors. Behind their glass panels are stainless steel troughs, coiled hoses hooked on the wall, charts and huge sinks. There's a lot of equipment, countless whiteboards, and taps. *So* many taps.

"Ollie, go haunt the staff," I say. "If anyone looks like they're coming in here, let us know."

"Will do."

"Thanks, mate, appreciate it."

There's a keypad. Heather has the code memorized. Sam keys it in and the buttons beep loudly. I'm sweating. The door makes a happy buzz and clicks open.

Everything is spotless. The long wall at the back is covered in tall doors, not the small, square ones for individual bodies, meaning several corpses to a fridge. There are another couple of those metal bed-sinks, which I guess is where they put the cadavers when they're working on them.

"Anything?" I ask Leonie.

She scans the walls, looking under tables and along the counters. "Nothing is glowing, no wards, ghost-lines or traps."

"No occultists working in the mortuary, then," says Mitch. "Thank fuck."

The soft hum of the cooling elements and the extraction is kind of calming. What's not helping my nerves is the solid half-wall of glass near the doors we came in. It seems to be a little viewing room. Anyone who steps in there will clock us right away.

"Out of curiosity, what's the jail time for breaking into a morgue?" I ask.

"We'd better hurry," says Sam. "Which fridge is he in?"

Heather points to the far end. "Second to last."

In my head, it was going to smell of decay, but opening the fridge I just get a waft of cold air and then a sweet tang, fetid, but not *really* bad. It's not even enough to make me gag, though Mitch is looking a bit peaky.

Five trays to a fridge. Top two slots are empty. The bottom three are full. I pull out the drawer Heather gestures to. It rumbles on its tracks. I slide the zip on the body bag down a few centimetres and—

Oh god, that's *rank*. I stagger back, arm over my nose to stifle the stink. Sam gags and turns away.

We've found a body before, but he was the best part of a

century dead and partly mummified; the smell had settled. This is fresh, dampened by the cold but it still coats the back of my throat and churns my stomach.

Dark hair, heavy bruising to the forehead and cheekbones, mottled skin … wait. I should have checked the tag. "This isn't him."

I think it's a lass.

"What?" Heather pushes me aside. She's as grim-faced as I've ever seen her, and she's pretty unshakeable when it comes to medical stuff. "They moved him? Bollocks." She goes to grab the zip, then stops. She must be rattled, it's not like her to forget she can't touch anything. "I'll check the whiteboards."

Zipping up the woman's body bag, I slide her back in the fridge and lock the door tight.

JD's in the fourth fridge along, slot four. Unknown male, mid-thirties, date of death noted and a case number attached, which means the police are investigating. Sam unzips this one. Mitch takes a big step back. I prepare myself for the worst but JD's been on ice since he died.

I focus on the deep scratches around his lips and chin and can't help a shudder. His mouth looks like he tried to eat glass. The mess continues down his torso – jutting bone, pale flesh, dappled bruising – all tidied up as best as they can manage, stitches dark against pallid skin.

I'm no expert, but it looks like he's already been autopsied, organs weighed and measured, like some ancient ritual to prepare him for the afterlife.

Only, *he's* not here. Again, not saying his soul had to stick around or anything but, looking at how messed up his body is, it's weird that he just petered out. Maybe he did pass on, or maybe something's different because of how he died.

Hopefully, we're about to find out.

We start with Sam's famed herbal mix. Two sparks of the lighter and the little heap flares and spits, wisps of smoke curling as he carefully wafts it over the corpse. Not enough and it won't reveal anything. Too much and we set the fire alarms off.

We check JD's hands carefully in case he touched something magical and that's what made him a target. No old symbols, no broken glyphs, nothing.

"Negative." Sam sweeps the herbal ashes into a damp cloth and stashes them, the lighter and the dish back in his pockets.

I wave my arms about, trying to disperse the smoke.

"You're up, babe." Mitch nudges Leonie. "Show them how it's done."

The theorem she inks into her palm with a sharpie is one she's been working on with Viola for a while. Burning herbs for revelation and clarity make weak and broken theorems appear, but strong magic won't show. Leonie's theorem draws out *active* power, the kind that needs a soul source to work.

For a second, I worry she's going to cut herself to syphon into the theorem. Leaving DNA evidence on a suspicious dead body is a bad idea, but it seems marking the glyph on her skin is enough. Unflinching, she lays her palm on the part of JD's chest that's the least damaged. For a second, the air around the corpse shimmers like hot air over tarmac. Leonie sways. Mitch puts a steadying hand on her back.

"Anything changed?" Her voice sounds strained.

We look again; chest, arms, hands, legs, his head. No secret theorems come swimming to the surface. No new marks on his skin at all.

"What about discolouration? Or…" Leonie's breathless. The drawing feeling of syphoning into a theorem, like a hook under your ribs, must be pulling hard on her. Leonie's gonna need a Red Bull and a nap after this.

"No change," says Heather.

With a gasp, Leonie snatches her hand back, breaking the connection.

It suddenly hits me that Heather died at this hospital. Years ago, her body lay on one of these trays. She was stored in one of these fridges. The thought makes me cold. She's so alive to me, I sometimes forget that she's not.

Ollie comes tearing through the wall. "Company incoming!"

8

†HEN †HERE WERE †WO

here's nowhere to hide. In the movies, people slip under sheets, pretend to be dead and always get away with it. Real mortuaries use body bags. Not helpful.

There's only one exit and that door is about to be opened by someone who won't hesitate to press charges. That leaves all four of us ducking into the corner behind the last stainless-steel table, putting the long sinks and cabinets to our backs. Yeah, this is a crap hiding place. Whoever walks in here will spot us in half a second.

Ollie paces at the door. "They're getting close."

"Leonie, now would be a great time to test that invisibility theorem," says Mitch.

"Technically, it's not *true* invisibility—" There's sweat on her forehead.

"Semantics." Sam's crammed under the sink behind me. "If it'll stop us getting arrested, it's worth a try."

"Once I set the theorem, don't move or it will break," Leonie warns. "And it doesn't hide sound either so keep quiet."

We bunch close together as she scrambles to draw an unbroken oval around us with the sharpie. Mitch hands Leonie his pocketknife and, slicing her thumb, she marks a series of hurriedly sketched glyphs that glow against the pale floor.

"Five seconds," Heather warns, looking through the narrow pane of glass on the doors.

C'mon, Leonie.

"Three seconds."

Leonie's hand is shaking as she starts on what I hope is the last glyph.

"One."

The door swings open. Leonie lifts her bloody thumb from the floor. The theorem snaps into place, settling over us like a cold breath.

The footsteps stop and a clipped female voice says, "Why is this deceased patient here? Sorry, Neelam, one moment."

Shit. Shit. Shit.

She walks back into the corridor and I hear: "Julie, can you check the logs for whoever was last in here?"

The woman left behind in the fridge room – Neelam, the other lady called her – steps into view. She's British-Indian, mid-thirties, with full lips and thick dark hair cropped to her earlobes. She tucks back a stray strand and I notice she's wearing a lanyard like Heather's. A doctor, then.

What's she doing here? Her business is with the living.

Crossing the room, she looks over JD's exposed corpse, then glances back over her shoulder to where Heather and Ollie are hovering. Shivering, she scans the room. Something flexes in the air when she looks right at us. My breath hitches. Mitch squeezes his eyes tight. Leonie glowers, maybe forcing her will into the theorem to keep it from breaking.

Look away. Don't see us.

Heather's staring at Neelam like she's seen a ghost.

Is that irony?

The pathologist or technician, or whoever she is, strides back in. "Sorry about that, they're looking through everything to see what happened." She's a white woman dressed in dark blue scrubs, fine silver threads in her hair. "Leaving the deceased lying exposed is not our normal practice."

"Wendy." Neelam sniffs the air. "Can you smell burning?"

Shaking her head, Wendy walks—

Ah, bollocks, right towards us.

I can feel Sam's fearful breathing in my ear; I want to draw back against him, make myself smaller somehow, but we can't move. The woman comes closer … closer … she's going to bump right into us—

She stops at the long sink, the flare of her scrubs a centimetre from Leonie's knee.

Don't move, don't speak, don't breathe loudly.

Opening the overhead cupboard, Wendy pulls out a box. "I

don't smell anything." She's standing on the edge of one of the glyphs. "But my senses haven't been the same since covid."

The snap of a pair of latex-free gloves. She's so close I could reach out and touch her. If she takes even the tiniest step to the right...

"He's still unidentified?" asks Neelam.

"Police are making enquiries, though they don't have any leads. The coroner has ordered a full report." Spinning on her heel, her shoe smears the side of the glyph and Leonie makes a soft whimpering noise. Her face shines with sweat.

I'm in a bad position. My stumps are cramping painfully. When Leonie cast her theorem I was too busy panicking to think about how I was sitting. Now I'm stuck with my muscles screaming bloody murder. If I move, the spell will be broken, quite literally, but I'm not going to be able to hold this position much longer.

"These injuries..." Neelam motions to the torso. I catch a hint of a tattoo under her rolled shirt sleeve – a crystal and a flower stem.

"Forty-three fractures including all of his ribs, front and back," says Wendy. "Lacerations to his mouth and throat. Extensive bleeding in his kidneys and liver. His spleen didn't just rupture, it liquified. Multiple brain bleeds and, finally, his heart gave out." She shakes her head. "I can tell you one thing. It wasn't a traffic collision."

"Because of the oral lacerations?"

"That, and..." Wendy blows out her breath, as if she can't believe what she's about to say. "Looking at the bruising

73

patterns, the fractures, it's like he was hit by a car but … from the *inside* out."

Neelam's brow goes up. I sneak a glance at Heather, careful not to move my head. She looks heartbroken. Neelam's care for her patients probably reminds Heather of when she was able to make a difference to people's lives. It must be hard for her to see so much pain in the world and not be able to fix it.

"Have you ever seen anything like this before?" asks Neelam.

Wendy gestures to the fridge down the far end, the one we opened first. "Sadie Sudarma."

That name cuts through me. I typed it in an email to the head of archaeology just yesterday. Sudarma can't be that common a name, can it? It's not like Liu, Jones or Patel. But if it's the same person then we just accused a dead girl of theft.

"She shares the lacerations to the mouth and throat," Wendy goes on. "Although they're not as extensive, much of the damage in the thoracic and abdominal cavities is similar." Zipping up the body bag, she slides "unknown male, mid-thirties" back into storage. "I've alerted the coroner. The lab is rushing toxicology and the police have opened an inquiry."

My thighs are screaming. Any second now, I'm going to slip. If it wasn't for Sam pressed against my back I would've fallen already. Beside me, Leonie's breathing is shallow. Keeping the theorem stable is probably exhausting. There's a way I can syphon into the spell and share her burden, but it means moving.

Stripping her gloves, Wendy tosses them into the nearest

74

bin. "I'd bet my career that whatever killed Sadie Sudarma also took the life of our unknown man, though I couldn't begin to guess how it happened."

Neelam turns away.

"It's hard to lose a patient, but there really was nothing more you could have done for him," says Wendy. "I'm amazed he made it to hospital at all."

"I know, it's just..." Neelam grimaces. "Never mind, I'm tired. It's been a long shift."

"When was the last time you went home and got some proper rest rather than sleeping in one of the on-call rooms?"

Neelam doesn't say anything. Wendy's expression softens. "I heard you took the Manchester job."

"I've been thinking about a fresh start for a while."

"Well, we'll miss you here." With one last glance around the fridge room to make sure everything is in place, Wendy leads the way. "Come on, let me buy you a coffee."

As they pass Ollie and Heather, Neelam pauses, tensing.

Heather dips her gaze, like being too close to the doctor is hard. *They knew each other.* Of course! I think of the tattoo I saw on Neelam's arm – the plant is a sprig of heather.

Wendy holds the door open, waiting. With a last look over her shoulder at the bare patch of wall where Heather is standing, Neelam leaves. The door swings shut with a click. Their footsteps and voices retreat down the hall.

Leonie releases her theorem and wipes a thin smear of blood from her nose, face shining, eyes bloodshot. Sam gasps, slumping to the cool floor. I wince as I stretch out my legs to ease the cramp as Mitch helps Leonie up. She's weak as a noodle.

None of us have wet wipes, but we find some disinfectant in the cupboard above the sink and clean up the blood glyphs. There's nothing much we can do about the sharpie on the floor. That's going to confuse some people.

"Is it just me, or does it sound like there are two victims not one?" whispers Sam.

I glance back at the whiteboard, looking for the name Sadie Sudarma. *The student who stole all those bones.*

Does that have anything to do with her death?

Ollie slips out to monitor the corridor and signal when it's safe for us to sneak past reception. Sam helps Mitch support Leonie, who's bloody knackered. I hang back with Heather.

"How do you know that doctor?" I ask.

She doesn't answer right away and for a moment I think she's going to deny it, or lie, then she steadies herself. "Neelam and I used to date."

"She's your ex-girlfriend?" I ask, surprised.

"Yeah."

"Why'd you break up?"

Heather looks at me, mournful. "I died."

9

ᵻHROWING ᵻHE BONES

"**M**elted cheese is probably the best thing humankind has ever invented." Sam nabs another slice of cheese on toast off the plate beside his laptop.

We left Leonie sleeping upstairs, tucked under a quilt made in the colours of the bisexual flag, fairy lights strung overhead like stars. Burning through back-to-back theorems makes your bones feel like water and gives you a pounding headache as punishment. She won't wake up for hours.

Sitting at the table between Sam and Heather, Ollie snorts. "You can work magic but you think *cheese* is the pinnacle of human discovery?"

"No, I think *melted* cheese is the pinnacle of human discovery." Sam raises what's left of his slice in a salute. "Seriously, Mitch, this is what I call magic."

Setting up in someone's kitchen when they're passed out

upstairs should be weird, but there's no one else home today. Mr Agyemang is at work. Al, Leonie's younger brother, is at school and her older brothers are away at uni. Plus, Mitch has basically lived here for years so it feels normal. His own family don't give a crap about him.

I've half an eye on him as I stack dirty bowls and knives into the dishwasher. Normally he'd chime in about now to tell us that the perfect cheese on toast is all about sprinkling sage on top, or something. But he's silent as he swirls whipped cream on to a hot chocolate for Ollie.

Is he worried about Leonie? She'll be fine, she just needs a good rest.

"Oi." I nudge him. "You good?"

"Yeah, yeah, I need to text Chef that I'll be late in."

"Go now, we'll be all right."

He glances sideways at me. *Don't you want me here?*

Bollocks, I don't mean that. I'm not trying to push him or Leonie away again, I'm worried about his *job*. While most people our age are out with mates on the lash, he's working long hours in a hot kitchen cooking up fancy food, but he's going to *be* someone someday. Like Gordon Ramsey or Jamie Oliver.

Mitch can be a moody git sometimes, but he's been off lately whenever the restaurant comes up. Before I can ask him what's going on, he picks up his laden tray and makes for the table. He's brewed coffee for Heather and a big pot of tea for the rest of us. I'm not much into hot drinks but there are exactly two people in the world who can make a brew that I'll drink: my dad, and Mitch – milk, one sugar, not too strong but not like watery piss either. Perfect.

Maybe Mitch's old man is being a dickhead again. Mitch would talk to me about it, if he wanted to. Wouldn't he? We hang whenever he's free, mostly studying magic or sorting out ghost stuff. But sometimes we'll listen to music, binge a show on Netflix or bake. We work well together: he cooks, I clean.

Closing the dishwasher, I give the almost pristine kitchen a final once over and slide in on Sam's other side. He shuffles his chair closer to me, pressing his knee to my thigh.

Like exercise, cleaning keeps me calm. With the kitchen done, I've nothing to do but worry. Mitch isn't himself and the sight of Heather's glum expression makes me uneasy. She's been quiet since the hospital. I bet it has everything to do with running into Neelam.

On the way back to Leonie's, I pulled Ollie aside to ask if he'd known about them. "Oh, it's *her*!?" he'd said. "Blimey, I mean, I knew Heather had *someone*, but I thought it was another ghost. I never thought she was haunting an ex but it makes sense; it's not like she's good at letting go, is she?"

"She's not?"

"Er…" He'd flourished a hand at me. "Exhibit A."

And it all clicked into place for me. The mystery that is Doctor Heather Noble unravelled a little bit more. Every night Heather goes back to her old life to curl up beside the woman she loved – *loves*.

The woman she left because of me.

I should have trusted her.

We'll miss you around here.

No wonder Heather's been off these past few weeks – she's tethered to the hospital and can't leave the city. Manchester is over an hour away. When Neelam goes, she can't follow.

I hate that I feel a tiny bit of relief. It's selfish, but the idea of losing her is more than I can handle. I'm not daft. I know all my living mates will move away for uni, or work, one day. Yeah, I don't *have* to stay in York but the ghosts here need me, so I kinda do. I always reckoned Heather would be here too. As long as I've been a seer, she's been part of my life, like a big sister. What would I do without her?

Trying not to spiral, I anchor myself to the pressure of Sam's knee; the smell of cheese and chocolate; Ollie's smile as he watches the marshmallows on his drink sink into the whipped cream; Mitch pouring the brew and the sound of Villiers arriving in a flourish of silk and steel.

"Two dozen souls called Sophie and not one attired in white," he huffs, pacing the patch of floor by the window with its view on to the garden and the leafy quiet of York Cemetery. "I fear I owe Mister Broomwood an apology. I assumed he hath not fulfilled his pledge to search, but I declare that such soul doth not reside in this city."

With no trace of magic on JD's body, and no idea who he really was, we're no closer to working out what the hell is going on. Sadie Sudarma is the only useful lead we have. We're hoping there'll be some evidence where she died. Something magical the police missed because they can't see it.

Sam found a recent article about her in the *York Herald*. It's not much to go on but at least we know when and where she was found – a week ago, 2.30 p.m. The police reckon she was a hit and run victim dragged into a nearby abandoned property on King's Staith and left to die. No witnesses, no suspects.

Yeah, that's not what happened. Sadie was murdered by something spectral.

My gut instinct is that it's an angry, messed-up spirit, but the shadow entity's probably not a poltergeist released from a bottle trap, there would be much more collateral damage if it were.

Sam's dark hair is mussed. I want to wind my fingers in it. Instead, I polish off the rest of my cheese on toast. When in doubt, eat emotional support cheese.

Sam pulls out his phone and his expression brightens when he sees who's calling. The face that fills the screen a second later belongs to a cute lass, with large wide-set eyes, pale pink hair, and a new piercing on the bridge of her nose.

Leaning into Sam, I wave at her. "Hey, Miri, we need help breaking into a crime scene."

"Hmmm, business or pleasure?"

Miri and Sam connected in an online trans support group years ago and have become really good mates. She's helped him through a lot.

"Business," says Sam. "You get the article?"

Miri looks offscreen, probably at a laptop or tablet. "I did and I have a location, a property that's been empty for two years. Sadie was found upstairs, don't ask me how I know that. Sending you a pin."

Sam's phone buzzes. "How soon can you get us in?"

"Leonie needs a few days to recharge." Mitch blows on his brew to cool it.

"We don't have a few days," I huff, anxious. What if it attacks again?

"She'll want to come with and help give Sadie's family some closure if she can."

There's a framed photo of Leonie's mum on the sideboard. From the plumpness of Effia Agyemang's cheeks and her healthy smile, it must have been taken before she got sick. Her mystery illness resisted all treatments and slowly, steadily, stole her from her family.

I think of my Aunt Chrissie, fighting cancer, and of the meningitis that killed me as a kid. That's the thing about death. It sneaks up on you. Leonie knows what it's like to have someone she loves taken away with no real answers as to *why*.

Maybe that's why she wants to know the why and how of … well, everything. Maybe that's just how she is. Either way, she won't want Sadie's family to wonder what happened to their daughter the way she wonders about her mum.

"I'll need a couple of days anyway," says Miri. "Security is handled by a local firm. I'll find a backdoor into their system." She types something, her keyboard clattering. "Give me twenty-four hours. Once I'm in, I'll set off false alarms for the King Staith address day and night. I suggest you break in

Saturday. By then, they'll be so sick of seeing that flashing button they'll just cancel the alert."

"Will that really work?" I ask.

"Yes, but to ease your pretty little mind about it, Charlie, I'll find a way to remotely deactivate the alarm too."

"We owe you," says Sam.

"I know." Miri smiles sweetly. "I'll also dig into Sadie's digital footprint and see what I can exhume for you. Speak later, darlings, enjoy your illegal activities."

Waving, she ends the call.

"Breaking and entering again?" chimes a sweet sing-song voice.

Villiers lunges, whip quick. I startle, slipping sideways into Sam. Mitch spills his brew. We all swivel to face Viola, sitting prim and proper in the spare chair at the end of the kitchen table.

"My goodness." Raising her brows, she looks down the length of Villiers' freshly drawn rapier and bats the blade away like it's a pesky fly. "We *are* on edge today."

Flushing, Villiers bows to her. "Apologies, mistress."

Viola's nothing like a former occultist, at least none I've met. They all strode about with long dark coats and thunder in their eyes. Viola's vibrant, all puffy sleeves, tiny flower prints and old lace. With her neat waves and her pretty dress, she looks like she's going for a nice afternoon tea at Betty's. Her knowledge has saved us years of rooting through the occult section of every antique bookshop in York for something useful.

When Leonie got her part-time job at the shop, Viola was

one of the ghosts haunting the place. Apparently, Viola's not been there long, having recently broken her tether to the house in the suburbs where she grew up. I once asked her why she's chosen to haunt a bookshop and she just gave me a look like I'd asked her a trick question.

"A friend wanted me to read the bones for her." Viola taps the little silk purse she wears. "As soon as I heard the news I came right back. What happened? Tell me everything."

We do, starting with the morgue and what we discovered about Sadie and her thieving ways, then going back to the attack on JD and the modified wards.

"How is Leonie?" Viola asks.

"Worn out," says Mitch.

"You must be more careful; we can't have you all wilting when there's work to be done." She talks like she's our mum or something, but she's barely older than us. She died young. "Now, the shadow creature you describe sounds like a shade, it's a general term for a soul corrupted or controlled by magic. As for the wards, I presume Sam made a sketch?"

He flips to the right page in his pocket notebook and slides it down the table for her. "Leonie thought the perpendicular element might be indicative of a schism but the glyphs aren't consistent with any concordance we know."

Viola's brows snap together as she studies the modified theorem. "No, these are Ulrican, an auxiliary set of glyphs derived from the Lullian set. It's an alarm system, keyed into the primary resonance." She takes a moment, then shakes her head. "It's not subtly done but it's elegant, and effective. This theorem feeds off the original system, alerting whoever set it to your location if and when you use magic. My guess is they meant to confront you the next time you worked a theorem."

"But Leonie did and no one showed up," says Ollie.

"Perhaps they were delayed."

"Can you tell us who set it?" asks Heather.

"I have my suspicions but … let's confirm." From her little purse, Viola takes out the grisly collection of painted bones that she uses to read fortunes. They're her manifested object – singular, though there are eight of them, all different sizes and shapes and painted with tiny patterns.

Human carpal bones. Proper creepy.

First time I saw her "throw the bones" as she calls it, I asked how it works and got a lecture on astragalomancy as a niche branch of osteomagi. Proper confusing but I understood that magically speaking, bone is unique and excellent at holding and directing power. All I know is the knucklebones are a passive magic, tapping into the phantasmic essence that's naturally in everything around. Like Sam's herb mix, they don't need a soul source to work, though how Viola even begins to interpret the answers I've no idea.

Gathering the bones, she rattles them in her palm, whispers something under her breath and tosses them high over Sam's notebook. They fall and for a half-second it's as if the air catches and holds them. I blink and they're tumbling over the pages and wooden tabletop, settling into a map of the future.

We all lean in.

Viola chews on her bottom lip as she hovers a hand over

the table, going from one bone to the next, reading the signs. "As I suspected. This is the work of an old enemy. There are many practitioners who would have the depth of knowledge to make such modifications to your wards, but the use of the Ulrican auxiliary was developed by a particular group. Its presence is telling, and the bones confirm it."

"Good lady, hold us not in such terrible suspense," says Villiers, eager.

Viola looks pained. "The Hand, my darlings. This is the work of The Hand. They've finally returned to York."

10

WHAT REMAINS

"Everything all right, mate?" I ask Mitch as we stride side by side up the paved road winding through York Cemetery. We're not the only living visitors here today, but we are the only ones who expect the dead to talk back. It's a fair day, dappled sunshine but cold, the kind of weather that makes creepy places like this look peaceful.

The air is too still.

The Hand are back in York. I've been fizzing since yesterday, part excitement, part concern. Why haven't they already approached us? It's not like we're hiding. If they were our allies, they'd be puzzling things out with us, not sneaking around messing with our wards. They could be sussing us out before coming in with an offer, or something. If we talk to them, explain everything, then they could even tell us about mirroring—

"Yeah," says Mitch and I realize I asked him a question

then let my mind wander, which is a dick move. It takes me a second longer to clock that his "yeah" was proper unconvincing.

"You … want to talk about it?" I ask.

"About what?"

"Whatever's bothering you, because something is."

"Just restaurant stuff."

I leave the silence open and when he realizes I'm waiting on him, he shakes his head.

"Doesn't matter. We've got a murderous shade to deal with and dead bodies piling up."

I step in front of him, stopping us in the middle of the path. "Just because it's not about ghosts and that, doesn't mean it's not important. Look, you don't have to talk about it if you don't want to, but you're my mate. I care is all."

He ducks his head and nods.

"You not liking your apprenticeship?"

"I love it." He shrugs, looking out over the graveyard. "But we get coffee brought up at the start of every shift. I asked for a mocha and the sous chef took the piss, said it was *gay*. Who even uses 'gay' as an insult any more?"

"You told them you're pansexual?" I ask, surprised.

His laugh is dry and bitter. "God, no. They know about Leonie so they just assume I'm straight, and I let them because it's easier. But then I feel … invisible, and guilty because being straight passing is a kind of privilege. I should be standing up for the community, visible, like Sam is."

"Not if it's not safe you shouldn't," I warn.

He kicks a clump of turf. "I didn't even have the guts to go to Pride this year."

"Next summer we'll all go together, if you want," I offer. "Ghosts and all."

He nods. "Yeah, that would be good."

Being a trainee chef is pretty full on, but it's Mitch's dream. I don't want him to quit because of homophobic bullshit. He gets enough of that from his old man.

We start walking again. "I'm sorry you've got to deal with that crap. Can you talk to Chef? You said he's all right."

Mitch snorts. "Is Charlie Frith, king of 'I'll deal with it on my own' actually advising me to reach out for help?"

"Well, someone has to have a word with the lot of them. Imagine really thinking a mocha is the gayest beverage. That's an insult to the classic iced latte."

That scores a laugh.

We follow Ollie and Dante towards the chapel. It used to be a proud, Greek-style building until me and Sam accidentally set it on fire. What remains is a charred and blackened ruin. The site is surrounded by bright blue timber hoarding that blocks the destruction from view.

I keep well clear, standing back on the tarmac with Mitch as Ollie finds the ghost line, the invisible force field around the chapel that dead souls can't cross. He hammers his fists against it, pushing on the air. No matter how hard he tries, he can't get closer to the ruin than ten metres or so.

"Yeah, the closed cycle's still going," he calls. "Now can we get out of here before *she* shows up?"

"Gotta check the whole perimeter, mate."

A whispered Lord's Prayer floats on the wind.

"Ah crap," Mitch swears, probably debating if he wants to take his cryptolenses off.

"Here she comes," I warn.

"I'll protect you." Mitch pats my shoulder.

Slowly, a nun melts through the blue wooden hoarding. Her habit is pale grey, her eyes milky. She's not wearing a wimple and her shorn hair is patchy, blood glistening on her scalp. We're here every week to make sure the ghost line is intact and there's no risk she'll get out. She's a Hungry One so if she escapes, she'll come after me and Sam, attack and eat us.

Not fun.

"Hey, Agnes," I say, as casually as I can. I hate how fast my heart is beating. She scares the shit out of me. "How's ol' Sharp-Teeth doing? He coming out today?"

The other Hungry One trapped inside the line with her never comes out of the ruin. Ollie thinks Agnes drained his phantasmic essence out of spite and he's too weak to hold his ghostly form together. I think he's probably just sulking.

"Help me, please. My baby—" Agnes's voice catches, eyes pleading. She looks so pitiful, but I know better.

Mitch folds his arms. "We're not falling for that shit."

"Seer flesh and blood is a link to the living," she hisses.

"Yeah, we know," Ollie shouts at her as he feels along more of the ghost line. "But like Charlie tells you *every* week: it's not a cure-all for death. Remember that seer back in the early forties, the one you attacked and *ate*? Don't look so surprised, I've heard

90

the rumours. Everyone knows about it; you've got a reputation. You ate her. You're *still dead,* so what does that tell you?"

Needling broken fingernails against the air, Agnes starts to cry. "Please, Charlie. Charlie, let me out."

I couldn't even if I wanted to. I've no idea how the magic works. There's no mark on the gravel to show where the boundary is so I have to be careful not to cross it by accident. If I do, it won't end well for me.

Agnes's pleas become threats as we follow Ollie around the back of the chapel.

"In her research, has Leonie ever come across anything on how to join souls together?" I ask Mitch.

He hesitates. "Like … mirroring the way The Hand do?"

"Yeah, I mean, I know Viola says they're … dodgy, or whatever, but the actual mirroring sounds cool. Think about it, dealing with deathloops would be a doddle and Hungry Ones wouldn't be able to hurt me or Sam."

"That sounds dangerously like a restoration theorem," Ollie warns. Of course he's listening in. "Caleb Gates messed with The Hand's spells and traditions, so did Audrey— Sorry, Rachel, I always forget. Look how it ended for them. I wouldn't risk it."

He's right, but I'm just … *me*, and that isn't enough, especially now this shade is killing people. I'm sick of feeling like a failure all the time, of worrying that something will come for my friends and I won't have the strength or knowledge to fight it.

"You wouldn't want to pair up with me, then?" I yell back at Ollie, trying to keeping it light-hearted. "You could touch the physical world again, move with superhuman speed, maybe even drink hot chocolate?"

"Oh, well, yeah, obviously. Who gives a shit about backlash from a secret society of dangerous seers? I'd do it for the chocolate."

I actually have no idea if he's serious or not.

"You're really thinking about it?" asks Mitch, impossible to read as we step around gravestones Ollie can just float through.

It's my turn to shrug. "Not … I mean, we don't know how."

"But if you could?"

Yes.

"It would solve a few problems," I say, feeling the tips of my ears flush pink.

"You talked to Sam about this?" asks Mitch.

I stick my hands in my hoody pockets. "Nah, well … I mentioned it a couple of times over the summer, but he's dead set against it. Power corrupts ultimately … or something like that. I think it's because of Gates, you know, and the fact that Viola says they're a bunch of evil bastards, so I stopped mentioning it."

"You should tell him."

"It's not like it's gonna happen anyway, I don't want him to—"

Hate me.

I'm not ready to admit how much I want the advantage mirroring would give. Saying that I don't feel enough, that I feel weak and overwhelmed sounds way too much like fishing for compliments and I don't need empty reassurance. I need to *do* something.

"What?" asks Mitch. I realize I just stopped talking mid-sentence.

"I don't want Sam to worry is all. He's got enough to deal with."

We round the side of the chapel, Agnes trailing along on the inside of the line. She's quiet now, but still glowering like she can tear me apart through sheer will.

I shouldn't feel bad for her, she's a killer. Still, it must be boring being stuck here.

"Look, you want me to bring you some magazines or something?" I'm only half-joking. "I could read them to you, if you want."

In answer, Agnes spits at me but her saliva can't cross the ghost line any more than she can. Still gross.

"I dunno why you keep trying." Ollie shakes out his hands. Apparently touching the ghost line too long makes them tingle. "Some people won't change, even in the face of evidence."

Sister Agnes slams herself into the air, muttering angrily at someone behind me. Viola stands a little way down the path, staring at Agnes like she's seen her nightmare come to life.

The nun's nails scuttle at the air. "You look like someone I feasted on once."

Wrinkling her button nose in disgust, Viola sets her lips into a grim line. "Is she always this charming?"

"Yeah, Agnes is a real treat," I say. Viola looks proper uneasy, which is fair enough. The nun rattles most folks, dead and alive. "She can't really eat you, you know."

Taking a deep breath, Viola clutches her bone pouch against her chest. "I don't intend to give her the opportunity."

Sister Agnes bares her teeth.

Breaking eye contact with her, Viola tries on a smile and offers me her arm. "Boys, I need to speak to Charlie about his future. Give us a moment, would you? Don't worry, I'll return him in one piece."

As Mitch and Ollie head back to Leonie's house, Viola leads me to one of the mown side paths, heading deeper into the cemetery. Finding a quiet place, she climbs on to a tomb and sits cross-legged, patting the stone beside her.

I eye the spot warily. "You want me to sit on someone's grave?"

She looks back at the headstone. "I don't think he's going to mind."

"What's this about my future, then?"

Not like I have much of one.

What if I never pass my GCSEs and just keep having to retake them until some Hungry One puts me out of my misery?

I'm never going to be the academic type. I've got wards to deal with, a dangerous shade to find and The Hand to worry about.

And then what? Maybe she's about to tell me it's my destiny to be a cleaner or something. Actually, crime scene cleaner must be a job, and if I did that, I could help any souls lingering around their remains in the first few days.

Viola pats the slab again, a small, silent smile at the corner of her mouth. I give in and settle beside her. The grave is damp, not long since the last rain. A breeze plays through the trees, making them creak.

From her drawstring purse, she takes out her knucklebone set and passes them to me, like I'm a kid being shown the needle before an injection. Human wrist bones are a motley collection of shapes and sizes. The smallest is half the size of my thumbnail, but together they feel heavy in my palm. I give them back quickly.

"I threw the bones to discover what The Hand are doing here. There's only one mirrored pair, and they didn't come for the shade but to follow up on what happened to Dusan and Jan. They're interested in you."

I dig my nail into my knuckle. "They know about Liska?"

Her hand moves, grinding the bones in her palm against each other. The sound sets my teeth on edge. "Not your part in it, but they'll know he's dead. It was in the paper."

My skin prickles. Are we being watched right now? This is so overwhelming.

A scattering of browning leaves tumbles from the canopy. The breeze picks up, snaking around my neck. Shivering, I put my hood up and ask, "Why do you hate them so much?"

She blinks. "They're bad people."

"Yeah, you've said, but the only time I've met any of them they saved mine and Sam's lives so maybe they're not as—"

"They murdered me, Charlie."

"Oh, shit, wow…" What the fuck can I say to that? "Um … sorry."

Picking one of the bones off her palm, she turns it between her fingers. "Don't be sorry, be smart. My girlfriend, Edie, warned me not to trust them. I didn't listen and I lost her."

I swallow. It's kinda awkward to talk about, but I've got to ask. "What happened?"

Viola heaves a sigh and looks out over the gravestones. It's not that she's secretive exactly, not like Heather, I'm sure she tells Leonie all kind of things. But everyone has parts of themselves, or their past, that they keep locked up. I reckon The Hand is that for Viola.

"They came to York purely by chance," she says, voice almost a whisper. I lean closer to hear her. "They're largely nomadic so it was only a matter of time. My little coven had never heard of them. We were just a group of girls who longed for more than the world wanted to give us. Our magic was small, mostly passive and theoretical. Not a threat but—" She swallows. "There was a fire. I became a seer."

It takes me a second to process that. "Wait, you were a seer?"

How did we not know that? I guess because of all the mathemagics I had her down as a catcher type like Pete Rawley or Simon and Rachel Tussle, strictly an occultist.

"I was less prepared than you, and determined to understand what had happened to me," she goes on. "I'd not heard of seers or death-touched and I … got myself into trouble." We share a small smile. I know how easy it is as a seer to walk right into danger and not know it until it's too late. "Rachel Tussle helped me out – *yes*, I knew her, even considered her a friend for a time – but then The Hand found

96

out we knew one another. We seers are rare and they were desperate for me to join them, but they *hate* occultists because they trap the dead. But not *all* of them do. I refused to bow to The Hand's rules and in the end Meryem decided I was too dangerous—" Her lips pinch and she falls silent.

Meryem had her murdered, even though she was a seer.

"Do the others know?" I ask.

"Not yet." She's giving me this secret, but there's an edge to her voice, a warning.

"I won't tell them."

"Thank you."

Sunlight skirts the stone, swallowed by grey as the clouds roll in.

"You met Meryem, then?" I venture, knowing the answer already, but just wanting to keep her talking. She's never been this open with me before.

She nods. "It's inevitable that you will too."

"The bones tell you that?"

Another nod.

My breathing becomes shallow, fear or excitement, I'm not sure. Probably both. I can't believe The Hand killed Viola. If the bones are right then my path is leading me to them and that's terrifying, but if I can convince Meryem to work with us…

"Be careful, Charlie. Never trust her." Viola's tone is sharp, like she can read my mind. "Meryem's utterly convinced that she's correct, in *all* things. She's powerful, having been mirrored to countless seers over the centuries and her knowledge of the occult is unparalleled. Although she didn't found The Hand alone, she developed the three unbreakable seals—"

"Three *what*?" Viola's never mentioned any seals before.

"The magical foundation of their order." Viola pauses, as if deciding if she should tell me more. "The first seal severs. They use it to stop occultists tapping into soul sources, either their own or bottled souls. Just as ghosts can't use magic, neither can anyone sealed by the first seal. They can't even fuel magic. It's…" She shakes her head. "They survive, but there will always be something missing. They can never truly *live*."

"That's fucked up," I say.

"Meryem thinks it's the lesser of evils." Viola exhales. "The other two seals are used for binding souls together. The second is specifically used as the final step in mirroring."

I sit up straighter. "You know how mirroring works?" I ask, then wince, knowing I sound too keen but I can't let this go.

If what Viola says about The Hand is true I can't ever join an organization like that, and they're not going to share their secrets with me if I don't. They'd likely kill me first. But at night, in the dark, I remember the way Dusan merged into Liska, their eyes blazing sliver as they fought Gates with lightning-fast movements, levitating broken glass and stone, casting theorems against Gates.

I just want to pair up with one soul so that I can protect the people I love.

I need to keep them safe.

If Viola knows how—

"I don't know how mirroring works in any detail," Viola admits, puncturing my hopes. "But I know there are stages. First they carve a complex theorem into the seer's ribs—"

I wince.

"Yes, it's as comfortable as it sounds. That theorem opens the seer's body to possession, then the ghost they're mirroring with merges with them and the second seal is applied, linking them in a conterminous, mutually supporting bond until the seer's death."

"What about the third seal?" I ask. If Viola notices I'm sweating in the cold, she doesn't let on.

"As far as I know, it's only used in the rarest of circumstances. Once mirrored by the second seal, seer and ghost can separate, only coming together when they need to be at their toughest. With the third seal, there is no separating. Ever. Both souls are bound into one body for the duration of that body's life and the stronger takes control."

"You know *a lot* about The Hand."

A wry smile. "Know thy enemy."

God, we're so underprepared.

"So … between Meryem and the murdering shade, how fucked are we?" I ask.

"Leonie's shield charm is coming along nicely but…" Viola looks pained. "I'd tell you to lie low, however the bones have made it very clear it's too late for you to avoid this storm. I'm sorry for that and I'll do what I can to see you through." She covers my hand with hers. "I can see how much you care for your friends."

I do, and I owe it to them to make sure being part of my world doesn't get them killed. I feel like I just got Mitch and Leonie back.

Drops splatter from the canopy. Thunder rolls in the distance.

I blow out my breath, frustrated. "Before now ghosts couldn't touch Leonie and Mitch, I just had to worry about Sam and me. But that shade could kill us all. The Hand might too, when they catch up with us. And Sam, I've never met anyone like him and he's hurting and I'm worried that I won't be enough."

Why am I telling her all this? I clamp my mouth shut and pull my hand from hers. I should talk to Heather, she knows me better than almost anyone. But she's being weird and distant with me and I never realized Viola was so easy to talk to, or that I had so much to say.

Viola's smiling. "Love someone enough and you're capable of the worst things imaginable. You'll do anything to protect them. The same is true of loathing. Hate something or someone enough and you'll risk it all to tear them down. Loathing and love are terrible things. They seem like opposites, but they shape you the same way." She tilts her head softly, the gleam of sadness in her eyes. "I need you to remember that by the river."

"The river?"

"I rolled the bones for you all: Sam, Mitch, Leonie. I understand how they'll fit into things but *you*..." She sighs, clutching the knucklebones tightly. "The bones indicate the river, a terrible enemy and *you*. It ends at the river. I can't get a clearer reading than that, nothing that tells us exactly how it will all happen. But you're the heart, the crossroads where all the possible paths connect, your transformation is all but inevitable if we are to scourge York of this darkness—"

"Transformation?" I ask, shaking my head. That sounds well dramatic. "Look, I'm barely holding it together here—"

"Last spring, you saved York's ghosts from a deadly multiloop. Now the living are being killed unfairly and before their time. York needs you."

Need. Something about that lights a fire in me; it's good to be needed and, yeah, here in York I've a task for life. Some kids inherit their family business, I get ghosts. Fair enough, at least that's something, for all it's hard and scary and more than I can handle most of the time. It's my responsibility. I took that on, and I'll own it.

"What about Sam? Does he … I mean, do we stay together?"

A heavy raindrop hits my cheek and rolls, making me look up into a face full of rain. The sky grumbles again and the light smattering quickly turns into a downpour.

"Oh, drat," says Viola, leaping up as if the wet can mess with her curls. Instead, the droplets sail through her to strike the stone slabs at her feet.

It's only when we're back at Leonie's that I realize Viola never answered my question about Sam and me. Maybe it's for the best.

II

KING'S STAITH

"Nice quoins," says Ollie.

I gaze at the fancy house that matches the address Miri gave us. "Nice what?"

"The stone frame around the windows. It's a popular detail in York's architecture from early seventeen hundred."

How does he remember this stuff?

The building where Sadie's body was found is elegant but it looks worse for wear; red brick pitted by centuries of weathering and, being right on King's Staith, probably a fair few floods. According to Miri, it was a lawyer's office until a few years ago. Before then, the council had it, but it was built way back by a wealthy tanner and brewer.

Cumberland Street slopes towards the river, meaning the front part of the basement is exposed. Heavy grilles stop anyone climbing through. One of the openings is partly blocked by a plant but the other is clear. I get close, squinting inside—

—and lurch back as a wet hand tries to grab me.

"Whoa, that's grim," says Ollie.

The cellar is full of drowned ghosts, their skin puckered and bloated, hair slick against their skulls. Some of them look to have blended into each other. Water does weird things to the dead.

I curse, willing my heart to stop racing but Viola's warning echoes through my skull.

It ends at the river.

I've not told anyone what she said, not even Sam, and I don't plan to. It's a lot to process.

"They must have washed in when the river flooded and somehow got stuck," says Mitch warily. He should be at the restaurant but one of the lads in the kitchen made a homophobic joke so he put down the veggies he was peeling and walked out.

He could lose his placement, but he's determined, says he'll make a formal complaint to the college. He's got balls that lad. Still, he doesn't look keen to get any closer to the cellar.

They say a river is the lifeblood of a city. In York, it's the city's soul. The waters are a mass of dead, thousands of wan faces blurring, their hands grasping through the surface, edges undefined. The river is greedy, swallowing the souls of everyone who's drowned over the centuries.

When I first saw the ghosts in the water, I thought they were looped but Mrs Tulliver told me they're only tethered, tied to the river and each other in a way no one really understands. A few wander the banks, glassy-eyed and dripping, but their leash is short.

They scare the hell out of me, if I'm honest. I once saw them pull a free soul in, dragging her deep when she strayed too close. The river keeps what it takes, so I'm always nervous this close to the bank.

"No access into the upper floors anyway." Sam is closer to the cellar than I'd dare get, but he's faster on his feet.

"Side door it is," says Heather.

"I need to be back at the bookshop in an hour," Leonie reminds us.

The door on Cumberland Street is draped with a sagging strand of police tape. With the pub right across from it, it's as exposed as the unused front door on the Staith. There is no "round the back" so it's this way in, or nothing.

Leonie and Mitch wait a little up the way because a group of us hanging about would look suspicious. Sam messages Miri. She's been setting the alarm off all night. As predicted, the security firm in charge of the place isn't bothering to send anyone out any more, they just shut it off and reset. She'll set it off now and we'll get three minutes to break in before it arms again.

"Annnnd ... *go*," says Sam, pulling the crime scene tape off the door and bundling it inside his jacket.

Picking the lock would be easier with a proper kit but, if we're ever caught, a couple of bent hairpins are easier to explain away than a set of professional tools. Plausible deniability.

"You in yet?" asks Sam.

"Gis a sec," I say, twisting one pick and hearing the second to last pin fall into place. My hands are sweating. Almost there. If we don't get in, or if there's nothing here to find, then we've got shite to go on. Maybe the shade's done it's work. Or maybe it's just getting started.

Sam rocks on his feet, nervous. "One minute gone."

Heather hisses my name. Voices echo from the corner. Someone is about to come past and bust us. I've almost got it.

"Hold on," I say.

Hands on my hoody, hauling me up. Sam spins me about, pushes me back against the door I'm supposed to be breaking into and kisses me. Hard.

Oh.

Wow.

Not complaining.

Laughter. Sam tilts his head and I semi-open one eye to see a bunch of drinkers migrating from the pub opposite. Someone wolf-whistles, but they keep moving.

"Seriously?" asks Ollie when we break apart.

Sam looks up the street after the group. "It worked, didn't it?"

I stand there, probably with a right daft look on my face because that was … yeah. Heather winks at me. Clearing my throat, I get back to work on the lock as Ollie mutters something about, "any excuse".

Twenty seconds left.

Sam gets Leonie and Mitch's attention and they hurry our way.

Fifteen seconds.

The last pin is giving me trouble. If someone else interrupts us, we're done.

Ten.

The pick levers up, the pin drops into place and the lock clicks open. We're in. On the other side is a short entrance hall with steps leading up to a second door.

Five seconds.

Mitch and Leonie slip through and we shut the door just in time. According to Miri the alarm is on the top right of the front door. Now we're in, we're safe until we want to leave.

Inside, the main building smells of damp river and stale air. Sunlight leaks through dirty windows, dust shimmering in the dull beams. Behind the broken office furniture and ugly fluorescent strip lighting is the skeleton of a beautiful house.

"This place is huge." Leonie's voice echoes up a grand staircase that spirals all the way to the top floor.

I wince. Seriously, are we not going to whisper?

Then again, there's no one else here except the dead. A place this old is likely to be haunted. Let's hope the residents are friendly, because Villiers is off with Reid preparing a rousing election speech and Leonie's on strict instructions from Viola not to use any magic. She really shouldn't be up and about, let alone back to work or helping us out here, but she insists she's all right and she's even more stubborn than Sam.

Heather pokes her head through the open door to our left. The large front room is mostly empty except for some mismatched desks and discarded office chairs.

Sam's lips catch a smile. "This place would be incredible if it was renovated."

Movement above. A young-ish bloke in a periwinkle-blue frock coat and waistcoat floats down the stairs. My heart plummets. Kill me now. Anyone but him.

"How marvellous, you've seen reason." Periwinkle catches sight of Leonie and Mitch and his beaming smile stretches into something strained. "And you brought friends. Well, more hands make light work, as they say. Now, you'll have to use your imagination but I think delicate brocade in a blue-grey for the parlour—"

"The deathloop upstairs," I interrupt, remembering what he said back at Grape Lane. "Is it … new?"

A tense silence. Periwinkle narrows his eyes in suspicion, then his face breaks into an even wider grin. "Of course, excellent thinking. You *must* rid us of that first. It really is an intrusion having her here." He straightens his cuffs. "It will be impossible to properly sample colours in the upper front room with her lurking about the place, especially the way she looks. Dreadful. You'd better follow me, careful on the steps."

I hate stairs at the best of times, but here there are uneven treads, trailing wires, and mouldering carpet stinking with damp. Rotting wood creaks under our weight.

"That doesn't sound good," says Mitch, pressing against the wall.

"Keep to the edges," advises Heather. She and Ollie are right behind us. "One wrong move and you could go straight through the floor."

"Oh, I implore you not to damage the house further," says Periwinkle. "My heart couldn't take it."

"Mate, if the floor goes then *we're* the ones in trouble," I say, irritated. "You can just levitate."

Periwinkle puts a hand to his chest with a little gasp. "To have to float in one's *own* home."

Back pressed to the wall, Mitch edges up another step. "Oh, perish the thought."

Ollie turns his laugh into an awkward cough as we all follow Periwinkle on to the first-floor landing.

The deathloop is in the front room overlooking the river. I sense it before I see it, which is rare for me. Sam tenses and I know he feels it too.

"Spidey senses tingling?" asks Ollie.

"Just a bit." My breath mists, the air catching halfway out my lungs. Thick trails in the dust at the top of the stairs show where a fair few people have marched through here.

I can't help remembering the cracking ozone scent of the multiloop beneath Harrow house. Whatever we face today, it can't be as bad as that.

Wary, we move inside the front room, smelling dust, old wood and something cold and sterile that doesn't fit with the age of the building.

"Careful," whispers Heather.

Leonie gasps and Mitch almost whips off his cryptolenses as a young Southeast Asian lass with long dark hair, heavy eye shadow and dark red lips, materializes three metres from us.

Sadie.

I recognize her from the article. Here, her neck and limbs are broken, shoulder dislocated, chest misshapen where ribs stick out of her torn clothes. There's a devil on her chest, a printed T-shirt of some ancient evil. When she opens her mouth, blood spills over her lips. Fear in her eyes, and something else that scares me.

"I went to the theatre for the evening," says Periwinkle from the doorway. "When one's abode is decrepit, one finds other places to be. My friends and I returned to this."

I imagine the police zipping Sadie into a body bag, taking photos of the scene, sampling blood and fibres, all the while her soul is still right here, terrified and trapped.

Except.

Sam edges around her at a safe distance. "Charlie, do you see that?"

"Yeah." I can see *through* Sadie to the peeling plaster and half-shuttered windows. Ghosts are never transparent, not even the looped ones. There's something wrong with her deathloop. I blink fast and rub my eyes, as if that will fix the problem. It doesn't. What the hell is going on?

Leonie flicks her cryptolenses up to see the room without them, then slides them back on. "I can hardly see her."

"Same," says Mitch. "She's an echo of an echo."

First JD's ghost vanishes and now Sadie's loop is odd.

"Heather, any ideas?" I ask.

She looks as puzzled as the rest of us. "Outside influence maybe?"

We know one thing. Whoever, or whatever, killed JD also

murdered Sadie so we need to understand what happened to her. The answer lies inside her loop. If we can free her, then she can tell us what she remembers. If we can't, I'll still witness her death inside the loop and learn something.

Sam knows what I'm thinking, I can see it in his eyes. "I'm coming with you."

It's his choice, but I want to tell him no. He's not ready. I say that and he'll be pissed. He'll tell me he's fine even if he's not.

"You sure?" I ask, all I allow myself.

A hint of hesitation, but then he nods.

"You guys are—" Mitch blows out his breath, lacing his fingers behind his head. "Look, we'll be here if you need us."

Leonie's smile is tight but encouraging. If things go really wrong I trust them to get us out in time.

"Ready?" I'm asking everyone, but mostly Sam. Bracing myself, my hand slips into his, criss-crossing our fingers and holding tight.

"Think those happy thoughts," says Ollie, giving us a double thumbs up.

Sadie's bones crack and pop. My mouth is dry. I wish we'd brought water with us.

"Godspeed," says Periwinkle, his eyes shining.

Sam squeezes my hand.

"Die, and I'll be so pissed at you," warns Heather.

In. Free the ghost. Out. Simple as.

What could possibly go wrong?

12

BLACK MIRROR

The light changes first. Cool day makes way for warm lamplight streaking through the front windows on to worn carpet and flaking walls. It smells of damp without the blood and the bleach. Everything is quiet except the sound of my panicked breathing.

Fear is a solid tangle in my chest. I fight the urge to freeze. What comes next is going to hurt, but we have a job to do.

We.

Sam.

Sam?

He's not here. I'm alone. He definitely walked in with me so either something went wrong and one of the others pulled him out right away, or he's lost here with me. I call his name. Nothing.

"Help him sit against the wall." Heather's voice echoes

around me. "Sam, you're safe. Mitch, keep an eye on Charlie. If he looks distressed, pull him out."

Something's different.

Although I'm still *in* the loop I'm aware of the real world. Usually, I lose that. Whatever's happening, Sam's out. I'm here alone.

I could die.

No, my mates won't let that happen. I have to keep my focus.

A young woman climbs the stairs, nervous and tearful. She's carrying a small duffel with worn red handles.

"Sadie," I whisper, focusing on her. She looks so alive. It breaks my heart.

Checking her watch, she crosses to the windows in the front room, peering down at the Staith. If I stand any chance of getting an emotional reading, I need to get closer. When I'm behind her, she shivers, like I'm the one haunting her.

C'mon, Sadie, tell me how you feel.

She's meeting someone and she's afraid. And sad. So much sadness.

Scrambling in her pocket, she pulls out something that looks a bit like a magnifying glass. The short handle is wooden, but instead of a clear lens the black surface is polished mirror smooth. Holding it up, she catches her reflection but not mine. 'Course not. I'm not really here.

There's a flash of movement in the mirror, a sudden jerking motion that makes me jump. Quickly, she turns the dark glass with shaking fingers, angling it to look into every corner.

There – a skeletal face and glowing eyes engulfed in wreaths of smoke. Scattered shadows flit around it as it settles to sniff the air like a hound after blood. My tight breathing matches hers.

Fuck. Fuck. FUCK.

She drops the bag and tries to run. The shadow entity, invisible to me now that I'm not looking at its reflection, catches her midway to the stairs. She claws at the air, fighting as blood blooms around her mouth. Like something is levering open her jaw, trying to get in. I taste iron and spit blood. Bone cracks. She screams and thick inky shadows slide down her throat. She grasps at the shadows, fighting for breath. A tendril wraps around her hand and wrenches her finger back.

Sharp agony flares through my hand and I feel a pop. I bellow in pain.

From somewhere Heather shouts, "Get him out!"

An arm hooks through mine and I'm hauled into the daytime. Mitch holds me up as I drag in deep breaths and my vision settles. "You with us, mate?"

"I saw it." I wipe blood from my lips. My little finger pulses and I suck the air, trying to still my shaking. "I saw it."

But what the hell is it? Having seen it up close, I'm not so sure it's Caleb Gates. There's something about it that feels … ancient.

Sadie's looped soul is now so transparent she's just an outline. That's not the only thing that's off. Deathloops are cold. I should be chilled to the bone, proper frostbitten. Instead, I'm chilly at best. Somehow, that makes this more sinister *because it makes no sense.*

The strange pressure of the deathloop lifts. The last of Sadie's outline fades and she's gone. *Really* gone.

Sam moans. He's crouched against the wall, his breathing laboured like every gasp of air is some gargantuan effort. Ignoring the throb in my finger, I scramble over to him. "Hey, love?"

"It's a dream, just a dream." His breathing picks up. I've been where he is. He feels like the walls are crushing in and every part of him is washed with terror. I knew he wasn't ready to face a deathloop. I should have said something.

"No this *is* real." I gesture to our living and dead friends. "You're here with us."

He shakes his head. "You're *hurt*."

I hold up my sore hand. "Just a sprained finger."

"Broken," mutters Heather.

"OK, broken, but it's just the little one, look. I'm fine. Promise."

Sam squeezes his eyes closed and tears roll down both cheeks.

"Love, hey, look at me." I make my voice as even and measured as I can. "What helps you feel calm?"

He gasps a few quick breaths, eyes focused on my lips. "Painting."

Sam's notebook is sticking out of the front pocket of his jacket. That will have to do. I pull it out, flipping to a clean page. Leonie passes me a pen and I press it into Sam's hand.

"Draw instead," I say. "Can you do that for me?"

Nodding, he starts, shaky at first. I half-think he's going to give up when that narrow crease appears between his eyes, the one that means he's really focused. He's calmer, breathing evenly. Some of the tension in my shoulders releases. My finger really hurts but I tuck the pain away. I can handle it.

After the first sketch, Sam tries another, and a third. By the time he finishes the fourth he's not shaking any more. He looks up at me from under his mess of curls, eyes red-rimmed. "I'm sorry."

I press my forehead to his. "Hey, don't apologize for weird ghost shite, remember?"

When I look down, all of his sketches are of me.

My finger's swelling nicely but the break isn't that bad. I can splint it myself when we get home. Heather isn't happy about that, but we've bigger things to worry about and we have to move. For a start, Leonie needs to get back to the bookshop.

I try not to crowd Sam as we head downstairs because I know he hates the fuss, but I'm aware of every movement he makes. Periwinkle follows, congratulating us on a ghost loop vanquished. "Oh, to be able to entertain here again. We used to have the loveliest soirées—"

"You haven't seen a bag in the house, about yay big?" I mime the size and shape. "A duffel with red straps?"

Caught mid-flow, Periwinkle swallows the rest of his sentence. "I'm afraid not."

No bag means it was likely picked up by police and is currently sitting in evidence and out of our reach. Unless—

"How long were you at the theatre that night?"

Periwinkle thinks on my question. "Three hours at most."

"And no bag when you got back?"

He shakes his head. "Just the girl and her loop."

I wince, but not because of my finger. "Then someone else was here."

This wasn't a random attack. Sadie was a target just as much as JD was and someone did this, not a ghost or shade working on their own. Someone living.

An occultist.

Shit.

My stumps change shape through the day and the fit isn't the same as it was this morning. I need to take off a layer of compression on my left side. I'd rather wait until we're someplace familiar, but I've got to deal with it now. Sitting on the bottom step, I get the pins unlocked and manage to pull my left prosthesis off one-handed, sighing with relief as the ache eases.

"Who was here?" asks Sam.

"Dunno." I pull off the compression sock. "But Sadie was meeting someone. Whoever it was probably took the bag with them after their shade killed her."

Mitch leans on the banisters. The carved wood creaks dangerously and he rights himself. "What do we think was in the bag?"

"I'm going to bet stolen bones," says Ollie with a shrug.

"Was she stealing them for someone else then?" wonders Leonie.

"She was scared," I say, putting my prosthesis back on. Much better. "Maybe she didn't want to steal the bones but had no choice. Whoever she was meeting could have been threatening or blackmailing her to do it."

"And then they killed her to keep her quiet," says Sam, voice hard with anger.

"How dreadful!" exclaims Periwinkle.

Magically speaking, bone is unique.

Sadie steals a bunch of ancient bones and then turns up dead, killed by a shade. Yeah, not a coincidence. But what's in it for the occultist? Money? Power?

"We need to figure out what the bones are for before someone else gets hurt." Tucking the dirty compression sock into my pocket, I dig out some ibuprofen to take the edge off my broken finger. I've no water, but I manage to swallow a couple of tablets dry. "Sam, can I borrow your sketchbook?"

He hands it over, along with the pen. I'm no artist, but I draw the big magnifying glass object Sadie was holding. "She used this like a mirror to check behind her for the shade. She tried to run but—" I go quiet. I don't want to sink back into that memory.

"That *is* a mirror." Ollie makes a face at my terrible drawing. "Ancient Egyptians made them from polished copper, bronze or silver, sometimes they had figures of gods on the handle."

"This one was plain," I say, "And it wasn't metal. Stone maybe, or some kind of darkened glass."

"The oldest mirrors ever found were made from obsidian," says Leonie.

I know that stone. Last spring, Sam's dad used spelled obsidian globes to move a deathloop. "That can affect ghosts, right?"

"It has strong phantasmic properties, yes," says Sam.

"Charlie, you said the mirror *reflected* the shadow shade." Leonie chews on her lip, uneasy. "If obsidian mirrors have been around for thousands of years, then maybe they're a precursor to cryptolenses, the ancient way our ancestors saw ghosts."

Mitch sighs. "Well, it's not here now so whoever took the bag probably also took the mirror, right?"

"Yeah. And left Sadie to rot," I add darkly.

13

STICKS, STONES AND BROKEN BONES

We call it a day. Leonie goes back to the bookshop. Mitch gets a text from Chef and heads off to smooth things over at the restaurant. I tell him to call us if he needs backup. Me, Sam and our ghosts retreat to Grays Court.

When we arrive, the yard is packed with soldiers of the Ninth Legion Hispania, The Sixth Legion Victrix and assorted deceased citizens of Eboracum. Armour gleaming, they line up for inspection before their usual march around the grounds of The Treasurer's House next door. Through them, new guests are unloading fancy suitcases from a swanky car. It makes my head spin.

Actually, that could be the pain in my finger. It's not feeling great now the adrenaline is wearing off.

A Roman soldier halts us as we head inside. He looks a bit frazzled. "Have you seen Lucius and Octavian?"

"Sorry, no," says Sam.

"Oh, bother. They're late."

Muttering apologies, we head upstairs towards Sam's room. Heather and Ollie trail after us, talking about shades and obsidian mirrors and missing bags.

I just walked in a deathloop for the first time since the multiloop, on my own, and I'm not dead. Yeah, it was a weak and half disintegrated one but, still, I'm kinda chuffed.

Everything else though – the bag, the bones, the shade – *fuck*.

Poor Sadie. No one deserves to die like that. The bones are a real lead, though. If we can find them, we might find who's behind this.

Voices sound along the corridor. I recognise Lucrezia's velvety tones and a second voice – another woman. Grabbing my shirt, Sam hauls me through the nearest doorway, pushing me against the bookcase inside the door.

"Wha—" I stammer. His lips are close to mine but I don't reckon *that's* why he dragged us in here. Still, while we're…

Behind us, someone clears their throat.

The room – some kind of lounge for the hotel's guests – is packed with ghosts. Roderick, the Elizabethan barman from The Snickleway Inn, is standing in front of the fireplace, looking surprised. His audience all swivel to stare at us.

Sam steps away from me, blushing. Mrs Tulliver, the former landlady of The Snickleway Inn, gives us a merry wave, her old cat Seamus draped sleepily over her shoulders. She's sitting with a cluster of ladies, including the lady of the house, Faith Gray.

"Seers, you are very welcome, indeed." With a fine woollen shawl wrapped over a muslin dress, Lady Faith looks like she's stepped out of the Jane Austen movies my mum and Aunt Chrissie love. "Roderick was just reciting a fine sonnet of his own composition."

We've rudely barged into poetry night. Very smooth.

"Er, we can't stay," I stammer as my finger throbs. We'd leave, but the door is blocked by Ollie and Heather.

"It's just your mu—" Heather shudders as Lucrezia and her companion stride right through her and Ollie.

Ollie makes a face. "I hate it when they do that."

"Nothing here," declares a middle-aged white woman with long dyed blonde hair, heavy lipstick and dark arched brows. "I'm certain the presence is strongest in your suite, Lucrezia."

Mrs Harrow is smart in all black, a small hat with a net veil half-obscuring her face. She looks like she's going to a funeral.

It clicks who the other woman is. Claire Cole. She's wearing an extravagant dress threaded with gold that wafts around her as she trails ring-adorned fingers over the corner of a nearby armchair. The ghost sitting in it – a wealthy gent in a black doublet and hose – eyes her suspiciously.

Nothing here? I bark a laugh born from pain and irritation. All it does is turn Claire's piercing eyes on me and Sam.

"*Mi amore*, whatever are you doing here?" Lucrezia asks Sam. From the look on her face, she thinks we snuck in to snog behind the door.

Unfortunately not.

The medium offers her palm and I take it, thankful that my broken finger is on my left hand. We shake and she doesn't let go. "It's wonderful to meet you, Charlie, is it?"

"Yeah."

Her accent is generic south of England, bland and breathy. It makes me itch. "I've heard that you also have a natural connection to the dead."

Define natural.

"I … guess."

The twenty odd ghosts in the room are watching us with a mixture of annoyance and amusement.

"I too have a divine connection, Charlie. I've seen through the veil since I was a child." Claire's smile lifts slightly on one side, like she has a secret. There's a sliver of cream peeking out from beneath the high neck of her collar. A chunky necklace, maybe? "Do lost souls seek you out, Charlie?"

Why is she saying my name all the time? I already know she's talking to me. I wish she'd let my palm go because this is getting weird.

What if she's from The Hand?

I pull away so fast she gasps, taken aback at my rudeness.

"S-sorry, static shock," I say, which is total bollocks but I'm not touching her any more, which is a blessing.

I'm being daft. She walked through Ollie and Heather, so she's not a seer and she can't be with The Hand. I'm getting paranoid.

Claire smiles and wrinkles her nose in a way I'm sure she

thinks is cute. "Sometimes my power can be overwhelming," she tells Lucrezia.

"Is she serious?" asks Ollie. He looks at Claire, looks at us and then starts "wooooooing" in her ear.

No reaction.

Sam's told me all about this type of spiritualist. If they predict something right, it's because they're a powerful psychic. If they get it wrong, then the spirits were feeling shy that day, or the client didn't part with enough cash for them to make a connection.

Poor Roderick looks pained. Poetry night can't continue with us yammering on back here. "We should go, we're interrupting poetry night for the dead."

Claire gives Lucrezia a tense glance, then blinks hard as she plasters on a fake smile. "You are mistaken. There are no lingering spirits here."

Sam snorts unkindly. "Are you seriously trying to gaslight my boyfriend? He can literally *see* them."

Claire's lips tighten, as do the thin lines around her eyes. She's pissed off.

"There's being a little bit wrong and then there's missing…" I lean around her to count. "… twenty—" Mrs Tulliver clears her throat. "Sorry, twenty-one ghosts, including Seamus. He's a cat."

Sam shakes his head. "That's just *embarrassing*."

As we pass Claire, heading for the door, she lets out a little gasp. "Charlie, the energy coming from your heart space…"

"Save it," I snap. "You're a fraud."

A mischievous grin plastered on his face, Ollie reaches up and ruffles my hair.

Eyes widening, Claire Cole takes a step back as the door closes behind us.

The curtains in Sam's room are drawn and the heater is on.

"You all right?" I ask him as soon as the door's closed.

He throws his coat over the chair. "Mother will soon move on to a magical chakra water that balances your hormones or vibrating stones that summon ley lines and Claire will be gone."

At least neither of them brought up Sam's dad again.

Wrapped up in the smell of sandalwood soap and oil paint, I just want to retreat under the covers, but there's no chance of that. We need to find out more about this shadow shade, see if we can work out what it wants, or what the person who created it wants.

Heather and Ollie didn't follow us, so we can't have a Team Spectre meeting, but there's still my finger to fix. Sam watches as I feel around the swelling, sucking in my breath as the pain spikes. Nothing grinds, and the finger isn't wonky.

"It's a clean break," I say. "We can splint it with a lolly stick."

Sam riffles through his art supplies. "The best I can offer is a pencil. You seem like an HB kind of a guy."

Sam keeps medical tape and other first-aid supplies in the bedside table. Drawing back the curtain for better light,

I direct him to place the short pencil along the outer edge of my injured pinkie. While he gently tapes it in place I hold as steady as I can, breathing in the smell of his hair and counting the freckles on his cheeks to distract me.

"I ... had a letter from the clinic." There's a hopeful note to his voice as he smooths the tape round my nail, making sure there's nothing to snag. "They've set a date for my top surgery."

"Really?" Finally, some good news. "When?"

This must be what he wanted to talk about at dinner and I'm so bloody chuffed for him. I can't stop grinning.

"The end of January next year." His expression is full of everything all at once – hope, fear, anticipation. "I can't go through the recovery here, it's not practical." He suddenly looks very tired. "I was worried. Without a house I might have to push the date back—"

That can't happen.

"Hell no, you've been waiting months." I decide right then that I'll speak to Mum and Dad. Sam can move in with us for a few weeks. He can have my bed. I'll sleep on the blow-up mattress on the floor. I can take care of him. "We'll work something out—"

"I don't want to impose so I've actually—"

"No arguments, OK. I'm your boyfriend." I'm not having him get stuck in that whole bullshite of feeling like a burden. "Look, I've been watching all these videos on YouTube about how to be a good caretaker after top surgery. You're not alone in this, Sam, I'll look after you."

As he hears the promise in my voice, whatever he was going to say next falls away. "You mean that?" he whispers.

"Yeah, I fucking mean it."

The look on his face is the kind of thing that people cross oceans for. Suddenly his brow falls and he's close to tears. "I'm really sorry I left you in the loop alone."

"Sam, don't."

"You got *hurt*."

"Not because of you."

"You talk to them and I help ground you." He folds over the end of the tape so that it's not lost on the roll. "I left you in there alone. I let you down—"

"Nope," I say firmly. "If you're just going to be a dick to yourself then you can shut up, Harrow." I hate how he second guesses himself all the time now. He used to be stubborn, passionate and confident to the point of being a cocky prick. He still is, sometimes, but it's tempered. "You shouldn't have gone in at all. I knew it, and I didn't say anything because I can't tell you what to do."

"You literally *just* told me to shut up."

"I'm a complex person, me."

He laughs, but it's a sad chuckle. "I'm sorry, I just … watching you face it without me brought everything back. Sometimes I—" He falters. "Sometimes, I dream that you die." He can't meet my eyes. "The nightmare always starts the same. I'm back at the house, but it's not my house any more, it's a field full of corpses. All the bodies have your face and your ghost is gone. You didn't stay with me and there's nothing I can do to save you."

I dig under the pile of books on the coffee table for one of his clean handkerchiefs, cup his chin as best I can with my sore hand and blot his tears. More of them fall, faster and faster.

He sniffs. "Sorry, that sounded profoundly creepy, didn't it?"

"The first time we met, you stalked me through York. Creepy is your general baseline." I wink. "It's a real turn on."

A watery laugh. I kiss his cheek, then rest a forehead against his temple and look down at his handkerchief. It's monogrammed.

They haven't found a new place yet, but Sam took the time to buy embroidered handkerchiefs. Why am I so surprised? The lad wears cravats and bowties most days. Honestly, that just makes me fall for him even harder.

I don't think he realizes I'm always having an internal breakdown over everything he does. It's not normal to be this into someone, is it? I know it's a leftover thing from a couple of months ago when I had to worry about him every waking moment and looking after him was all consuming.

PTSD isn't something you just get over.

But he's improving. I don't have to obsess over each small expression any more, or the way he holds a spoon, or paint brush, or how I really like his hands. I think I like them as much as he hates them. They really get to him – he thinks they're too slender and delicate, which is why they're usually shoved in his pockets – but to me they're strong. An anchor to grasp when I feel like I'm spiralling.

Sam is so much to lose.

He's afraid of *me* dying and I'm afraid of *him* dying, and that might legit happen. Not in some distant future when we're two old men winding each other up in an old folks' home, but tomorrow. All it'd take is the wrong ghost, at the wrong time.

If I mirrored with Heather, or Villiers, or any one of our ghost friends I could keep us all safe. According to Viola my path and The Hands' are destined to cross. So, I convince them to show me their secret second seal, or I find another way. I bet Leonie could do it; she's great with difficult theorems.

Mirroring. It always comes back to that.

But what would I become?

It would be worth it. For him.

For the second time in a few days I feel myself choking back the words, "I love you."

I want to say it, but … no, not yet. I can't.

"Sam?" I lean back and he looks up, expectant. "Kiss me?"

He meets me halfway and time stops. It sounds cliché, but that's how it feels. Everything else melts until it's just me and him and the beam of sunlight we're sitting in.

Someone clears their throat. Villiers and Reid are hovering in the doorway.

"Apologies, masters," says Villiers. "Mistress Noble hath informed us of poor Sadie's fate and your encounter with the fiend. We came to suggest you speak with Master Buckle."

I know him. Marmaduke Buckle, died at eighteen and used to haunt the house next to The Snickleway Inn before he broke his tether and went off on a bit of a tour. A couple of months ago he came back home and Mrs Tulliver introduced us. I've not seen him since he went up Whitby way.

"He hath seen something similar to this shadow fiend you speak of," says Reid.

Sam wipes his eyes. "Really?"

"Aye, he hath agreed to meet you upon the morrow."

I exchange a hopeful glance with Sam. We need answers.

"Thanks for setting that up," I say. "Villiers, how's your speech coming?"

Throwing his short cape over one shoulder, he titters. "As you know I am a *superb* spokesman. When negotiating the union of His Royal Majesty King Charles and Queen Henrietta, I enchanted the entire French court with my superior wit."

It's Reid's turn to clear his throat.

"However," Villiers goes on, "after some pertinent … critiques from Mister Broomwood, I have revised my address. Perhaps thou wouldst do me the honour of hearing it?"

Sam slides to the floor and leans back against the side of my armchair. "Go ahead."

As Villiers starts to speak, I slip my fingers through Sam's curls.

Love someone enough and you're capable of the worst things imaginable. You'll do anything to protect them.

Viola's right.

I'll do anything.

14

MARMADUKE

Marmaduke meets me, Sam, Mitch, Heather and Ollie outside a café on the corner of High Petergate.

"All right, mate?" I ask as he crooks one of his crutches under his elbow to shake my hand. "How was the coast?"

"Cold and damp," Marmaduke chuckles. He's got a prominent jaw under ruddy cheeks, his fuzz of strawberry blonde hair messy in contrast to his neat, finely made clothes, linens gleaming white. In life, his family had plenty of brass.

It's cold out, so we head inside for our chat. The café door has a shallow step. I lift the front wheel of my chair on to it and pull myself forward using the door frame, jarring my finger enough to make me grit my teeth. Using my chair with a broken finger is hard, but my stumps are too sore for me to wear my prostheses today.

Mum nearly hit the roof when I went home yesterday with

a pencil taped to my hand. She had Dad drive me to the out of hours clinic to have a proper splint put on. Heather didn't say anything, but I could hear the "I told you so" all the way across town. The nurse who saw to me said we did a bang-up job of the temporary splint, so I don't know why everyone's making such a fuss.

Inside the café there are marble tabletops, green walls hung with old prints, and a long glass fronted counter full of scotch eggs and quiche. We settle by the window, pushing two of the free tables together to make room on the end for my wheelchair.

"Would you like to order now or would you prefer to wait?" the waiter asks, eyeing the supposedly empty seats where the ghosts are sitting.

"Oh, we're all here," says Sam with his polite-but-firm smile.

Hot chocolate with cream and marshmallows for Ollie. Heather and Sam are on coffee. I go for orange juice. Mitch grabs a croissant and a brew. I ask Marmaduke what he fancies and he seems kind of startled, eyeing the waiter with concern. To his credit, the lad doesn't seem fussed that Sam's asking invisible people how they want their coffee, which makes for a nice change. Marmaduke orders a fancy herbal tea.

It seems daft to order ghosts anything, it's not like they can drink it. But they can smell the steam, enjoy the warmth of the mugs and feel like they're part of the living world again, even just for a moment. That matters.

Marmaduke's crutches are getting in the way, so I offer to lay them on the floor behind him. Even though I've used

Villiers' rapier plenty of times I marvel every time I touch a manifested object.

"My thanks, Charlie." Marmaduke settles into his chair. "Might I see the likeness thou hath made of this foul shade?"

Sam flips through the sketchbook he brought. From the page, the shadow entity is a jumble of charcoal smoke, skeletal limbs and angry eyes. Marmaduke is quiet a full minute, assessing, then he clears his throat.

"On the edge of Loch Assynt in the Highlands, the local souls tell stories of a long dispute between two families, the Murdochs and the Budges. Although both were loyal to the same clan, they could not settle their differences. When the young Murdoch heir was murdered, accusations were levelled upon a hot-headed Budge. He was acquitted, but is then said to have boasted of the deed, not knowing the boy's mother was a powerful witch."

Marmaduke motions to Sam's sketch. "She called forth an abomination of bone and shadow and sent it out to slaughter every Budge for miles." He pauses for effect. "Even the children."

Bone and shadow?

"Does this thing have a name?" I ask.

"They called it a wraith. It climbs inside the living flesh of a person, breaking their body and consuming their soul until they no longer exist in either life or afterlife."

Wraith. The word echoes somewhere deep inside me, raising the hair on my arms.

The scratches around JD and Sadie's mouths – from spectral claws as the shadow ghost climbed *inside* them. No wonder their throats and tongues were torn up. Snapped ribs, shattered bones, melted organs. I shudder and the café seems smaller somehow, no longer safe and cosy. I check the exits.

Ollie whistles. "Even the dead have ghost stories to tell."

"Surely tis mere legend," says Marmaduke.

"Tell that to JD and Sadie Sudarma up in the mortuary." Heather's forehead creases with worry. "No ghost should be able to hurt them, but it did."

A tray bangs the edge of our table, startling me. The waiter mutters an apology. Mitch helps him serve drinks to the empty seats.

"Can I get you anything else?" the waiter asks.

Adjusting his cryptolenses, Mitch flashes him his winning smile. "That's everything, thanks."

The lad's cheeks flush pink. I gulp my orange juice to hide my smirk. Yeah, Mitch looks proper fit in glasses, and he isn't even flirting, he's just being Mitch. When he turns on the charm he's got his own kind of magic.

Marmaduke leans into the steam rising from his posh tea, inhaling deeply. It's in a proper pot with a strainer. The minty apple actually smells all right, way better than coffee.

There are all kind of legends in the ghost community. Like the old rumour that consuming seer flesh and blood will restore a ghost to life. It's a load of bollocks, but it started from a kernel of truth – that possession *is* possible. The Hand certainly figured it out.

So there's likely something to this ghost story too.

Breaking their bodies. Consuming their souls.

"Heather, you said JD's soul sort of just disappeared when he died?" I ask.

She sits forward. "Yeah, it flickered like a broken light bulb for half a second and then fragmented."

"Like Sadie's deathloop fragmented?" Everyone looks at me. *The wraith drains them until they no longer exist in either life or afterlife.*

Marmaduke looks troubled. Ollie swears under his breath. Mitch picks at his croissant, shredding it into flaky strips on the little plate as Sam says what we're all thinking: "So, the wraith *eats* their souls as they die?"

Yeah, exactly right. That's why Sadie Sudarma's deathloop was weaker than it should be. It wasn't a soul, it was the dregs left over after the brew is drunk. An echo of an echo, nothing of her left to save, the rest has been *consumed.*

"That is a fate I'd wish on no one," says Marmaduke, leaning into the comfort of minty apple steam rising from his pot of tea.

"What does it want, then, this wraith?" asks Mitch.

Marmaduke's voice is steady. "It was a spirit of revenge formed from the bones of the witch's dead son. She trapped his soul, corrupting him into an instrument of death to avenge her loss. As for the shade, I know not if it feels or wants for itself."

The tension in my chest breaks. It's not Caleb Gates. If bones are needed to summon this thing, then I know for sure he was cremated. There wouldn't be anything worth working with in his ashes. I can let that idea go for good.

Sam's making notes in the margins of his sketchbook. "Did the ghosts you spoke to say anything about *how* the witch used bone to summon it?"

"I know not how it was called forth," says Marmaduke. "Nor did any other. It is old knowledge."

"Maybe they have magic bone rings, kind of like the Nazgul?" says Ollie. "You know, Ringwraiths."

Sitting back, I cross my arms. "How can a ghost wear a ring?"

"Er … *magic*, obviously."

"What are these naz gool you speak of?" asks Marmaduke.

"Fictional." Sam downs his coffee. "We're dealing with something real."

"Forget how it's summoned," I say. "We need to know how to *stop* it."

Marmaduke shakes his head. "According to the legend it will not stop until its vengeance is completed. Only when every man, woman and child of the Budge family was dead, did the wraith melt into Loch Assynt and vanish forever."

"I don't want to alarm anyone," says Mitch, "but I'm pretty confident the wraith isn't in the loch any more."

Heather grimaces. "Maybe it's not the same wraith. If someone found out how the Murdoch witch summoned that kind of shade then they could replicate the process."

"The stolen bones," I say, thinking of Professor Purcell. It makes sense. Same magic, different occultist. "Sadie must have taken those remains for the summoner. When they had what they wanted, they called the wraith to kill her so she can't tell anyone who's behind it."

It couldn't have happened exactly like that, but we're on the right track.

"Who was she going to tell?" asks Ollie.

"Us?" says Sam. "Or more likely, The Hand. If they're in York, maybe they're already tracking it."

"Viola said they're tracking us," I say.

Mitch has his phone out, flicking through something. "If it's a spirit of revenge, what did JD do to make someone want him dead that badly?"

"Not just dead," says Heather. "Destroyed both body and soul."

Marmaduke shakes his head. "It takes an evil most foul to go against God and extinguish an immortal spirit."

"And a lot of power, I'll wager," says Ollie.

"Maybe JD knew who the summoner is, so just like Sadie, he had to die," I suggest, thinking out loud.

"I'm *sure* Leonie ordered in a rare book on Scottish ghost stories and folklore a few months ago." Mitch is still scrolling his phone. "She sent me a pic of it when it came in because it was well pretty, gold on the cover and everything."

"Coincidence?" Ollie shrugs. "Folks in York like ghosts. It's kind of our thing."

"Here, look." The photo is of an open book showing an etching of a loch framed by dark spectres. On the opposite page are two broken family trees headed Budge and Murdoch. Yeah, that's more than a coincidence.

"Can you remember the title?" asks Sam.

Standing, Mitch grabs his coat off the back of the chair. "No, but we can easily find out."

15

BOOKS AND BONES

Goslings and Waite, the bookshop where Leonie works weekends, is on the other side of Minster's Yard. It's a neat double-fronted building with "Rare second-hand books, manuscripts and documents" etched into the window in fancy letters.

Marmaduke says goodbye, thanking us for the tea and we head inside. The steps are higher here, and the doorway even narrower than at the café. I can't get my chair in so Sam gives me a boost. Ollie and Mitch both breathe deep, look at each other, and crack a grin.

Yeah, fine, bookshops smell nice. They're sort of sweet, like vanilla and grass and something woody. Aside from a couple of prints behind the door, every other wall is taken up with stuffed bookcases, the genres written out on little index cards clipped to the shelf in plastic holders.

There are a few other customers caught in the hush and shuffle of casual browsing. Like most bookshops, the place has a fair few ghosts, including Viola, but right now I can only see an old man with a fancy fob watch snoring in one of the armchairs in the front room.

I bet Viola's in her usual spot. I want her opinion on Marmaduke's wraith theory. Now we can put a name to the shade she might realize she's got the perfect way to banish it.

Ollie's already dived into the classics section, gleefully reading the spines. I wish I had the brass to buy him a whole library. I really need to find a proper part-time job. Problem is, I don't have experience in anything except talking to the dead, and the ghosts make everything more complicated.

I can think of plenty of ways to make money as a seer, but none that aren't an unethical clusterfuck or straight-up illegal. When I was a kid I wanted to be Spider-Man. Clearly, being a superhero is out, plus, I don't think they get paid anyway.

Behind the front desk, the reedy man with salt and pepper hair glances up and beams. "Mitch, nice to see you."

"Jasper mate, you remember Charlie and Sam?"

"Of course." The bookseller gives us an awkward smile. "A pleasure to welcome you back."

I don't come here much, least never in my chair. With uneven floors and narrow doorways, this place is like a warren, rooms and nooks extending off a long gallery with a rickety staircase that goes all the way to the attic four stories up.

Jasper taps his fingers on the desk. "I presume you're here to see a certain young lady on our payroll."

"We won't distract her," I promise, not wanting to get Leonie in trouble.

Jasper tilts his head back and roars up the narrow staircase. "Oh, Wendy, there are three lost boys here to see you."

Leonie comes tottering down behind an armful of books. She dumps the stack in an empty armchair and tucks a couple of her corkscrew curls under her silk scarf. Mitch gives her a peck on the cheek and Jasper pretends not to notice.

"Actually, Sam's interested in Highland ghost stories," says Mitch, ruddy cheeked.

"You brought me *customers*," Jasper beams. "How delightful."

Leonie narrows her eyes, knowing something's going on, but not able to ask. As Sam and Jasper chat ghost lore, Heather fills her in on Marmaduke's story, the wraith and the book we're after. When Jasper invites her to show us to the paranormal section of the shop, she says, "What about that book you got in from Edinburgh a few months ago?"

Ollie rewards her with the finger guns and a wink. "Smoothly done."

Jasper frowns, thinking, then his eyes brighten and he snaps his fingers. "Ah, yes, illustrated endpapers and the most exquisite leather tooling. Hmm." He starts to click through the database on his computer.

Leonie leans over to peek at the screen. "Who ordered it, a regular?"

"Not really. She came in a handful of times over the summer, but I haven't seen her for a while. Nice lass, studying history or archaeology or something like that."

"Her name wasn't Sadie, was it?" I ask.

"Sorry, can't say, customer orders are confidential." Jasper gives me an apologetic shrug. "Aha, *A History of Highland Apparitions and Hauntings* by Edwin McNish." His crooked grin is triumphant. "Printed by a small press in Saint Andrews in 1873, a run of only a hundred and fifty."

It was ordered in the summer, weeks before the wraith appeared. Whatever's in that book, it's not likely there's a simple recipe for a vengeful shade on page forty-six. Whoever's behind this has been building up to this for a while, maybe months. Plenty of time to perfect the theorem and find their targets.

"Can you get hold of another copy?" asks Sam. "I'd be interested."

Jasper raps his fingers on the desk again. "I can call around and see if anything is still available. The last edition we sold was around the eight hundred pound mark, so depending on the condition—"

"I'll pay a deposit," says Sam quickly.

Jasper tries to hide his surprise and fails. He takes Sam's name and number so the shop can notify him if they secure a copy. Maybe this book is the key to everything, but what if it's not? Eight hundred quid! Luckily Sam can cover it, but that's got to be a bit steep for most folks, especially a student.

Jasper's called into the Nature and Botany section to advise a customer. As soon as he's around the cabinet and out of sight, Leonie slips into his swivel chair and brings up the record. "Ordered by … yep, Sadie Sudarma."

My thoughts whirl. She's definitely our bone thief, and the bones are probably connected to the wraiths, as is the book Sadie ordered. But all I felt in her loop was fear and sadness, there was no anger.

"She's not the summoner," I say, confident. "The wraith killed her. She's a *victim*." I don't know why I'm so keen to defend her. Maybe because I saw her die.

"I agree. If there *were* bones in the missing bag then none of them could be the seed of the wraith that killed her," says Sam. "Even if she's involved, she's not working alone. JD was the real target."

"As were Graham Geoffrey, Naomi Petty and Irma Lane," says Heather, moving out of the way of a customer.

We all look at her.

"The other attacks," she explains.

"That was some gang, though," I say, confused. "I mean, none of them died."

Heather takes a deep breath. "No, but I went to see them and all three have scratches around their faces and broken ribs."

The wraith's signature. The feeling rolling around in my gut is strange and uneasy. More victims complicates things, but we've more chance of making a connection too.

"Each attack got progressively worse," says Heather. "I

think it's always been the wraith and whoever is summoning it has just been perfecting their control."

Sam takes out his phone and starts to message someone.

"Your girlfriend wasn't in the morgue to find out why she lost a patient, was she?" I ask Heather. "She was doing some sleuthing of her own."

Heather hesitates, looking away. I know she hates I've brought Neelam up. Maybe she thinks I'll judge her. Haunting your ex isn't exactly healthy.

"Neelam's looking into it on her own time. I'm afraid she'll get herself into danger without knowing the whole truth of what's going on." Heather holds up her hand before I can speak. "And, no, I don't want you to tell her about me, or any ghosts at all."

"We've got to find whoever's doing this first, then," I say. "Shut them down."

Heather shakes her head. "It's too dangerous. Between the threat of The Hand and a wraith on the loose, you don't need another target on your back. I won't always be—"

She falls suddenly silent.

"Hey, Villiers is teaching me fencing and I'm getting a bit better at mathemagics. I'm not defenceless."

Her brow softens, frown smoothing to the barest pinch between her eyebrows. "I know, it's … we'll talk about it later, yeah? I just worry for you, all of you."

Sam slips his phone back into his pocket. "Miri's on it. If there's a connection between the first three victims, she'll find it."

"What about JD?" asks Leonie. "How does he fit in?"

We really have no idea at this point.

Time to find Viola.

They keep all of the weird occult books in the back room on the ground floor. Getting my chair in there is a proper faff. Mitch, Sam and Leonie have to scoot a tiered glass cabinet of expensive first editions over so that I have enough space to squeeze through.

The low-ceilinged room has a threadbare armchair and a little couch where Viola's curled up, rolling her knucklebones in her palm. "There you all are. How was your meeting with Marmaduke?"

She talks about him like they've met, when they haven't. She's not very social, claiming she's worried what other ghosts will think if they learn she was an occultist. I get it. They might not take too kindly to her if they think she once trapped souls, and ghosts can hurt each other badly when they want to. Her solution is to hermit. Unless she's off reading the bones for that one friend of hers, she's here, surrounded by books.

Sam sits next to her and flips through his sketchbook. "We have a suspect, well, a lead at least."

"Oh, goodness," says Viola when she sees his drawing of the wraith. "You are frightfully talented, Sam. That thing is ghastly."

"We know what it is." Sam explains everything Marmaduke told us about the wraith from how it's made, to how it kills.

"It consumes souls?" Viola doesn't take her eyes off the sketch.

"It's a spirit of revenge," says Ollie.

She's unnaturally still for a long moment. Then, she blinks, wets her lips and sits back. "How terrible."

I park my chair at the end of the couch.

Heather perches on the arm of the other chair, Ollie having claimed it. "Have you heard of anything like this before?"

Viola shakes her head. "This is obscure osteomagi blended with nescropic theory. A very different kind of shade."

Bringing up Sadie's Instagram, Sam scrolls through her grid of aesthetic graveyards, funerary urns, skulls and vintage anatomy models. Images of Sadie with friends in bars, shots of graveyards, a dig site somewhere, Sadie with a trowel in hand, and several of her holding human skulls.

"She's very into … death," says Heather.

A photo flashes past. Recognition flares inside me.

"Wait, go back—" I say. "There. That one."

Clicking on it, the image fills the phone screen. It's of Sadie with her arm around a pretty white lass, their chins tilted down, eyes at the camera. Behind them is a wall of skulls and bones.

"Tagged as the catacombs in Paris," says Sam.

"The remains of six million people were dug up from Parisian cemeteries, moved into old quarry tunnels and arranged in pretty patterns." Ollie's miscellaneous knowledge always comes through. "It's the largest underground ossuary in the world."

Taking Sam's phone, I zoom in. "On her arm, see the straps there? That's the bag Sadie was carrying the night she died."

"You're sure?"

"Very."

I keep scrolling, finding more pictures of Sadie with the same lass. They seem close. She's tagged. I hop over to her account, Jory Chambers.

"Yeah, I don't think they were roommates," says Mitch, leaning over my shoulder.

I don't need to see the photos of Sadie laughing, reaching back towards Jory, rainbow light reflecting off a polished bird skull sitting in their joined fingers to know they were a couple. I feel it, just as I feel the faintest echo of fear from Sadie's memories.

She was afraid for Jory when she died.

"She's an artist." Leonie has Jory's social media up on her own phone. "With a website."

It's basic but sleek with a gallery and a short personal profile that states she's "*interested in the liminal as places of transformation and purpose*".

I like the way Sam talks about his art. He keeps it simple. This feels deliberately confusing and well up itself. I click on the gallery link at the top and scroll past some weird, cutesy taxidermy. What do dead mice have to do with liminal places?

Wait.

A piece of what looks like body jewellery comes up. Then another. "Holy shit." I turn Sam's phone so everyone can see.

"Are those human bones?" asks Leonie.

I zoom into the image – a necklace of twelve finger bones interwoven with gold wire – trying to see if there are serial numbers marked on them. I can't see anything, but that doesn't mean they're not on the back and out of view.

"Maybe Sadie was stealing bones for art, not magic," says Sam. I appreciate him trying to side with Sadie, but there's something about these bones that bother me.

"Viola?" I prompt.

She leans in slowly, almost reluctant. "They're impresa, designed to hold and direct magic."

"Like a ghost bottle?" asks Mitch.

"Nothing so sinister. They're often used as good luck charms."

"Can impresa be used to do something bad?"

"Of course." Viola takes another long look at the photo. "To know for certain, you'd need to see the bones in person."

I navigate to the contact page of the website. "Jory has a booking form for appointments at her home gallery... Ah, shit, turned off."

Sam shrugs. "We could go over there and claim we've booked."

"No way," says Heather. "Not if there's a chance she's the summoner."

I expect Viola to chime in and disagree – *It's far too late for you to avoid this storm* – but she's quietly thoughtful instead.

I know we're messing with something proper dangerous but we can't wait around for someone else to die, not when we could save them. It's been a week since JD died. Maybe he was the last target and it's over, but there's a nasty catch in my throat telling me there's more to this. We haven't seen the last of the wraith.

"How's that shield theorem coming along, Leonie?" I ask.

"Will it hold back a wraith?" asks Mitch.

Viola nods. "If at full strength and if cast perfectly, a shade of any kind should be deflected, as will any theorems meant to stun or seal."

"I'm almost there with it," says Leonie.

"Almost isn't good enough," snaps Heather. "Getting between hunter and prey is a bad idea. I don't want you to visit Jory until we know more. All right?"

Viola meets my gaze, the tiniest trace of a smile at the edge of her mouth. The knucklebones clatter in her palm, past and future mixed up together. She's already read my path. She knows what I'm about to do.

I look Heather dead in the eye, and lie.

16

THE HOUSE OF DEAD THINGS

Jory Chambers stands in her doorway, arms folded. Since the photo of her at the Paris Catacombs, grief has worn at her edges, sinking in her cheeks and painting dark bags under her eyes.

Leonie smiles, trying to act casual. I'm so used to her wearing glasses that she looks less like herself without them. But the last thing we want is to tip Jory off that we're on to her before we can suss her out. Before they took their cryptolenses off, Leonie and Mitch checked the outside of the house and the narrow street for signs of magic. Nothing.

Peering in the front window, Ollie mutters something about "tiny hats". He wanted to go in and scout, but I wouldn't let him. I'm too nervous about ghost traps.

"Art thou certain you wish to provoke Mistress Noble's ire?" Villiers whispers, knowing I can't answer him without giving myself away. He insisted on coming in Heather's place but has spent the whole way here trying to convince me this a bad idea.

It is, and it's a dick move. Heather's visiting Neelam at the hospital to see if there's any update on the first three victims. She didn't exactly forbid me from … OK, she did. "Don't even think about going over there until we hear back from Miri," is pretty direct, but she's not my mum and it's my job to keep the city and its souls safe. I have to get to the bottom of this or what use am I?

Looking at Jory in the doorway, she doesn't feel like a threat. Her thumb is raw round the nail where she's been chewing on it and she just looks so … sad.

"Can I help you?" she asks.

"Er, yeah." I try to hide my nerves, smiling to match Leonie. My mouth is dry and my palms are sweating. Get her talking, then I'll try and move the conversation towards the untimely death of her girlfriend without her shutting down or guessing that we suspect her.

Easy.

And if she *is* the one summoning the wraith and takes offence to our snooping then, well, we'll improvise and learn all we can before we're brutally murdered. God, I am so anxious. I need to start thinking positive.

I motion to me, Sam, Leonie and Mitch, "We're here about—"

Ollie points at something just visible through the black lace netting over the window. "There are squirrels drinking tea with a hedgehog."

"Squirrels drinking tea?" I blurt.

Ah, bollocks.

Sam edges in front of me, trying to smooth things over. He's looking sharp today, a nice tweed blazer under his usual waxed jacket. "We made an appointment on your website."

Jory drags herself upright from where she was leaning against the door jamb. "I haven't checked my email in a week. It's a bad time." She falls silent, waiting for us to piss off voluntarily.

"We're really interested in the squirrel piece," says Sam. "Is it still available?"

Jory shakes her head, but then steps back. "Yeah, fine, come in."

Sam goes first. I follow, careful not to trip on the welcome mat.

The house is narrow the way a lot of terraces are, like someone built them all in a row and then gave them a big squeeze. The hall is painted black and hung with big canvases. It makes the place feel even more compressed.

Ollie motions to the stairs. I give him a slight nod and a look to say, *Be careful*.

I'm glad I wore my prostheses today. Getting through these tight doorways in my chair would be a nightmare.

Jory shows us into the front room which is less a living room and more of an art gallery full of taxidermy – sparrows wired around a bleeding love heart, a fox head wearing a flower crown and mice taking bubble baths. I recognize a few from her website, but most of them are new.

"This is everything I have for sale. Squirrel Tea Party is

in the window there, prices on the tags. I'll leave you to have a little browse. I won't be five minutes."

Jory disappears upstairs and we're left alone in a room of dead things.

Squirrel Tea Party is a long miniature table set with tiny plates covered in fake cake and sandwiches. Around it, five stuffed squirrels sit in wicker chairs. They're wearing hats and waistcoats. At the head of the table a hedgehog in a bowtie pours tea.

"I have *so* many questions," says Mitch, examining it.

Villiers squints at a mouse in a bathtub. "Methinks this one has a certain charm."

"Oh my god, is that a mummified cat?" Leonie leans in to poke what does look a lot like a mummified cat.

"Yeah, they used to put them in the walls of old houses," I say. "That's why we're blessed with those two terrors down at the Starre."

In cabinets either side of the chimney are what we came to see; bone impresa disguised as jewellery. Ribs, fingers, spinal columns, feathers and teeth all crafted into crowns or necklaces, earrings and gauntlets.

Remembering what Professor Purcell said, I look for little numbers marked in ink knowing it's possible Jory destroyed or removed the dig numbers. This close, some of the jewellery has larger symbols painted on in a pale, barely visible wash, or shaped into the wiring that's holding them together.

"Glyphs," whispers Sam, keeping his voice down for a change.

Slipping on her cryptolenses, Leonie takes a look. "Yeah. Not active, though."

Mitch points to some triangular patterns along a rib bone necklace. "Iron, copper, quintessence, all taken from old alchemy."

He's been reading into potion making because he wants to see if it's possible to bake health and happiness into desserts and cakes. I imagine him having his own restaurant one day, or maybe a bakery with a little something magical in the mix.

"What's the diagnosis?" I whisper. "Yay or nay for practising occultist?"

Villiers hisses a warning as Jory appears in the doorway. She's changed her ratty jumper for a black polo layered with necklaces – crystals, beads and a simple bone pendant made from what looks like a human fingerbone wrapped in a wire hilt. Her hair is down, falling around her face in choppy waves.

"Are you … collectors?" she asks.

"Looking to be," says Sam smoothly.

Adjusting the mouse in the bathtub on the shelf, Jory straightens up the label. "How did you hear about my work?"

"Popped up on Insta," says Mitch.

"We really liked your commentary on death as a mirror of life," Leonie adds.

"Is that so?" She doesn't sound convinced.

"This piece is particularly striking." Sam motions to Squirrel Tea Party and says something about *Alice in Wonderland* and capturing the everyday moments and making them strange.

Jory stares at us for a few seconds. "You didn't come here to talk about art."

"I'm seriously interested in this piece," says Sam, his voice straining at the edges. "In fact, I'd like to take it."

I turn a gasp into a cough. He saw the price tag, right? Mitch pats me on the back, and I tap his arm in thanks as I wince an apology to Jory.

She folds her arms across her chest. "I turned off my appointment booking form because my girlfriend just died. You're not here to buy art. What do you really want?"

In the excruciating pause that follows a thousand lies run through my mind, all dafter and more unconvincing than the last. Jory doesn't look worried that we're here, just irritated.

Are you collectors?

She didn't mean collectors of art, she meant collectors of *something else* that she doesn't want to name before we do.

Ollie ghosts through the wall, sees us all standing about looking tense and says, "Books on osteomagi, tools, the works."

Any doubt that Jory's an occultist evaporates.

"We're here about the wraith," I say plainly.

Sam goes rigid. I think Leonie stops breathing. Mitch makes a startled, deflated noise and glowers at me. Villiers cracks a grin, he likes this tactic. Ollie just waits, watching Jory's expression flicker from wariness to confusion.

"The … what?"

"A terrifying shade summoned with bones that crawls down people's throats and murders them." I gesture to the stands of jewellery dripping in occult symbols. "Sound familiar?"

"I don't mess with that stuff." She's shaking. "My impresa are imbued with glamours, luck, foresight and admiration, that's all."

Being bold, I pick up the necklace made from a rib bone, spinning it over. "Human, right?" There's the ID number, half-hidden under a fresh line of gold glyphs.

"They take magic better than animal." Jory bites her lip. "They're *old*, all the human bones I use are. I … I didn't kill anyone!" Red-rimmed eyes blink back tears. "I can't deal with this." She turns on her heel and disappears into the back of the house.

A nod from Villiers and we follow.

The space isn't huge: a U-shaped kitchen with red cabinets making up a breakfast bar that divides the cooking area from a dining table. French windows open on to a poky concrete courtyard, unused except for a washing line and bins. The far wall is taken up by an oversized dresser cluttered with books, framed postcards and weird little sculptures.

Jory's leaning against one of the mismatched chairs arranged around a small dining table, crying.

"Dramatic, isn't she?" says Ollie.

To be fair to her, her girlfriend did just die.

"Hey, we're not going to hurt you," Leonie soothes. "We just have some questions about Sadie and the bones she took."

I'm surprised this house isn't haunted. This would have been a working-class home back in the day, whole families crammed into a two up, two down. Plenty of lives lived – sweat, tears, blood, laughter – these walls would have seen it all, but the space feels empty, like something is echoing here.

I feel sick and wrong.

Realization floods Jory's expression. "Did *she* send you? I already told her we're not going to—"

I hold up my hand, cutting Jory off. The air in here suddenly smells earthy. My skin itches.

"Spidey senses," I mouth at Sam.

He nods, on edge. "Something's coming."

A clicking noise, like a huge insect is in the walls. Or the sound of claws scuttling on stone. Shadows bloom in the corner of the kitchen. Villiers' blade sings as he draws it, putting himself between us and danger.

"W-what's going on?" asks Jory, voice high and tight. She's clutching one of her necklaces as if it's a talisman. For all I know, it can protect her, but the rest of us are fucked.

We need to get out.

17

RATS IN A CAGE

A skeletal claw reaches through the ceiling and the wraith hauls its body into the kitchen, its form wrapped in sinuous smoke that turns oil slick as it moves. Pausing with the focus of a predator, its glowing eyes fix on us, no, on Jory. She can't see it, but it sees her. It sniffs the air. Deep, guttural grunts as it rocks back, swings and releases—

"Move!" I don't think, just push a chair aside and launch myself forward, catching Jory round the waist and slamming us into the dresser. Something tugs on my arm and releases. Sam yells. Air bursts from my lungs and my broken finger sears. Plates, a vintage radio and bones mounted in glass domes smash on the floor where we cower.

It can move through walls, but it can also touch the material world.

No time to think on that. Beside me, Jory's scrabbling to

stand as I gasp for air. I have to get up and get us out. Inside, the wraith has the advantage.

Who am I kidding? Outside, it also has the advantage because we can't fight it. At least we'll have room to move. Right now, we're rats in a cage with a rabid dog.

"Go!" Ollie bellows.

I scream at Jory, pushing her to move as the wraith drops on us, a jagged blur of shadow, stinking of earth, ash and dust.

On all fours, Jory scurries under the kitchen table, the bone pendant around her neck swinging wildly. I follow but the angle of the feet on my prostheses makes it awkward. On the other side of the table, Ollie helps me up.

Blood drips from Leonie's hand. She's hurt – no, she's cut herself to mark a glyph on her palm. The wraith is above us, swiping at Jory. Sam pulls her out of the way just in time.

"It's only going for *her*," he confirms.

Jory's not the summoner. She's the next target.

Villiers slashes his rapier into the smoky cloud. His short cape flares as he spins to aim a cut to the wraith's head, the sword sticking in whatever ghostly flesh lies beneath the smoky clouds. It screeches in anger, high and long, the sound grating inside my mind. Mitch and Leonie cover their ears.

If I die today, Heather's going to make my afterlife hell.

And Sam…

A surge of fresh panic sings through my blood. *Keep him safe.*

Villiers strikes, finding something in that writhing mass

to hack into. The wraith screeches again, the sound like nails on glass. Sam rattles the handle on the French doors. Locked. *Shit*. Ollie's on the other side, scouting out the courtyard for an escape. No point if we can't get the door open.

"Where's the fucking key?" shouts Mitch, slamming his weight against the glass. The doors don't budge or break.

Jory's searching around the kitchen in desperation. "It's normally in the lock."

We look in bowls and on hooks and anywhere that's close. Nothing. And we can't get to the front door because Villiers and the wraith are between us and freedom.

Parrying blade to claws, he grunts with the effort. He's fast, but so is it.

It should be *faster*.

In Sadie's deathloop I saw this thing really *move*. It's got to be playing with us. In half a second it will strike at full speed, claw Villiers aside and leap on Jory. Her throat will stream with blood, choking her, bones will break, organs fail, ribs pop open, and heart give in as it drains her soul.

All we can do is watch her die.

With a roar, Villiers stabs his blade into the wraith again. It staggers, claws raking the wall as it slinks through the plaster and vanishes.

Jory sobs. Mitch curses. I can hear my laboured breaths.

There's a slash in the sleeve of my puffer jacket; the wraith's claw must have caught me as we fell. It's gone right through, though not deep enough to get my skin. My jacket is torn to shit.

It might be after Jory, but the wraith is a danger to anyone standing in its way.

Sheathing his rapier, Villiers smooths one side of his curling moustache and turns to soak up our admiration. "Tis slain. Vanquished by *my* hand, for I am George Villiers, defeater of evil and defender of seers—"

"Er, shut up a sec." Ollie points to the hallway. Pressure builds, clagging the air with shadows.

Mitch wipes his brow. "A valiant effort, George, but I think you just pissed it off."

Ah, bollocks.

There's a hand in mine, an arm at my back – Sam. Fear in his eyes, but determination too. He's not backing down, so neither will I.

The wraith swings itself through the door frame, glowing eyes narrowing at Jory. Leonie screams a word, shoving her hand in front of her. Magic spills from her palm and a transparent circular shield emanates like a projection between us and it.

The wraith snaps against the barrier. Leonie grits her teeth, moving her shield as the wraith stalks left. "Something's wrong, the charm isn't stable. It won't last."

"Purification," mutters Mitch. Leaping over the breakfast bar he starts rattling through cabinets, pulling out packets and tossing them at us.

Sam picks one up. "Salt?" He looks puzzled, then hopeful. "Of course, it's protective *and* purifying."

Leonie gasps as the wraith slams into her shield again. The charm flickers.

"Salt doesn't do shit to regular ghosts," I say.

"What about *that* makes you think it's a regular ghost?" snaps Ollie.

The shield fails, silver light fragmenting. Villiers steps in, rapier drawn, and goes flying, a deep slash of claws over his chest. It swoops in with a growl. Sam and Mitch chuck fistfuls of gritty crystals that strike the wraith full on, crackling and flaring with light. The shade pulls back with a pained shriek.

"It's working!" I grab a bag of salt off the counter.

"More!" Leonie shouts, throwing a fistful with the hand she didn't slice open.

The wraith retreats and we push forward into the hallway, heading for the front door. It's injured, but that only makes it feel more dangerous. With a weakening screech, it falls back into the gallery room.

Now.

My legs burn; I'm pushing my prostheses to their limits. Jory gets the front door open, hurrying on to the street. Sam follows, calling my name, but I need to know Mitch and Leonie are out too. They are. My back is to the hallway but I feel the wraith gathering, stalking me as I stumble outside.

"Charlie!" Villiers chucks his rapier, hilt first. The weight sends it arching towards me. I think something confused about physics and wonder how an object made from phantasmic essence can have weight. And then I'm reaching for it, unbalanced, but I catch it without falling.

The hilt is solid in my hand as I turn to meet a roar of billowing smoke and gleaming eyes. A single thrust. The blade slides deep into the heart of the wraith, acrid smoke bubbling as its own momentum carries it on to the sword.

Its scream is an inhale that sucks the air into a breeze. Billows of smoke contract into a tiny point on the end of the rapier as the shade collapses in on itself with a wail. In seconds, the hallway is empty.

Pushing past me, Sam pours his last bag of salt over the front of the house from corner to corner. It's a nice gesture but we're talking about a thing that can move through walls here. If we're going to contain it, we need to circle the whole house. Impossible, it's in the centre of a terrace and we can't traipse through the neighbours' homes trailing seasoning and apologies.

Plus, it'll take a lot more salt than we have.

Sam catches me around the neck. We press sweaty brows together, each feeling the solid weight of the other. Alive, but not safe.

"That was close," he whispers.

My breaths heave, pulse racing. The ground under me feels unstable so I hold on to Sam. For some reason I remember the first time I saw him, waxed jacket, dimples, the shock of white amongst his dark curls, and how he spun me off balance. My heart feels like it's caught somewhere in my throat because now he's the axis of everything.

I put that in danger by coming here. I put *him* in danger.

"Let's get out of here," he says.

Staggering on the road, Villiers clutches his chest and sags into Ollie's arms. The short lad struggles to hold him up.

"Tell my beloved James I ended mine afterlife in defence of noble friends," Villiers wheezes, then frowns, looking down at the slashes in his doublet. He pats at the wound. Realizing the cuts don't go deeper than the fabric, he rights himself. "Oh, tis but a scratch."

Ollie rolls his eyes.

Someone *is* lying in the road. Jory – on her back. Did she faint? Her skin is grey and sweating, like Leonie's when she uses too much magic. I search for a pulse and nod.

"Help me with her."

Mitch takes Jory's arm and shoulder. Sam hurries to support her head as we lift her to sitting. I tap her gently on the cheek with the back of my hand. "Oi, Jory?"

She stirs, then lurches to consciousness, eyes wide and panicked.

"Whoa, chill, it's gone. You're all right."

Clutching the bone ornament at her neck, she tears herself away from us, backing against a car. "Wha— What the fuck was that?"

18

REASONABLE PRECAUTIONS

The face of the bloke at the front desk when we stagger into the lobby at Greys Hotel is part-horror, part-alarm that slides fully into confusion when Sam slumps against one of the elegant chairs and asks, "How much salt does the kitchen keep on hand?"

Whatever Sam and his mum pay to live here, it's enough to send the man scurrying. Within five minutes the staff bring us a wholesale size bag of salt, arrange for housekeeping to change Sam's bedding and promise to find a camp style bed from somewhere.

"I can stay at the Premier Inn," says Jory for the fifteenth time.

Seeing as she escaped her house with only what she's wearing, no phone or wallet, I'm sure Sam's generosity is something she can't turn down. But I get it. I'm not good at taking charity either.

"You can't go home tonight," Sam repeats patiently as we follow him upstairs.

"But Charlie" – she swivels to look at me – "it's Charlie, yeah? He killed it."

"Technically, it's already dead," Ollie mutters to Villiers.

We reach Sam's floor, the corridor warmed by sconce lighting, thick rugs and antiques. Sometimes there are roman legionaries on the march, but not tonight. The silence is piercing.

"It's not gone for good," I warn Jory. In Marmaduke's story, the wraith didn't stop until it had dispatched everyone on the summoner's hit list, which now includes her. It targeted Jory for a reason, which means she knows something. We keep her alive, ask her what she knows and catch who is behind this. Somehow. "We need to be prepared for another attack."

"I pledge my sword to protect the lady in her slumbers," says Villiers, swishing his cloak like he's about to pose for another of Sam's portraits.

Wiping sweaty hair off his forehead, Sam unlocks his door. "Villiers says he'll defend you."

Jory swallows. "Th-thanks?"

On the way over, Leonie reluctantly let her look through the cryptolenses to see Ollie and Villiers for herself. "Death-touched working with young occultists *and* ghosts. That's a first," she'd said, ignoring Leonie's protests over being labelled an occultist.

In Sam's room, Leonie draws the curtains and Mitch flicks on the lights. Packing up paint pots and brushes, Sam pushes his easel into the corner. "If we move the bed we can salt behind it, full circle."

The bedframe is solid. It takes all five of us to heave it away from the wall. A horrible groaning noise echoes from the legs and for a worrying second, I think we've broken a carving or scraped the floor, but it seems all right. To clear enough space we move piles of books and shift a stack of paintings over to the wardrobe.

"You did all these?" Jory asks Sam, pawing through the smaller canvases. "They're really good."

There's a soft flush under Sam's freckles. "The dead don't show up on film so painting their portraits is my way of keeping them alive, just a little."

Helping move the canvases, I pick up a portrait sketch of Heather. Her lopsided expression looks unimpressed, but also like she's secretly having a laugh. There's something about her that's hard to pin down. She's gonna be so pissed when she finds out we went over to Jory's behind her back. I swallow the gnawing guilt. It tastes bitter but I can't regret what we did, even if it put us in danger. We saved Jory's life.

I shouldn't have lied to Heather about it, though.

"Do you have friends or family you need to call?" I ask Jory.

"I … no. My dad died when I was a kid and Mum … moved away a few years ago. We're not close. Sadie was all I had."

"Sorry."

"Sam, can I use a page of this?" Leonie holds up one of

his notebooks. She looks as tired as Jory, her eyes red and bloodshot from using her shield.

"Go ahead."

"Thanks." Selecting a pencil from the pot on the dresser, she curls up in one of the armchairs by the window.

A knock on the door sets me on edge. It's just a porter with the camp bed. They only have one available which isn't ideal, but we'll make it work. He's reluctant to let us set it up ourselves but eventually Sam convinces him to leave. Villiers hovers, guarding the door as Sam hauls in the folding frame. Mitch brings the bedding and I get the mattress.

"Me and Sam will sleep in shifts," I tell Jory. "One of us will always be on watch."

We flip the frame, locking the three sets of legs in place.

Turning it over, Sam tests its sturdiness by sitting in the middle and bouncing. "I know it's a bit weird to have people you just met sleeping by you, but until we know how to stop a wraith, you're vulnerable."

Jory perches on the end of the main bed. "You don't have to do this for me."

"Does she think we're just going to let her die?" asks Ollie. "Harsh."

"Yeah, apparently. Look, we're not gonna abandon you," I reassure her.

"Thank you, honestly, I owe you." She looks between us and clears her throat. "I should probably tell you everything."

"That would be appreciated," says Sam.

She clasps her hands between her knees. "Sadie studies bones, their magical properties, use in rituals and rites, all purely theoretical. And I make practical wearable art with a bit of something extra. We're the perfect match." She winces, realizing what she's said. "*Were* the perfect match. Sorry, it's all pretty raw. Her parents live in Essex so I had to identify her body."

"That's shit," says Mitch.

"Yeah." She sniffs.

Nudging Sam out of the way, I slide the mattress on to the camp bed. "Do you always use human bone?"

"No, but human remains have enhanced phantasmic residua, meaning I need to put less of my soul source into the working if I use them. I don't syphon external soul sources so it's worth it."

"Residua decreases over time," says Leonie, without looking up from whatever she's writing. "Why steal old bones?"

"Because I don't want to get into grave robbing," snaps Jory. "Even ancient human remains contain more residua than animal."

"So Sadie stole them from the uni," I say simply.

Jory's jaw tenses. "Only once, *months* ago—"

"Months?" I exchange a look with Sam.

"A ghost at the department saw Sadie take bones only a couple of weeks ago, right before she died," he tells Jory.

"No, we agreed she'd stop—"

"We think she was threatened." Mitch's voice is gentle. "Or blackmailed."

I sit on the bare camping mattress next to Sam, easing my legs out. "The police report's total rubbish. Sadie went to Cumberland House voluntarily."

Jory's shaking. "I don't understand—"

"She was meeting someone and had a bag with her that was likely full of stolen bones. She used an obsidian mirror to check the room for souls so she knew about the wraith."

Jory blinks, sitting back. "That ghost glass was her great grandmother's. How did you know about it?"

"I saw it in her deathloop—"

"She's still here?" Jory leaps up.

Mitch catches her arm. "She's not."

"But if—"

"The wraith is a soul eater," I say. "Sadie's loop was weak, just an echo. What was left sort of … dissolved. She's gone."

Relief flits across Jory's face, hardened a second later by grief as she lowers herself slowly back on to the bed, sniffing.

Mitch makes a face at me that says, *You could have handled that better.*

"Sorry," I add, too late. "Jory, it's likely that whoever summoned the wraith killed Sadie to cover their tracks. They want you dead too, so you must know something—"

"I don't!" She wipes her eyes on her sleeve. "Sadie and I didn't keep secrets from each other. If someone was threatening her then she would have told me."

"Unless she was trying to protect you," says Mitch softly.

Her face crumples. Covering her head with her hands, she breathes deeply. When she opens her eyes again, there is steel in them. "I know who it is. There's a medium doing a show at York Royal."

"Claire Cole?" asks Sam.

Jory fiddles with the bone impresa at her throat. What did she say it was for? Protection. Cute, but it's obviously useless against the wraith.

"We went to her show when it first opened just for a bit of fun, but she's an occultist. She wears a bone impresa, similar to mine but ... darker. Dangerous. Magic I'd never fuck with."

I remember the flash of cream under the high collar of Claire's dress. Bones at her throat.

"Her impresa lets her read minds," says Jory. "She's not actually psychic, she uses magic to invade people's privacy and influence them. She must have heard us thinking it, because she confronted us after the show and she was *nasty*, calling my impresa weak because my work brings subtle, positive effects to wearers. I thought you might be working with her and she'd sent you to make good on her threat."

Back at the house Jory was scared, but anger carried her through the chaos. Now, she seems broken and alone. With her adrenaline gone, all that's left is hollow pain. I know how that feels.

"What threat?" I ask.

"Her reputation and career are everything to her and she made it clear that us just *existing* was a risk to her. Sadie thought it was just bullying, you know. Big bad occultist likes to push us dabblers around."

The nerves start to twitch in my left leg so I get up and grab the bag of salt. It needs to go in an even, heaped line around the bed and cot. As protection goes it's pretty basic, but it's the best we can do.

Maybe JD and the other victims found out Claire Cole's use of bone impresa and threatened to expose her, so she sent a shade after them. It's clear she knows the basis of osteomagi, so summoning a wraith isn't a huge stretch.

Sam edges the camp bed to the inner side of the new salt circle, careful not to break the protective line.

"God, I can't live inside a salt circle for the *rest* of my life." Jory draws her knees to her chest.

"We'll find a way to stop Claire and her pet wraith," I say, faking confidence I don't feel. Thinking of Sister Agnes and Sharp-Teeth in their cemetery prison, I ask, "Could a ghost line work? The wraith is a soul so it won't be able to cross it, right?"

Ollie raises a hand. "Er, we can't cross it either. That's a problem."

Standing, Sam parcels out bedding for the camp bed.

Mitch starts to stuff a pillow into its case. "And, it will take time to lay down, *if* we can work out how it's done."

Leonie sits back in her armchair. The paper on her lap is covered in scribbles. "I think I've worked out what went wrong with my shield charm. I need to run it by Viola first thing, and practise, lots of practice."

We can hold the wraith back with salt and manifested weapons like Villiers' rapier, or charms like Leonie's shield, but I know that sooner or later it will get through and kill Jory and whoever else gets in its way.

Our best hope is convincing Claire to stop killing people. If we can't do that, then we've got to break her connection to the magic and hope that does the trick.

But how?

The first seal used by The Hand cuts people off from their soul source, stopping them using magic. But it also forces them to live a kind of half-life. Could I ever do that to someone?

Yeah, if it will save lives. It could be the only way. Viola knows what the seals do, but we've no idea how they work or how to cast them. Maybe we need to approach The Hand and ask for help. Viola will warn against it, but we're running out of options.

"When the wraith attacks again we need to be able to *fight*," I say. "Not just ward it off for a bit."

"You're right." Sam passes me the corner of the duvet cover. "George, you were amazing and you totally saved us tonight, but we need more manifested weapons in play."

Villiers floats over from his position by the door. "I am friendly with Robert Savage who hath a ceremonial mace, and Hugh de Selby, Robert Aske and Will Bowes, all who carry blades as befitting gentlemen. I shall appeal for their aid in this matter. Mayhap we can raise a force to defend those in danger from this fiend."

Suddenly there's movement past the bathroom at the front door. We all freeze. Villiers draws his rapier but it's only Heather, Dante at her heels.

I wince, knowing what's coming.

She takes one look at me and Sam wrestling with a duvet cover, Villiers standing guard, and Jory sitting cross-legged on the bed inside a circle of salt and asks, "What the hell did you do?"

"How pissed is she?" Dante's sitting between my knees, his foppish head bent back to gaze up at me as I rub his snout.

With a sigh, Ollie slumps on the camp bed. "String you upside-down in a well by your ankles kind of pissed. If you're *really* lucky, she might forgive you by the time you're thirty."

There's a pause while I process the threat. "I don't have any ankles."

"She'll improvise."

I wrinkle my nose. "I'm too handsome to stay angry at, right?"

"No, mate." Ollie stands. "You hurt her feelings and she's scared for you."

"She lied to me about Neelam."

"Seriously? That's not even the same thing. Look, she's annoyed at me too but, already being dead, I'm unlikely to get myself killed after she gave up everything to give me a second chance at life."

I deflate, because he's right. Here I am taking selfish risks when Heather sacrificed a future with the lass she loves for my sorry arse. I am such a dick. The worst part is Heather was spot on. We waltzed into a situation we weren't prepared for. It's a miracle we survived.

"Where is she?" I ask Ollie.

"Helping Lady Faith look for some missing legionaries. Lucius and the bald one."

"Octavian?"

Ollie shrugs. "You've seen one Roman legionary you've seen them all."

It's weird that they've not shown up. The Roman lot are a pretty tight-knit group. I hope they're all right, the last thing we need are missing ghosts on top of everything else.

Sam, Mitch, Leonie and Villiers are happy to stay with Jory, so I head downstairs with pockets full of salt. Convincing Dante to stay in the room was impossible. Often, he likes to lope off and explore but tonight he sticks close. I wish I had Villiers' rapier but he needs it to defend Jory in case the wraith shows. I hope he can persuade some of his mates to help us out. We need more blades, axes and bows on our side.

Heather's sitting in a windowed nook overlooking the gardens. Quietly, I perch next to her. The legionaries are on patrol. I can hear their singing from here, something in Latin that helps them keep up pace and morale.

I tuck my hands in my hoody sleeves, nervous. With the light behind us, my reflection haunts the glass but there's an empty space beside me; the dead don't have reflections, except in obsidian mirrors – ghost glass, Jory called it.

Heather doesn't turn, sigh, or say anything. Maybe she's going to yell at me. That would be fair. Actually, I'd like her to start shouting because this silence is worse.

When she does talk, her voice is whisper-quiet.

"Neelam never puts anything in the dishwasher, always leaves it on the side." She pauses, the words coming slowly. "But all the books in the house have to be organized by subject and date of publication. She's a total tea snob. She has this favourite teapot, a blue cat with a white face and flowers all over it. Made in the nineteen fifties or something, *so* ugly." She smiles, her eyes glistening.

I wait, watching her caught between love and grief, as she remembers the small things that make up a person. A life.

"I really hate that teapot." She finally looks at me. "But I wish I could make a brew for her in it one more time."

A tear tracks down her cheek. I catch it on my thumb, in awe. *Ghosts don't cry, not often, not unless...*

"I shouldn't have gone to Jory's behind your back." I gasp. "I didn't think it through—"

She catches my hand in hers, her tear crushed, head tilted like she's seeing me for the first time in a long while and is surprised by what she finds. "You did, Charlie. I know you. You thought about it and you did it anyway." Her hand flies up, cutting me off before I can protest. She's right. I need to own that. "You made a choice and you saved someone's life. If you all hadn't been there, that lass would be dead and we'd be no closer to finding out who's controlling the wraith. You took a risk and it paid off and I'm proud of you."

"So … you're not angry?"

"Oh, I'm fucking livid. You could have died and of all the things in my afterlife, you're my favourite."

I test a shaky smile. "Better than unlimited free cinema?"

"Way better." She looks back out at the garden. "I should have told you about Neelam sooner."

I shrug, trying to pretend that it doesn't bother me. "I get it, lost love and all that. It's personal."

"There's more to it." Heather's brow softens like she's going to deliver bad news. "It's something I've wanted to—" My phone vibrates and Heather clams up. "You should get that."

I swipe away the Team Spectre group chat notification. It can wait. "Is your something about Neelam leaving? Because if we can break your tether to York General then you can visit her whenever you want."

Hurried footsteps echo up the corridor. We swivel to see Mitch, ruddy cheeked and tousled. "Sam says to please get your cute arse upstairs. Miri's found a link between the first three victims," he blurts. "As suspected, they all bought tickets to see renowned psychic and clairvoyant Claire Cole. Her last show is *tomorrow* night."

19

PLAGUE AND POMP

York Theatre Royal is impressive, all fancy arches, tiered details and little turrets. And that's *before* we get inside to the sleek floors and pillars boxed in by huge plate glass windows.

This place was built on the site of Saint Leonard's, a medieval hospital that saw thousands of souls die in its walls. Heather and Villiers scouted the building earlier today to give us a rundown on the resident ghosts: a bunch of plague victims who are apparently weird but not dangerous.

I spot one on the stairs. He's slender with sunken eyes, and is wearing nothing but a linen smock that falls to knees dappled with scabs and sores.

"Creepy," mutters Sam.

If I was on my own, I'd steer clear, even if Heather says they're all right.

Behind the box office, Claire Cole smiles at us from a giant poster with "Final Performance" plastered over it. Direct and knowing, her image has one eyebrow cocked. The slight smile on her dark red lips promises she knows the answer, for a price.

We've armed ourselves with as much salt as we can carry. Sam's pockets are so stuffed I'm sure the ushers will think we're trying to sneak in snacks. We collect the tickets from the box office, one for me, Sam and Leonie. Mitch is at the restaurant today. He can't miss more work or he'll get kicked off the course. He lent me his cryptolenses though; I may need to see magic today.

Jory wanted to come, but showing up when Claire wants her dead is just plain daft. She's back at her place in a ring of salt, fresh protections all over her walls. Villiers rallied his allies so she has an armed, ghostly guard stationed front and back. Reid and Villiers took some persuading to stay with her rather than protect us tonight, but Jory's the one in *real* danger. The worst Claire can do in a room full of witnesses is set her sights on us. If she does, we're ready with some theorems of our own.

We've not heard from Jasper at Goslings and Waite yet, and we really need to know how to stop the wraiths. *A History of Highland Apparitions and Hauntings* is our best bet. Viola reckons Claire must have Sadie's copy at the theatre, away from potentially prying eyes. Who knows what incriminating occult stuff Claire keeps in her dressing room, but right now she'll be *in* there. We have to wait until she's onstage.

We could just go up there and talk to her, but Viola thinks it's a bad idea, just like she shot down my suggestion of trying to find The Hand and ask for their help.

An announcement chimes through the bar and there's a mass scraping of chairs and clamour of voices as people get up to cluster queue beside the entrance to the auditorium.

We're not the only teenagers here, there's a young lass up front with her mum, but most folks are older. A middle-aged woman clutching a photo of two little girls chats to a younger man about his dead wife, putting a comforting hand on his shoulder when he admits he lost his wedding ring wild swimming in Wales and is worried his late wife will be upset.

The doors finally open. The auditorium air is stuffy. All the seats are rich red and there are fancy boxes decorated with cream carvings. Three galleries around the sharply sloped stalls and high above us is a glittering chandelier.

This place is posh. If Claire Cole has filled it midweek for five weeks running then she's *seriously* popular. Didn't Sam mention something about a TV show? I wonder if they're already filming. Maybe that's why she's doing all this, for fame, or notoriety.

But no, that's not the purpose of a wraith.

It's always revenge.

Our seats are mid-way down the stalls near the side. Sam thought it would be easier to slip out unseen from there. They're only using the stalls, but they've dimmed the lights on the upper tiers and somehow that makes it feel intimate.

We're banking on there being enough people in the audience that Claire won't be able to get a good read on us. We're under strict instructions from Viola to think thoughts like, *Gosh, isn't this medium amazing*, and, *I totally believe she's contacting the dead.*

No way can I keep that up for long.

We found a map of the theatre floorplan online so I know the way to the dressing rooms. After that, Heather can take over. It's all going to work, it's going to be fine.

And if it all goes to bollocks?

It's unlikely Claire would risk giving herself away. Her first three victims were attacked away from the theatre. We're not expecting her to try anything here, but we need to work out how and why she's targeting members of her own audience.

The big red curtains over the stage are already drawn. There's no intro or music. The lights dim some more and she steps onstage to rousing applause. She's dressed in a gauzy black dress with billowing sleeves, long hair a waterfall of blonde-silver, hands up to pacify and greet us in one. Her lipstick is blood red like in her promotional poster, but that photo must have been taken a while ago. She's wearing heavy make-up and a bright smile, but even from where we're sitting I can see the bite of pain and exhaustion behind her eyes.

I bet it's the overtiredness of using a lot of magic and not tying into an external syphon. That's something at least. Claire is fuelling the wraith herself rather than using bottled souls.

"I've got two little girls here, see, two young loves standing together." Her voice swells inside the theatre, teeth flashing white. "They're saying the letter G."

The woman from the queue slowly rises in her seat. "My ... my name is Gloria."

"They're your babies, aren't they, my love?"

Gloria nods, trembling hands clutched around the photo of two children.

With the scooped neckline of Claire's dress, I finally get a look at the bone impresa at her throat. It's bigger than I thought, a high necklace of wire wrapped bones, mostly fingerbones in a row, studded with some kind of stone.

Claire's reading minds *right* now. I plaster a look of daft admiration on my face and watch the audience, trying not to stress. Don't think about how cruel she is playing with people's grief, taking advantage when they're desperate and—

Shit.

I mean, she's so convincing, and amazing and I'm so jealous of her genuine connection to the afterlife.

I glance at Sam beside me. He's sweating. In the next seat along, Leonie has her phone out, typing something, the soft glow from the screen up lighting her face.

Too obvious, we'll draw attention to ourselves. Claire's still talking to Gloria, but soon she'll be scanning the audience for someone new.

Sam gets out his phone as a notification flashes up.

> **Leonie:** I can't see any magic coming off the necklace, but it could be subtle, or cloaked.

We nod discreetly at Leonie.

Claire senses her second "ghost" of the evening, a young woman mourning her husband. "I see deep water and something lost."

The young man I overheard talking to Gloria hears all about how his dead wife loves him and wants him to forget about the ring. "It's safe in heaven with her, love, OK? You're not to trouble yourself any more."

Sliding my hand over Sam's, I squeeze twice. He squeezes back. Now is good. Heather's by the door, waiting. Ollie will stay with Leonie in the auditorium making sure that if Claire leaves the stage, we know about it.

We're on the end of our row, so it's easy enough to stand up and slip to the door.

"Bathroom?" Sam whispers to the usher.

"Out and right," she motions, opening the door for us. As light from the foyer streams through, a few people turn our way.

"There's another spirit here," says Claire's voice behind us. "She wants to communicate. I see a purple flower and she's calling a name." Closing her eyes, she waves her arms toward the audience, as if someone is guiding her, then pauses. "Neelam. Is there a Neelam here tonight?"

Heather stops like she's walked into a ghost line. I hesitate too, knowing I'm still letting in light and drawing attention to myself.

At the far side of the theatre, a familiar dark-haired woman stands. "Here."

Doctor Neelam Iyer.

The usher makes it clear I need to sit down or get out.

Claire beams. "I have a message for you, from Heather."

Heather makes a worried, wounded noise. I want to scream at Claire. *Yeah, Heather's here, but she's not talking to you, is she!* It doesn't matter if Claire's using magic, she's still a fraud.

The usher's getting frantic. Grabbing hold of Heather, I shove her into the foyer with a worried looking Sam.

"Neelam *can't* be here." Heather clutches my arm. "What if she becomes a target? We have to stop the show."

"How?"

"Fire alarm, evacuate the building."

"And miss our chance to get into Claire's dressing room?" asks Sam. "Neelam will be safe if we can stop the wraith completely."

Heather curses under her breath, then she squares her shoulders and marches through the glass doors to the left of the auditorium.

Sam does a bang-up job of distracting the usher watching the entrance to the back of house and me and Heather sneak past into a tangle of low lit corridors, my nerves are a buzz of static. I quickly learn that theatres are a maze, most of it stairs. I bloody hate stairs. The big plastic pot of salt swings awkwardly in the front pocket of my hoody as I climb. There are eight dressing rooms, scattered on multiple floors. They don't put the names of the performers on the doors but, lucky for me, Heather knows where we're going.

"There's nothing obvious lying about up there," she says as we climb *another* set of stairs and turn on to a short corridor. "But there's a wardrobe I can't look in."

The dressing room door isn't locked.

Inside is small but bright, set up for one person. A window overlooks the roof of the Oratory next door. It smells of hairspray, make-up and a hint of perfume. Slipping on Mitch's cryptolenses, I scan the room, being careful not to look directly at Heather.

No obvious hints of magic.

The bin is full of bloody tissues. Interesting. Maybe Claire gets nose bleeds, or maybe it's a side effect from using magic.

One wall is a long vanity with a collection of make-up, a battered old urban fantasy novel, and some pills – iron supplements, vitamin B and something called ashwaganha.

Heather frowns. "It's a shrub, thought to be an adaptogen, used against emotional and physical stress."

"Murdering people must be exhausting," I whisper.

"As she's using magic to do it, then, yeah."

I put the bottles back.

A brightly lit mirror reflects the old wardrobe on the opposite wall. Beside it, there's a metal bar where Claire's hung a couple of spare dresses. The wardrobe is a nice piece, all dark wood and fancy carvings. If I was going to keep something special in this room, that's where I'd put it.

Like the dressing room door, it's not even locked. I brought my picks for nothing.

There's not much inside: Claire's handbag – wallet, keys, mints, tampons, lipstick, a dowsing pendulum, tissues and a bunch of receipts. A scarf, gloves inside the coat. Nothing of interest in any of the coat pockets.

"No book," I confirm, quietly annoyed.

We're going to have to break into Claire's hotel and riffle through everything there before she leaves the city. Maybe Sam could feign interest, apologize for my rudeness and take Claire and his mum to dinner. That would give me, Leonie and Mitch a chance to snoop about.

Problem is, Claire's impresa will warn her of Sam's deception.

I'm about to shut the wardrobe when I catch sight of a dark enamel tin on the shallow, high shelf at the top.

Clawing open the lid I find a bunch of random clippings and papers. Most are memorabilia from past tours. There're newspaper articles, all good press, old promotional pamphlets – not all Claire's. I find one dated 1998 for an evening in Blackpool with the amazing mystic, Clarissa Vizgirda. There are photos too.

A younger Claire, eyes closed, wearing a fringed dress Stevie Nicks would kill for. Claire hugging an audience member whose face is puffy with tears. Claire in a cowboy hat, standing on an outdoor stage addressing a huge crowd, a blood red sky behind her.

"Stop, look there." Heather points to a face in an image of

Claire and a circle of people all holding hands. "That's Irma Lane, one of the victims."

"You sure?"

"Years younger but, yeah, I'm positive."

I spread the photos out on the vanity for Heather to look at, quickly checking the time on my phone. We've been gone ten minutes. I wonder if Sam's still keeping that receptionist talking.

"There she is again." Heather snaps her fingers. "See?"

A photo of a small theatre, the image taken from the stage, Irma Lane's face smiles out of the second row.

"And that's Graham Geoffrey, victim number one." He's standing behind Claire in a fancy living room, with an expression of awe and admiration. "I bet Naomi Petty, the last victim, is here too."

Claire knew them all.

"Why would she attack her fans?" I ask. All three are still in comas.

My phone flashes with an incoming call. Swiping up to answer, Miri doesn't give me a chance to say hi before she asks, "Is Sam ignoring me?"

I cup the receiver to hush my voice as best I can. "He's distracting ushers."

"You're at the theatre?"

"Yeah, you got something?"

"Claire Cole is more than an accountant's daughter from Hull," Miri says quickly. "She's changed her name and identity to avoid allegations of theft stretching back two decades."

Wedging my mobile between ear and shoulder, I thumb

through the enamel box, pulling out the leaflet from the nineties. "She wasn't ever Clarissa Vizgirda, was she?"

"And Constanza de la Court, Farnia Faneau and Isobel Cotton. That woman has ripped off a lot of grieving people." I can hear the disgust in Miri's voice.

"We've found photos proving the wraith's first three victims have been coming to her shows for years."

"Oh, she knew them." Miri sounds confident. "I had to trawl a lot of accounts to find the trail, but Claire *paid* them all considerable sums over the past few years."

"They *work* for her?" I say, too loudly. Heather winces. We shouldn't have this conversation here.

One handed, I swipe the photos back into the box. Claire will know someone's gone through her stuff, but I can't worry on that now.

If three of the wraith's victims were employed by Claire, that means Neelam is likely safe. Claire isn't killing off just anyone who attends her shows, it's more targeted than that.

"If you ask me they're part of the con," says Miri.

Of course. The old woman in the crowd – Gloria – was talking to that guy about his dead wife, and then Claire goes and picks him immediately, even telling him all about his lost ring. Graham, Naomi and Irma were *plants*, canvasing the crowd for titbits they could feed back to Claire to make it all seem so much more real.

Shoving the box back in the top of the wardrobe, I say goodbye to Miri and let me and Heather out of the dressing room, closing the door with a soft click.

The corridor is empty and the other dressing rooms silent.

"Why would Claire need to use plants if she can read people's minds and influence them?" I ask Heather, wincing as I catch sight of her through the cryptolenses.

"Maybe she's not as powerful as she pretends."

"Fake it till you make it," I say, starting back down the stairs, careful not to trip.

Heather follows. "That would explain why she blackmailed or threatened Sadie into helping her raise a wraith. Real power."

But *revenge*?

"Why would she want people on her payroll dead?"

"What if they threatened to expose her?" says Heather.

If they knew about her old identities and crimes then they'd be even more of a threat and if they'd been working for her for years, it's likely they did know.

They're your babies, aren't they, my love?

It's possible Gloria's the next victim. I pick up the pace. My trainers make shuffling noises on the steps.

"*Charlie.*" Heather grabs my arm.

I stop. Three plague ghosts are waiting on the landing below, blocking our way. They crackle and flicker, proper scary-looking. I'm still wearing Mitch's cryptolenses. I pull them off and the souls settle into a solid form.

"It's coming," the taller ghost says mournfully.

That scent again – ash and earth.

Ah, fuck.

20

†HE LAS† SHOW

I t's here.

I barely register the pain in my lungs as I follow Heather's flustered instructions towards backstage. An usher tries to protest as I speed past, aiming for a small, glowing box in the wall. Curling a fist, I smash the glass. The piercing wail of the fire alarm surges through the theatre.

I need to find Sam and Leonie.

"Everyone out!" I bellow as I tear through the simple black cloth and on to the stage.

A third of the audience are already on their feet. Ushers on the doors take charge. Daylight cracks through the warm glow of the lights. They're evacuating. Good.

My throat is thick, chest aching as I catch my breath.

Sam, where are you?

I spot his dark, floppy curls. A beat of relief. He's with Leonie, people jostling them as they push against the flow, heading for the stage, and me.

And Claire Cole.

She's at the front of the stage, staring at me with shock and outrage. I clock the moment she recognizes me, anger twisting her features.

"Please, everyone, sit back down. It's sabotage, there's no emergency." The alarm rolls over her voice, hammering us with its sharp wail. No one pays her any attention.

I shove Mitch's cryptolenses back on. The bone impresa at her throat spiders with dark glowing lines that crackle into the galleries, slinking into the darkness there.

"She must be calling it," Heather shouts in my ear loud enough to hurt. Ghosts can see the syphon in action too, but not regular folk. No one in the audience is pointing in wonder; they're all set on getting out.

The wraith boils from the shadows of the gallery. Eyes in a bone skull, bared teeth. I bellow again. Sam and Leonie have seen it too, expressions frozen in horror.

I scramble for the steps from stage to stalls, jarring my prostheses and making me inhale sharply, but I'm already bolting along the front of the orchestra pit, ignoring the pain.

Someone is in the air – Gloria – floating as high as the balconies. The photo of "her children" falls from her hand, floating to be crushed underfoot by onlookers. The wraith sniffs at her, growling deep in its core.

The evacuation has all but stopped, punters pointing and

gasping, stumbling into the stalls, tripping over seats. *Run.* I've no breath to shout and the fire alarm is still screaming.

Neelam is below Gloria and the wraith, hand to mouth, her eyes wary. Is this part of the show?

No, it's bloody not. Move!

No time to even think before—

The alarm falls silent.

A sound like bone breaking. Gloria's body jerks. *Crack.* Blood pours from deep gouges in her face. Head lolling. Teeth. Meaty tongue sheered and pumping gore. Her lungs expel blood splatter. Warm wetness rolls down my cheek. Someone catches my arm, pulling me back from her. Heather.

The wraith climbs *inside* Gloria's mouth, squeezing clawed bone and twisting shadow into her gullet. She drops, plummeting into the now empty space below her. Everyone is screaming but I still hear the crunch as her face shatters, trailing jawbone and sinew. The wraith burrows deeper, unstitching her body from the inside out as it feeds on her soul. Her throat ruptures, ribs popping, dark blood seeping through her coat.

The scent of cedarwood soap cuts the tang. Sam slides a hand over my cheek, smearing the wet there, pushing me away. Leonie has her shield up, pale silver and rippling with power.

We back against the stage, away from the confused, terrified audience flooding towards the far door. No one seems to think of the backstage exit.

Claire's still onstage, expression carved into horror, tears streaking her make-up. Doesn't she know what she's doing? She sways, as if dizzy. Blood trickles from her nose. The dark threads from her bone impresa thicken and twist.

"Charlie!" Sam points to a dark shape clawing its way down the stage curtains.

There's a second wraith.

The sight of it slams into me.

Breathe.

Edge away nice and slow. They move like lightning. If they attack us now, we're dead.

But the wraiths aren't here for us, and Gloria's dead. Who else does Claire want to get rid of? I think through the photos upstairs, desperate to remember the faces. I'm not like Sam with his impressive visual memory and I'm too scared to think properly.

The wraith reaches the bottom of the curtain. Then it's gone. No, there. Onstage, sidling towards Claire. It snakes surround her, nuzzling in a way that's almost affectionate—

Dark coiling smoke launches itself into the auditorium. Fabric tears, spilling foam stuffing. Metal twists as it rips through the stalls. The wraith's strength is staggering.

I look back to the stage. No, the second wraith is still with Claire, the first wraith is feasting on Gloria, so the wraith tearing up the theatre must be—

A third.

Fuck.

A guttural and agonized shout. The third wraith drags a man from the press around the far door. People have fallen, blocking the way out. Oily shadows pry open his mouth as he kicks at the invisible force holding him. Blood rolls down his chin. Bone snaps, his neck twists as his body breaks at the spine, contorting to all fours, head back and mouth wide. The sound of his bellow, the hunger in his voice. The anger. Then he falls back over the chairs and disappears.

Was he a plant too? Maybe, but if he's not then … oh, God, please no. Claire's not targeting her failing network any more, she's letting her pets go after anyone they like. An undercurrent of desperation ghosts beneath my skin, mingling with the dread and fear.

The stage is empty. She and the second wraith are gone. Where?

Backstage. The only other way out.

I scrunch my eyes closed, not wanting to see more people die. My head spins, terror threatening to shut me down completely. There's no time to freeze up. We have to stop this but we're underprepared, *again*. I need Villiers and his mates with their weapons. We should have brought a whole Roman legion with us, not pissed about underestimating how bat-shit ruthless Claire Cole is.

We have to go after her. She's the only one who can stop this.

Neelam's beside the ruin of flesh that was once Gloria, as if there's *anything* she can do to save the poor woman. The first wraith oozes out of the corpse, sniffing the air. Its work is done. Gloria's dead, soul consumed. But it's not leaving. It sidles around Neelam with a sound like grinding teeth.

She can't see it or sense it. Doesn't know that death is only an arm's length from her.

In a blink, Heather's between them, shoving the shade with an angry yell. Tearing her stethoscope from her neck, she uses it like a whip to keep it back.

"Fuck, yeah, Heather!" cheers Ollie.

I've seen that hard determination in her eyes before – in the cemetery back in the spring when she faced down Sister Agnes and Sharp-Teeth to protect me and Sam.

My eyes burn. Dragging the plastic pot of salt from my hoody, I pop the top funnel so a stream of crystals can escape. Not much of a weapon, but it's what we have. Sam does the same. His nod is determined.

We move at the same time.

Sam's faster. Nimble. He throws an arc of white that dissipates into the air around the wraith. It screeches, flinching away from the salt sparks as I put myself between it and Neelam. Heather slashes with her stethoscope again. With a livid screech the wraith swipes out and catches her in the face. She goes flying. I bellow her name.

Behind me, Neelam gasps. I realize she's been talking this whole time, spouting questions, and I've barely heard her. The wraith slashes at Sam, but he ducks and stumbles away. A twist of my wrist and I'm shaking salt over everything to clear a path. I've Neelam at my back and Sam by my side. Ollie has Heather. There are nasty slashes across her face but no blood. The cuts are as dark as shadows.

Blackness closes in. I blink it back, slipping to the floor.

My head knocks against a metal chair leg on the way down. There's carpet under my cheek and my arm is wet.

Don't look. Not yet.

"Charlie!" Heather screams and hauls me to my feet.

"What the fuck?" Neelam gasps. "What the fuck? What the fuck?"

The theatre tilts, spinning lights as my head throbs. It's hard to talk. Bile burns. I'm gonna be sick. Sam throws more salt at the wraith, fending it off.

"Stage door," I croak.

Another sharp scream, cut off by gurgling.

Don't look back.

Silver light. Leonie lit by it. She looks like angels do in paintings, but angrier, determined. Ollie gives me a boost back on to the stage. It's higher up than I remember. I reach back for Sam's hand. My arm burns. There's a slash in my hoody sleeve. The gash in the fabric is wet. I'm bleeding.

Fuck.

My gaze connects with Sam's and I find the strength to haul him up.

Turning, he helps Neelam as I roll on to my back, gasping. The ceiling spins. Leonie has to drop her shield to climb but the second she's on the stage she whispers something and the magic unfurls again. She holds the shield up and out. Got to get up.

Up.

Leonie has me. There's sweat on her forehead. The silver light extends and thickens.

Shadows. The wraith is here, claws extending.

Into the wings. Heather. Ollie. Sam on my other side.

"Keep going," he urges. His voice is distant, like a dream.

Two soldiers, one with a long pike, the other a bow, stare at us barrelling towards them, the wraith on our tail. Ghosts. Part of Villiers' brigade?

"Shoot it!" Sam screams.

The archer scrambles to our aid, sliding an arrow into the notch on his bow and drawing back. With a twang the arrow sails past my left ear, a little close for comfort. Behind me, the wraith howls.

Ladders, winches, unused stage sets for a different show. The smell of fresh cut wood and paint and turpentine is smothering. Everything is bathed in harsh white light.

Sam's pulling me away. No, we have to get—

A wraith drops in front of us, blocking the exit. It boils with anger and hunger.

I'm out of salt.

Leonie pushes forward, meeting the monster as it slams into her shimmering shield. She grunts with the effort, feet sliding on the smooth flooring. Bone claws spike around the sides. It's going to pry the shield off like the lid of a can.

"You'll stretch it too thin," Sam warns Leonie. "Let me help."

The light widens into a dome. Leonie's eyes are closed. We huddle – Heather, Ollie, Neelam, me. Sam and Leonie stand solid, arms up, palms open as the monsters slam down again and again.

There're two wraiths on top of us now.

Our defences start to crumble. Blood drips over Leonie's lips and chin. Nosebleed. She's tiring too fast. Sam's tied himself into her theorem, his palm bloody as it wraps around hers. She can't hold the shield much longer, even with Sam giving what he can.

The world rings with noise and I know there's a fight and people are dying but I can't get up. If I could, I'd tie myself in too; blood, a simple glyph. We've practised it. It's the only way to keep the shield strong until help arrives.

Help isn't coming.

The Hand, a voice at the back of my mind hopes. *They're in York, they'll come.*

And when they do, will we be the enemy?

That's better than dead.

Ollie cheers. Bare feet and linen and enraged voices. The plague ghosts flood around us. Leonie whimpers as she falls against me, sliding on to the dirty floor where I'm lying. Her eyes are closed. I reach for her. Her shield is gone.

A face over mine.

Sam. His lips on my cheek. He says my name and I think I say his.

Stuttering light.

Voices.

I look down. Blood, most of it mine. The top of my left sleeve is shredded. The wraith got down to skin this time, actually way deeper. Funny how I don't feel any pain there but the back of my head is throbbing.

Where are Sam and Leonie? Heather's face swims into view, deep cuts on her cheek and forehead. Why doesn't she bleed? Oh, yeah, she's dead.

I try and focus on what she's saying.

Take the hoody off.

She needs to see my wound. I try, I do. In the end I just tear the fabric, exposing more of my arm and the curved gash carved through it.

Not good.

I cover the wound with my hand, thinking to stop the bleeding and a smarting erupts up my arm. I think I scream. There's salt on my palms. I curse as I try to breathe through the agony.

I need to get up.

"Stay down." Neelam's above me. So is Heather, their faces side by side and their voices distant. They're both talking at me.

Heather presses the edges of my wound together and holds, staunching the flow. Her touch is cool on my hot skin. Neelam blinks, drawing back, confused. What does she see?

"Heather," I whisper. "Heather."

Their faces blur together, becoming one as the lights go out.

21

UNSPOKEN

God, I really hate hospitals. There's that chemical tang to the air, constant coughing, machines beeping, alarms blaring, people in pain and ghosts everywhere. I hope none of them bother me because I'm knackered.

And I stink.

There's so much blood. It's in my hair, matted and drying. My hoody and trackies are stained with it.

Sam was here, dark bags under his eyes, but he's gone for an X-ray. His shoulder dislocated again. Leonie collapsed. The wraiths didn't touch her, but keeping that shield going was too much. Even with Sam's help, she pushed herself and burned out. But she saved our lives. Her and the plague ghosts. Apparently, they swarmed the wraiths and the monsters retreated, disappearing in seconds.

Heather's gone to find out what she can. People died, I know that much. My prostheses feel heavy and my hip and head throb. I can't handle this. The cubicle sways. I grip the gurney and suck in air as pain flares beneath my bandages. I shouldn't be sitting, but if I lie back down I'm afraid I'll never get up again.

Ollie's here. He lets me lean on him for a bit as he chats, talking too fast. I close my eyes and see flashing lights, Heather and Neelam above me, the blaring alarm, the smell – death has a smell. God.

I want Sam. I want to go home.

Has anyone called Mitch?

A nurse has already assessed my wound. It runs from the inside of my arm above my elbow to the outside below my shoulder, missing my arteries by a centimetre. I'll need stitches before I can go anywhere and they're worried about concussion. Now the immediate danger of me bleeding out is over, it's taking me a fair while to be seen again, even though I came in with a police escort.

Good, that means I'm not dying. Or maybe it's just a busy night.

Yeah, it's busy. *Three* wraiths attacked the York Theatre Royal.

Where the fuck is The Hand? Stopping occultists like Claire Cole is what they do, so either Viola's lying and they're not in York after all, or something else is going on.

"That rozzer still out there?" I ask Ollie, my voice hoarse.

He sticks his head through the curtain drawn over the cubicle. "By the water cooler with your dad."

Dad. The look he gave me when he rushed in – relief

sliding over his anger. I don't reckon he's pissed at me, it's the fact that I'm back in hospital, all cut up, and no one can explain what happened, least of all me.

"Doctor incoming." Ollie rights himself. "It's *her*."

Neelam pulls back the curtain, pushing a cart stacked with equipment and sterile bandages. "Good evening, Charlie, my name is Doctor Iyer."

"Yeah."

You were at the show.

I don't say it, but we both know it. Is she even supposed to be working right now? Maybe they need all doctors on hand, or maybe she's just like Heather, absorbed by the job.

They've cut the sleeve off my ruined hoody and T-shirt so she has no problem assessing the laceration. "I'm going to numb the area so you won't feel the stitches."

Needles don't bother me, but I still look away. Prepping the sutures and curved needle she'll need, Neelam keeps glancing up at me, as if she wants to say something, but can't bring herself to.

Ollie's wary, watching her closely.

"Does this hurt?" She tests the skin around the cut. I shake my head. "Great. This looks worse than it is, I promise you're in safe—"

Heather steps through the curtain. Doctor Iyer stumbles over her words. Heather stares at her, frozen. They both snap out of it at the same time. Neelam inhales, moving away from me with a shiver. I give Heather a puzzled look as she walks around the gurney, putting space between them.

"You all right?" I ask Heather, so drained that I forget not to talk to the dead with the living present. There are jagged cuts to her cheek and forehead, the wounds dark.

Wraiths can hurt other ghosts.

Neelam looks up, surprised. "Yeah, just—" She shakes her head, tears rising in her eyes. "Tonight's been … a lot."

"Four dead," says Heather. "Fifteen injured, some by the wraiths, some in the crush to get out of the auditorium. Leonie's still unconscious."

"Shit."

"Yeah, it has been shit." Neelam clears her throat. "Sorry, that was unprofessional." Steadying herself, she starts to stitch my arm. It's a weird feeling, pressure not pain. I keep my eyes on Heather, who's tracing the cuts on her face with probing fingers. I want to ask her if they hurt, but I can't.

"Weird night," I say to Neelam.

"You can say that again." She ties off the first stitch, cuts the thread and starts on the next. "I, er … at the theatre, you said a name, do you remember?"

Heather.

Neither of them has let go. It's not just my friend holding on, it's Neelam too. Death isn't the end of love, it amplifies it.

I flinch, pulling on the suture.

"Am I hurting you?" asks Neelam, concerned

I swipe away tears. "No, no, I'm fine, just … in the theatre…"

"Don't," hisses Heather, cutting me off.

"I'm gonna go." Motioning to the corridor, Ollie ghosts through the curtain leaving Heather glowering at me.

Is she so set on punishing herself that she'll let Neelam leave York without taking the chance to say a proper goodbye? If Neelam knows about her then it might be good for them.

Maybe she can't face telling Neelam that she gave up her life for a random kid. She chose a stranger over the woman she loves. That's not exactly true. She gave up her life for mine because she thought it was owed. Now, I owe her back.

"I said Heather."

"*Charlie!*" snaps Heather.

But maybe *I'm* wrong and telling Neelam the truth isn't the right thing for either of them. I don't get to decide that, even if I want to help. Where's the comfort in knowing someone you love is living an afterlife parallel to you, but you can never see or hear them?

"She's a mate from school." I look down because even though I get a lot of practice at it, I've never been a brilliant liar.

"You said her name like she was there."

"Head injury. It's all pretty hazy to be honest."

Neelam focuses on the next few stitches, silent. When the last suture is tied off, she looks over her work. I can see her wanting to ask again. She knows what she saw – my skin depressing under the pressure of an invisible hand as Heather staunched the wound, her bloody fingerprints appearing on my skin.

Neelam saw it, but she can't *say* it, even though she was at a medium's show so possibly believes in the supernatural.

Instead, Dr Iyer applies a bandage, tells me about wound aftercare and how often to change the dressings. Then, after checking the bump on the back of my head, she gives me a run down on concussion symptoms, warning me to come back if I feel nauseous, dizzy or if I have trouble staying awake.

She draws back the cubicle curtain. "Are you here with anyone?"

Ollie's outside. I look at him and not Heather because if I do I'm going to give something away.

"My dad." I point.

He's talking to Lucrezia, which always worries me. I wonder if Sam's back from X-ray. Seeing the curtain of my cubicle pull back, Dad excuses himself and heads this way.

Neelam tries to smile. "Great, well…" Heather comes a little closer and her breath hitches. *Sensitive to the spirit world.* Neelam's like my sisters – she can feel Heather's presence and some of her emotions, but she's not a seer. "Good luck, Charlie."

"Thanks."

Doctor Iyer strides away with the cart. Heather releases a long breath.

"I can talk to her for you," I whisper.

"No."

"But maybe—"

"I said no, Charlie. Leave it alone."

And then Heather's gone, the air empty like she was never there.

Even though we didn't get home until the early hours, the police knock on our door by ten. I've barely slept. Broomwood, Heather and Ollie kept watch all night, but I was never going to settle. Dad kept popping in every couple of hours, worried about concussion. Every time I closed my eyes I saw billows of smoke, blood and bone.

Sam's not faring much better. We facetimed for hours, trying to piece together what happened at the theatre. He was sweaty and shaking all night, exhausted from syphoning what he could into Leonie's shield to keep it stable, but unable to sleep thanks to the fresh ache in his shoulder. His arm is back in a brace.

There's more than one wraith. This is so beyond what we can deal with. I don't reckon we have a choice but to appeal to The Hand. They literally specialize in hunting down and stopping occultists.

Sam's not so sure.

Just because there are dangerous shades on the loose doesn't mean they'll give us a pass for what happened with Gates. I get it, but at this point what choice do we have? But we have no idea how to contact The Hand and Viola won't help us. Ollie suggested that laying another ghost trap to set off their alarms would probably do it. Not a bad idea but I want to talk to Mitch and Leonie about it first.

We were about to try and sleep when Villiers and Reid came charging into my room at three this morning going on about a wraith attack at Jory's. There was nothing they could do; they fought hard, keeping the wraiths back but one of them made it inside. The house is a mess and Jory's gone.

All of our protections fell apart. We did everything we could, and Claire still won.

We failed.

The officers showed Dad their badges at the front door but they're dressed in civvies, not uniforms. Detectives, apparently. Mum's working at the salon, so they ask him to be present because I'm under eighteen.

There's been no update on Leonie's condition yet. Mitch isn't answering his phone. I want to call the hospital again but they've already told me they can't share any details unless I'm family, especially as we're all part of an active police investigation.

They're interviewing everyone who was at Claire's final show. The detectives ask how I'm feeling, basic stuff like my name and date of birth, and they inform me of my rights and ask me to take them through the events of yesterday.

I'm stumbling and vague about most of it because I can't tell them half of what happened. I know it's suspicious to give such shoddy answers and claim I can't remember. This all went down yesterday, it should be fresh in my thoughts, and it *is*—

So much blood.

What if Leonie's not all right this time? She pushed too far, *way* too far. I should have done more, tried a theorem at least, but it takes so much focus I find it hard to use magic under pressure.

It would be different if I was mirrored.

My brain is too addled to keep the lies smooth, even with

Heather prompting me. Once or twice I seriously mess up and they jump on it.

"It sounds like you think Charlie had something to do with what happened," Dad cuts in.

"We're just trying to ascertain the facts," says the lady detective, her face unreadable.

I wish I had Sam's confidence, or Mitch's charm. I just clam up, which looks bloody suspicious. Maybe I'll get charged for murder. That'd be class that, criminal record before I'm eighteen when I've done nothing wrong. Dad will kick up a fuss if they try it, then they'll arrest him too. He doesn't deserve that.

Probably sensing I'm spiralling, the detectives change angle. "What can you tell us about Jory Chambers?" And that surprises the hell out of me.

They ask me for a timeline: when we got to her house, what art we looked at, what the conversation was about. Again, I keep it vague. The bloke detective takes out a folder and spreads several photos over the coffee table in front of me.

"We visited Miss Chambers' property this morning after a neighbour called with a noise complaint and found the house like this."

Photos of Jory's kitchen with the deep gouges made by the wraith on the wall. I can't help touching my arm where its claws caught me at the theatre. Screams echo in my ears. Clamping my eyes shut, I try not to chuck up.

The next image is of taxidermy animals on the floor of the front room, broken glass and wood, crushed bone, gouges on the walls.

Dad clears his throat. "Charlie didn't have anything to do with this."

"We're not suggesting he did, we're just concerned for Miss Chambers' wellbeing and are speaking to anyone who has had contact with her in the past week," says the lady detective. "Charlie, if you have any information regarding her whereabouts, I promise she's not in any trouble and neither are you, we just need to find her to make sure she's safe."

The last photo is of Jory's open front door. The hallway beyond is a mess. My mind is a whirlwind. No body, no blood, no sign that Jory was hurt. If the wraith didn't *kill* her then where is she? The ward alarms did their job and Villiers and his ghost brigade held the wraiths off for a bit. Maybe she had a chance to escape.

Then I spot something that sends my head into even more of a spin. Tucked partially under the stairs is a familiar duffel bag with red handles. The one Sadie had on her when she died. It's back in her house.

How?

I peer closer, trying not to be too obvious. My head throbs. I haven't had enough sleep to deal with this.

There's no way that bag could be at the house.

"Do you see something?" asks the bloke detective.

I drop the photo back on the coffee table. "No, sorry."

The detectives leave with a warning that they'll likely ask me to come down the station for a follow-up interview. Ollie trails them to their car in case they say something useful. Maybe I should ask Reid and Villiers to haunt the station for a while? It makes sense to keep tabs on the investigation, in case the police actually turn up something.

I make for my room, mind racing.

"Was that *the* bag?" asks Heather, following me. The cuts on her face made by the wraith's claws are still healing. Dark and thin, they look like a tattoo.

Closing my door, I lean against it with a sigh. "Yeah, or an identical one. Maybe Claire took it back to the house last night. If it was found in her possession, it links her to Sadie."

Except the police don't know about the bag, so it doesn't.

Unless we've got this all wrong and Jory was the one Sadie was meeting the night she died. But *why*? They lived together. The wraiths tried to kill Jory. It doesn't make any sense.

I sit on my bed. Something else is bothering me about the theatre. Before, Claire ordered the wraiths to attack late-night in dark streets with few witnesses. Why would she suddenly summon three of them to tear into an audience at her own show?

Even if the attack goes unexplained she's bound to get some backlash. I bet they'll cancel the rest of her tour off the back of this. Whatever her motive, it's got to be worth the fall out. Plus, it's made the international news. If The Hand didn't already know something weird is going on in York, they do now.

I'd have thought the mighty Meryem would show up at a magical massacre. Maybe Viola's wrong about them being back in the city, but I doubt it. They're sticking to the shadows, and that worries me more.

I prefer my potential enemies where I can see them. I'm gonna have to trip their alarms, try and make contact.

"However the bag got there, if Claire took Jory it's because she needs her," says Heather.

"OK, but what *for*?" I ask. "If she wanted revenge for something, why not just kill her like she did Sadie?"

Heather shakes her head. "I've no idea."

I hear the front door close. Getting up, I peek around my half-drawn curtains at the two detectives heading down the cul-de-sac towards their car, Ollie following.

The photos of Jory's house showed the floor covered in broken taxidermy and a few crushed bones, but not enough to account for all the bone impresa Jory had displayed in there. *That's missing too.*

Where's my phone? I search through the messy duvet on my bed.

For the first time in years, Dad opens my door without knocking. "Lad, what's going on?"

"Nothing." I can't deal with him right now.

"If you won't tell the rozzers the truth then you need to tell me. Whatever you've got yourself tangled up in, this is serious—"

"You can't fix this," I snap, hating the hurt in his eyes. He's only trying to help but all he can do is make it worse. I can't be worrying about him and Mum with everything else already going on.

My phone is under my pillow. Grabbing it, I find some cash in the drawer and push past Dad. He follows me into the hall. "You're not leaving until you tell me what's going on."

"Just drop it, all right."

A voice message from Mitch is waiting on the group chat. *Finally.*

Dad goes on. "Charlie, talk to me. I want to help."

Pausing by the front door, I take a deep breath.

Imagine I tell him the truth, right here, right now. Then what? Either he thinks it's some kind of delusion and tries to get me psychiatric help, or he rejects me outright. Let's say he believes me and doesn't want me gone. He'll still ask me to stop doing what I do because it's dangerous.

I can't change what I am. When I came out as gay he promised to always be here for me. But seeing the dead? No part of him knowing the truth about that ends well for us as a family. I've no choice but to walk away from the man who's always had my back.

It cuts deep.

I grab my cheap earbuds off the entryway stand and keep walking as I press play on Mitch's message. His panicked voice sounds in my ears, blocking out whatever Dad's saying as he trails me out the front. My attention is divided but I get the gist – Leonie's seriously ill. Mitch is at the hospital with her family.

Our landline rings and Dad ducks back inside, shouting at me not to go anywhere.

Sorry, Dad.

I message the chat. On my way.

"Everything OK?" asks Heather, knowing full well it's not.

I don't have much cash, but it's enough for the bus. At the

end of the cul-de-sac, Ollie comes rushing over. "Yeah, the rozzers don't believe you, mate. They'll be back to ask you down the station today for sure. Also, Claire Cole's under investigation for fraud; they were going to bust her soon. Get this … she's missing too."

She's been accused of fraud in the past. Changed her name, started fresh. I bet she's burning bridges because she's not planning on living as Claire Cole for much longer. Take revenge, disappear. Whatever she's got planned for Jory, it's not good.

22

†HE PRIMARY AUGURER

On the bus, me, Ollie and Heather watch the news report on my phone, the volume low. There'll be a vigil outside the theatre for the four who died – candles and flowers and impossible questions. The reporter mentions that a "teenage girl is still fighting for her life in hospital".

Leonie.

We arrive at the hospital, heading to the critical care ward in time to see Mitch, bleary-eyed, pushing open the double doors like he's trying to take something down. Turning, he punches his fist into the wall, then leans his forehead against the plaster, cursing in pain.

I gently touch his shoulder. He flinches, cheeks reddening and fighting tears. "They think it's the same thing her mum had."

"It isn't," I try to reassure him. "It's magical exhaustion."

She's overstretched before. A bit of food and sleep and

usually within a day she's fine. But something is different this time. She still hasn't woken up. Either there was a mistake in the theorem, or expanding and maintaining the shield, even with Sam's help, was way too much for her.

Shit.

Mitch shakes his head. "I dunno, I can't exactly tell the docs about soul sources and syphons and theorems and all that, but the symptoms are the same as her mum's were right when she started going downhill." He swallows and looks away, maybe ashamed that he's crying, which is daft. 'Course he's gonna be upset.

Then I remember what Mitch's dad is like. He probably has to hide how he's feeling most of the time. Sod that.

"Mate." Cupping the back of his head, I pull him into a proper hug, not caring that the stitches at the top of my arm pull painfully. I half-expect him to push me away, but he doesn't. With a fist full of my hoody, he sobs into my shoulder.

"Charlie, she's my heart. She can't die. She just can't."

I hold him as he cries, deep wracking gasps.

"She's gonna be all right," I whisper again and again, blinking back tears. It's the kind of bullshit fake promise that I hate, but if I say it enough times it will become true because the world without Leonie in it isn't an option for any of us.

When we break apart, Mitch rubs at my shoulder with his bunched sleeve. "I snotted on you."

"S'OK." I give him back his cryptolenses. Wiping his eyes, he hesitates before putting them back on.

Sam arrives with Villiers, his arm in a brace, looking tired and shocked. He's on some pretty heavy painkillers but he's here. I kiss him, breathing him in, feeling the magnetic pull between us, so thankful that he's all right.

"How fares Leonie?" asks Villiers.

"Not good," Mitch wipes his cheeks on his sleeve.

Sam hugs him next. "We went by the bookshop but Viola's not around."

Villiers is restless. "Mayhap Mistress Viola called upon her friend and will yet return. We can but hope."

"If magic did this then there has to be a theorem that can help Leonie heal," says Sam. "I found a strength spell we could try."

"Sam, if you show me how, I'll cast it," I say. He raises his brows. "I didn't use any magic yesterday and I'm not on any heavy painkillers."

The ward doors open to a bald man with a close-cut grey beard. Leonie's dad looks like a decade just dropped on him overnight. Al, Leonie's brother, is behind him, wearing his favourite blue basketball shirt. He picked it up in China when he and his dad flew out to meet his birth parents earlier in the year.

"Hiya, mate." I pat Al's arm. "How you holding up?"

"Not good." He's in our year but we never went to the same school because he goes to a specialist academy for kids with Down's Syndrome. "She's sick like Mum."

Taking off his round glasses, Mr Agyemang scrubs at his eyes. "Thanks for coming, boys. I need to get a few things from home, and Al needs some air. Terry and Joe are on their way." He names his other sons. "It's a five-hour drive for Joe and I only got hold of Terry a couple of hours ago. Are you all right to stay with Leonie until we get back?"

"Of course," I say, and mean it.

Mr Agyemang's lips part, half a question on his tongue. He looks tired and distant, like he's falling apart.

Guilt sits in my throat. We can't tell him the truth, just as we can't tell my folks what's really going on.

I treated my dad like shit when he was just trying to help. *I'll make it up to him. Somehow.*

They normally only admit two visitors at a time but the nurses let all three of us in, well, six, if you count the dead. Beyond the nurse station is a corridor with smaller wards off it. One way out, right down the end, fire escape. Breathing deep, I search for ash and earth, but there's only a blank medical smell.

Glancing at Sam, he meets my eye and I know he's doing the same – marking the exits, thinking about a quick escape in case we need it. I was in such a hurry to get out of the house, I didn't even bring any salt.

Leonie's in a private room off the main corridor. We gather round her bed. There's a tube giving her extra oxygen, a machine tracking her heartbeat, and needles dripping vital fluids into her arms. She looks like a stranger; her face is thinner and her skin has lost its vibrancy, like someone switched off the light inside her.

"Mistress Agyemang." Villiers hovers his palm over her hand, as if he can take it to comfort her. "We are here, my dear friend."

Mitch kisses her forehead. The machines beep reassuringly.

"Do you think she can hear us?" says Ollie.

Heather's brow is soft, her eyes filled with worry. "It depends; many comatose patients have brainstem auditory—"

SNAP.

Not a sound. A feeling, like a door slamming. A force punches through my back. Pressure in my upper belly, rising to my chest, a nasty, smothering sensation that's uncomfortable rather than painful. It's in my limbs now, arms, hands, thighs, knees.

I can't move, can't cry out; the only control I have is my breathing, which is a fast-panicked pump, flooding locked limbs with oxygen they can't use because some unseen force keeps me in check.

A side glance at the whites of Sam and Mitch's eyes tells me the same thing's happening to them. They're standing so straight it's unnatural, arms by their sides, feet just touching the floor, like someone's hung them on a hook.

I've no idea what's going on, but we're trapped. Did we step on some kind of reverse ghost trap that only gets living people because whatever has us, it doesn't work on the dead.

Villiers can move just fine, drawing his rapier. Ollie curses. Heather reaches for me, saying my name. I fight to keep conscious as the world bucks and cracks—

We're not alone any more. There's a huge figure in the far corner – he has a miner's hat on and soot-stained coveralls. Someone else holds a dark shape in front of Heather's face. It's a book, open, with a small latch on one side of the cover. I can just see Heather over the top. She stops, like a moth caught by a light, gaze fixed on whatever's inside.

A whisper. French, maybe, if someone was trying to speak it without a tongue.

Heather's lips part, pupils dancing left and right over the pages. A sigh escapes her and she falls impossibly forwards, slipping *inside* the book.

I've seen souls sucked into bottle traps before. This isn't like that, no wailing torment, skin flaking from bone that crumbles to fragments, whirling into the confined space. Heather's in front of me, and then she's just … not. Whoever's holding the book steps around me, closes the covers carefully and secures the latch.

Fuck. Fuck, no. No, no, no!

My limbs won't respond to my thundering anger. I know my body's *there*, but it won't move. I blink. The tear sliding down my cheek itches. Sam's eyes are steely, veined red with strain as he fights whatever magic has us in its grip. Mitch's focus is on Leonie. She hasn't moved.

The clash of metal on metal. Near the door, Villiers fights the miner who raises a pickaxe with one hand. With his other, he has Ollie in a chokehold, caught in the crook of his elbow. Red faced, Ollie slams his boot into his captor's knee, throwing his arm and saving Villiers a spike to the skull. The bloke recovers fast, hauling Ollie off the ground with a yell as the small lad's feet kick wildly. Villiers parries the next swing, twisting elegantly, to slam his shoulder into the assailant's side, sending him lurching forward.

Ollie's free.

"Go!" Villiers shouts. "Tell James what hath happened this day and call upon our comrades to avenge us!"

Ollie doesn't need telling twice. With a last, worried glance at me, he vanishes.

Now the big bloke has two arms to fight Villiers. He seals the advantage by pulling a second pickaxe from a harness on his back.

The person who trapped Heather curses. She's a white woman, in her forties maybe, high cheekbones, piercing eyes, no-nonsense undercut with the longer hair on top plaited back from her face. Sliding the book into the deep pocket inside her black coat, she pulls out another. They're not books, I realize, when she opens it. It's a kind of double mirror – obsidian like the one Sadie had, but rectangular and mounted inside a case rather than on a wooden handle.

Whatever it is, it obviously works like a soul catcher's bottle, dragging ghosts inside and trapping them.

Run, Villiers.

My throat is thick, voice choked by magic. I want to scream at him. *GO!* He won't though, too bloody noble.

There's something on the woman's wrists, coiling under her sleeves, slithering around her hands. White snakes? No, something like silk ribbons.

Launching like spiderwebs they unfurl, leaping the distance to Villiers, winding around his arms, holding him fast. No, no! But the man doesn't strike with his axes. Instead, he grins and points to the woman.

Villiers' eyes catch on her, then slide to the mirrors in her hand and his reflections – two of them, each angled. The change is instant. He stills, suddenly relaxed. The white ribbons unwind, freeing him. He lowers his blade as the mirror yawns, its darkness unrelenting and deep. Harsh-sounding words, spoken by the woman again, and in the space of a blink, Villiers is gone.

Fury and fear spark a fire in my head. Whoever they are – soul catchers, occultists – I'm going to tear them to shreds. I can feel the muscles in my neck straining, but no matter what I do I can't break free. My next breath comes out as a grunt, frustration making my eyes sting. I'm so fucking useless, so weak.

The woman snaps her attention to me, eyes cold, then fixes on Sam. "*Two* undiscovered death-touched." Her voice is husky, and there's an accent – she's from somewhere down south. "They weren't in Jan's report, were they?"

Ice crashes through my blood. *Jan as in ... Jan Liska?*

Her companion hooks his axe into a harness on his belt.

"Gage?" she prompts.

"This one's the secondary augurer." He jerks his chin at Sam, then to the bed where Leonie lies, her chest softly rising and falling. "She's primary. Trace doesn't lie." His voice sounds like he's rolling grit at the back of his throat.

"Take her, then."

The man called Gage shrugs. "Not much point, she'll be dead soon."

As the horror of his words sink into me, I notice his eyes. Like every mirrored ghost's, they blaze silver.

23

†ALK †O †HE HAND

I'd chuck my guts up, but my body won't let me. I'm not in control. The woman with Heather and Villiers in her pocket is somehow able to command our movements, marching us through the streets of York under an invisibility theorem. If they've been cloaking themselves with magic The Hand could've been swanning about York for ages and we'd never know. Hell, the ghosts wouldn't even know.

Blinking away the shapes that dance on my retina, I search for Sam. He looks as peaky as I feel. Can he breathe? Are they minding his shoulder? Mitch looks worse for wear too, eyes puffy, cheeks red from straining against our bonds.

I remember my hollow promise to him less than a half hour ago – *It's gonna be all right*. Yeah, bollocks it is. We can't speak, so we can't explain that we're not the threat and ask for their help.

A wooden door opens. Where are we? We're led into a broad vestibule with carved stone and gothic arches. Everything smells of old leather, cold stone and candle wax. Up ahead is a set of wide fancy stairs but the banisters are dull and unpolished.

Ollie got away.

He'll tell Broomwood, Mrs Tulliver and the others what's going on, bring help … somehow. The ghosts'll find us, wherever we are … and probably end up trapped in mirror books themselves if they try and interfere.

Shit. I've got to break free from this, got to explain to them—

Gage the miner strides past holding a sack – no, a person – *Leonie*! They didn't leave her behind. A stab of relief followed by another flood of panic.

They said she was going to die.

"Infirmary." Gage dumps Leonie into the arms of a waiting lass with thick red hair. "For all the good it will do."

Leonie's head flops back. She doesn't wake up. Mitch is crying slow silent tears.

The hall is busy with people in long dark coats, or armour, or doublets who turn from lugging bags and boxes to stare at us.

A plain-looking man waits at the bottom of the stairs.

"Is she here?" the woman who brought us in asks him.

His pale eyes with nervous pupils flick to me and Sam There are ink stains on his cuffs.

"*Victor*, is she here?"

"Upstairs," he says in a voice that doesn't suit him; it's

confident and clear, but he looks like he wants to hide behind the drapes.

The woman shapes a sign in the air and my body starts to walk itself towards the stairs, Sam alongside me, Mitch behind. I'm sweating, my heart battering my ribs.

A sea of eyes follows us as we go, green, brown, blue, *silver*, all glowering. Their lips twist into hatred, or grim satisfaction. God, these people really loathe us.

"They're so … young," whispers a man in a dark plaid rolled-up shirt. As we pass, I notice one of his tattoos – an upright hand holding a flaming torch. It's identical to the tattoo Jan Liska had on his wrist.

"Young doesn't mean they're not capable," someone else hisses. "They gave up their right to childhood when they started killing people."

Killing people? What the fuck are they on about? We haven't killed anyone.

They think we *summoned the wraiths.*

The horror of that sets my mind railing against the tingle in my limbs and the dreamy twist to the air. This is *real*, and we're in danger and no matter how much the magic wants me to just relax and go with it, I won't fucking do it. They killed Viola for less than what they're accusing us. My throat strains as I try to speak, shout, make any kind of noise.

At the top of the steps, Gage nudges me. "Ariadne, this one's sweating."

The woman assesses me coldly. "Stop fighting. It'll be over soon."

A shudder of dread. What the hell does that mean?

The room we're marched into is vast and barrelled. Measly light filters through stained glass, bleeding watery colour over well-worn floorboards. The hand and torch motif is emblazoned two storeys high, the design stretched over the whole, huge window that fills the far end.

Subtle.

I strain my eyes, searching for a way out. Tiers of bookshelves, spiralling metal stairs to a mezzanine of more books, a cold fireplace filled with ashes. There, a door, heavy wood. Leading where? Dust sheets, stacked chairs. I think of the people downstairs carrying boxes and bags.

This is way more people than the one pair Viola said came to York. Someone called in reinforcements and by the looks of it, they just arrived. Are they here to help stop the wraiths?

I've *got* to talk to them, but my tongue is still heavy in my mouth. What if they don't bother hearing our side and just execute us on the spot?

Up ahead, beneath the window, is a long table with people around it, talking. As we approach they peel back and turn to stare.

My pulse sprints and everything tightens to sudden sharp focus.

There are seven of them. A severe, silver-haired bloke in a clean-cut suit that reminds me too much of Sam's dad to ever trust him. A teenage lass with Down's Syndrome in a cheerleading outfit. An elderly lady wearing coral lipstick and a look of thick disdain. A guy who reminds me of that fit duke character from a TV show Mum loves: light brown skin, stubble on his jaw, and eyes that could melt a heart at forty paces; he's just a lot less polished. A woman with weather-worn, salt-crusted freckles, a long messy braid, cutlass in her belt and silver eyes. The crusader knight in white and red also has a silver gaze.

In the centre behind the table, the stained glass blazing at her back, stands a petite woman draped in layers of expensive silk heavy with fringing and embroidery. Jewellery winks at her ears and throat. When she moves, it's with the confidence that the world will rearrange itself to her convenience. She fixes her silver-eyed gaze on us.

Something about them makes me think of Arthur and his round table. This table isn't round, though, and only one of them is a knight. I'm also pretty sure Arthur's supposed to be the hero, but I can't bet on this lot.

"These … children are accused of creating and letting multiple shades loose upon the city of York, with nine confirmed deaths?" asks the old lady. She's the only one sitting down.

"Punishments for such unforgivable crimes are swift and severe." The man in the sharp suit has a thick eastern European accent. "Regardless of age, or if one is death-touched."

Some things are unforgivable. They're going to murder us just like they murdered Viola. It doesn't matter that me and Sam are seers.

Fuck.

But it should matter that we're innocent.

"You reported four," the woman in fancy silks says to Gage and Ariadne.

"Apologies, Meryem, Haffla already took the primary to the infirmary."

Meryem?

I don't know whether to be star-struck or terrified. For a while she was just a name flung like a weapon between two men about to kill each other. Then I built her into a saviour who'd arrive in York and solve all our problems. When she didn't show up, yeah, I was pissed and disappointed. But then we met Viola and she told us some of the violent, terrifying things The Hand had done, and I was relieved she hadn't come to York looking for Dusan and Liska after all.

Meryem became someone to fear.

But also someone who could help us. If she wanted. I'm desperate, my nerves electric, muscles exhausted as I strain to talk, grunting through the magic, trying to communicate. The magic has me locked down.

"The girl doesn't have long." Ariadne shrugs as if Leonie means nothing. "Soul burn. She blood-bonded a self-syphoned soul source to not one, but *two* raw glyphs, no limitations."

The cheerleader starts to walk away but Meryem places a gentle hand on her arm. There's silence as the lass stares at Meryem. She's our age at most, probably a bit younger, with brown skin, a round face and dark hair tied high on her head with a red bow. She looks determined.

Meryem's lips pinch then she sighs. "Very well, Cassie, you can try."

As the cheerleader passes us I meet her eyes – plain brown – and find curiosity mixed with sympathy, the first kind look since we were marched in here. I think she's a seer, not a ghost.

"You should let them tell you their side of things at least," she tells the assembled Hand, then she's off, striding through the door in the wood panelling.

Meryem nods once. "Ariadne, release them."

The woman who brought us here snaps her fingers and whatever theorem is keeping us locked in place melts. I'm not centred. My right prosthesis is out of alignment and my knees can't hold my weight. I go down, scraping palms on the floorboards and sending pain singing through my broken finger and sore arm.

Mitch gasps, breathless and doubled over. "I think a little bit of piss just came out."

I get it. My body feels watery and drained, throat sore from trying to talk.

"We didn't summon any shades." I cough, my voice coming out cracked and broken.

Sam's on his knees, swaying like he's trying to keep his stomach inside his body, holding his damaged shoulder like it might slip out again.

I'm slammed by thoughts that aren't mine – *they betrayed me, abandoned me, promised me better and this is what I get?* Where are these thoughts coming from? The trickle of anger thickens, growing branches up my arms. Suddenly I'm filled with the ache of loneliness.

A growl. "Get up, augurer." Someone nudges me with their boot.

That word again. *What does it mean?*

I'm hauled by rough hands and the angry sadness melts away as quickly as it washed over me. *What the hell was that?*

Tobacco-stained teeth sneer at me. Gage. Did it all come from him? I don't reckon so. Then where? And *how*?

No time to stress on that right now.

"We didn't summon the shades," I repeat, angling myself in front of Sam and Mitch who are also on their feet, shaken. There's anger in Sam, it blisters around the curl in his lips and sits heavy in his glower. "We've been trying to track down the summoner and stop more people from dying—"

"Then you claim no responsibility for the death of Tomas Ribeiro and the disappearance of his mirror Sophie," the crusader demands. He's not wearing his helm, but he's plenty intimidating without it. Snub-nosed like me, he's got a hard, angular face weathered by battle. His silver eyes glint steel.

"We don't even know who that is," says Sam.

Mitch is close to tears. "Let us see Leonie, please."

Sophie?

The ghost in white that Villiers and Broomwood were looking for. That means she was *mirrored* to our John Doe – Tomas. No wonder he was asking for her when the wraith attacked him.

"Sophie and Tomas are two of our order," Meryem explains. "They came to England to follow up the death of one of our operatives and to seek out their mirror, who is *still* missing. I've lost four of my people here in York, two of them gone without trace. Tomas and Sophie were tracking a coven of young occultists active in the area: you." She gestures to us, a smooth movement that somehow feels like a threat. "I asked them to test your strength, then bring you all in for questioning for Dusan's disappearance. A day later, Tomas was murdered by a shade. Coincidence?"

"Yeah," I say, desperate for them to listen. "We didn't hurt any of your operatives."

Almost true, but explaining what happened under Harrow house isn't going to help us right now.

Viola was right about one thing. The Hand did mess with our wards, supposedly to test our strength, or maybe alert them that we were in the area. I bet Sophie and Tomas were hurrying our way to apprehend us, or whatever, when the wraith attacked them.

But I was so sure JD wasn't a seer because Heather's hands went right through him – so maybe something to do with how the wraith kills changed him. And what happened to Sophie? Broomwood and Villiers looked everywhere in York for her.

"Enough lies." The crusader glowers. "Tell us to whom the last trace belongs, admit to your crimes, and we might offer clemency."

What they on about?

"We don't even know what this trace thing is that you're following," I say. "If you could just listen—"

Mitch bolts, almost tripping over his own feet as he charges for the door midway down the room. A word from Ariadne and he's bound in white ribbons, one winding around his mouth to muffle his shouts. He struggles then slumps against his bonds.

Sam's yelling, but I'm just stunned.

That wasn't a theorem making me see things back at the hospital. Ariadne's a seer, but somehow she can *manifest* phantasmic essence. Can they all do it? Liska didn't but … wait, he had a baton like the kind riot police use. I never thought about it, because I never even imagined it was possible, but I bet that wasn't *real*, not in the material sense.

What else does pairing up with a soul let seers do that Viola never mentioned?

"Try the same and I'll have Ariadne bespell you," Meryem warns me and Sam, cutting off his protests.

"Please don't hurt him. Mitch is just worried about Leonie; we are too." I hate how scared I sound. "They've both been helping us protect the ghosts of York. That's what we were trying to do with the wards. We want to protect local souls from occultists, not trap them."

"The shades killing people are called wraiths," says Sam. "They *eat* living souls and I-I have a theory about what happened to Sophie. The wraith killed Tomas, drained his soul and because they were mirrored, it's possible that she was consumed too."

There's silence among The Hand. I'm in shock too. I hadn't thought of that. It's brutal.

"What do *you* know of mirroring?" asks Meryem. Everything is suddenly colder.

Ah, crap. We're not supposed to know about it. No one outside of their organization should know.

I twine my fingers through Sam's and hold on. "Let's focus on the wraiths, yeah? They're strong, dangerous and out for blood. The woman who summoned them is called Claire Cole. She's had her revenge, so we're proper confused as to what her game is. After the theatre attack, she kidnapped an occultist called Jory Chambers, who is all right – she doesn't bottle souls or anything like that. Please, if there's anything you can do for Leonie… She's saved ghosts, she's helping us and she's—"

"An augurer," says the man in the suit.

"Yeah, we don't know what that is—"

"She is not death-touched and uses powers that are not for her to toy with. Now she suffers. Cassandra will try, but she can do little to save your friend."

Cassandra's trying to help her? I risk a glance at Mitch, sweating in the magic ribbons that encase him. He meets my eye, hope shining there. Maybe, just maybe, there's a chance Leonie'll be all right.

"You must tell us everything. Start from the beginning," says Meryem, splaying her hands on the table. "Do not lie or omit information."

We both lie and omit information. Admitting all the times we've used magic is a terrible idea, so we gloss over the parts we can and focus on our investigation, telling them about Sadie and the missing bones, her deathloop at Cumberland House, our run-in with Jory and then searching for a copy of the book we think might contain build-a-wraith instructions.

Sam doesn't let go of my hand the entire time.

When we finish, Meryem addresses Ariadne and Gage. "Find Claire Cole and assess if hers is the missing trace behind these wraiths. Have Ardor call the muses. I want the archives scoured for references to wraiths and every detail of Claire Cole's life dissected. She must be found."

Gage and Ariadne nod, accepting the orders.

"The suspects were defended by three local souls," says Ariadne. "One escaped, but we contained the two others – neither are shades."

Meryem thinks for a moment, then flicks her fingers in a dismissive wave. "We don't have time to assess them at present. Shelve them."

Shelve?

"Whoa, wait. What the fuck does that mean?" I ask. "You can't just—"

The old woman stands and crusader knight steps sideways, melting into her skin, their limbs fusing as his form disappears within hers. Her eyes shift from blue to silver. I can see the shadow of him under her papery skin. It's as instantaneous and elegant as when Dusan possessed Liska under Harrow house, working together in slick harmony. Equal. Balanced.

Powerful.

I want that.

As one, the old woman and her mirror raise an arm, wrist twisting in a flicking motion. Breath explodes from my lungs as I'm wrenched backwards, losing my grip on Sam, to hang a foot above the floorboards.

Yup. Very powerful. It's elegant and amazing and I'd be even more in awe if I wasn't terrified for my life right now. With nothing to support them, the weight of my prostheses drag on my stumps. It bloody hurts, but it's nothing compared to the rushing panic as my lungs fight for air they can't reach through the overwhelming pressure of my rib cage. Are they using a theorem to steal my air? No, this is like telekinesis. They're crushing my chest with their minds.

I gasp and struggle, desperately trying to suck in a breath, every part of me screaming for oxygen. The edges of my vision speckle with darkness. I can't hold out much longer.

"Be gentle, Bathily," the budget *Bridgerton* bloke warns the old woman. "Death-touched aren't so common that we can go around breaking them."

"Hoping to try one on, Tempest?" the suited man sneers.

The old woman – Bathily – shares his cruel amusement, or maybe that comes from the crusader still possessing her. Either way, they open their hand and the pressure crushing my chest lessens.

I drag precious air into aching lungs. Sam says my name, but Gage stops him trying to help me. I can breathe but whatever magic has me keeps me stuck, unable to move.

"And this one?" Gage jerks a thumb at Mitch, who is still cocooned like a caught fly in Ariadne's web. "He's not death-touched."

"Seal him," says Meryem simply.

Seal?

As in the first seal? The one Viola says cuts someone

off from their own essence, forcing them to live a half-life, severed and unconnected? I don't get exactly what will happen, but Viola made it sound bad, really bad, like Mitch will become a kind of zombie, unable to connect with the world, no empathy, no love.

No, no way. They can't do that.

But they can.

"Stop!" I shout, but I'm helpless to do anything.

Mitch fights, but there's nothing he can do either as Ariadne plucks the cryptolenses from his face and crushes them beneath her boot, shattering the lenses and warping the frame. He blinks, confused, then the white ribbons wrap over his eyes and wrenches his head back.

"We've cooperated," begs Sam. "You don't have to do this."

Meryem is unmoved. "I'm afraid that we do."

"It will burn," Ariadne tells Mitch. "But only for a moment."

A fucking lie and she knows it. Every day after this will be a struggle. They're going to hollow him out and leave him broken.

Gage walks into Ariadne, stepping inside her skin and sinking on to her bones. Her eyes take on the silver in his. They raise a hand, a single, fluid movement like they're not a miracle breaking every rule I used to think I knew about being a seer.

The voice that rings from Ariadne's mouth is a blend of two people speaking as one. "You have been found guilty of practising theorems by self-syphoning and, for your own protection, are hereby sentenced to be sealed from magical practice by way of the first seal."

Their white ribbons pull open Mitch's zippered top, wrenching back the neckline of his T-shirt to expose his breastbone. They shape a sign in the air – no pen, no blade. Enclosing it in a circle swoop of their wrist, the pair pushes it into the bare skin below Mitch's throat. He screams through his gag, thrashing and shaking. Light flares around Ariadne's hand and when they pull back, the first seal burns on his chest – a shape like an elaborate S inside a double circle. It's as if she's branded him.

The helpless, desperate look on Mitch's face as he slumps against his cocoon kills me. This shouldn't have happened to him.

"He can't harm anyone now," says Meryem, satisfied. "Expel him from the aperture."

"A memory reset?" suggests the suited man.

No, god, no.

"Unnecessary, just make sure that he can't find his way back to the aperture." Meryem flicks a dismissive wave. "Lock the death-touched in containment."

24

WHISPERS IN THE WALLS

"Sam, stop." I catch his wrist, disrupting the glyph. Blood drips down his thumb and on to the hard-stone floor.

He twists out of my grip. "I can make it work."

"You're hurting yourself."

"I don't care!" His voice breaks. "Leonie's sick, Mitch needs us, they have Heather and George. I'm not just going to wait around in here until they take—" He swallows, lips trembling.

"I know, hey, I know." And *fuck* do I know. My brain is an alarm and I am two seconds away from losing it, but Sam's anger gives me something to focus on to keep the pieces of me from fragmenting.

We're belowground. There's no window and the air's stagnant and musty. "It's not much of a prison cell if we can hocus pocus our way out of it," I say. "Save your strength, love."

Love. A small word I've called him so often, but I see what it does to him now. I meant it to bolster him, but I realize too late that it reminds him of how much he has to lose. He stops fighting me, retreats, fading somewhere inside where I can't reach him. I need something to draw him out and soothe over his feeling of being trapped. Nothing feels good enough.

Sometimes when he's like this he wants me close; other times, he needs space and can't stand anyone near him. I don't know which it will be so I hover, uncertain, not wanting him to face this alone.

The last time we were kidnapped, his dad died.

This time, we might not make it out. The Hand are as brutal as Viola said they were. They don't even care that we're innocent, they still locked us up. I can't believe I thought they might actually help us.

"Sam, do you mind if I touch you?" I ask. "You … should sit down, is all."

There's a thin mattress on top of low wooden boxes. He sits without my help and I settle beside him, close but not touching. I'm desperate to take my prostheses off but it's not safe.

There's no solid cell door, just a wall of iron bars on one wall. Behind a chest-high screen is a scummy loo. There's some bottled water on the floor near the bars. The plastic looks out of place. Everything else could have been dragged from the past. Even the light fittings in the corridor outside the cell are old-fashioned glass globes burning with a low hissing flame.

Sam leans back, adjusting his arm so it's more comfortable in his brace.

There has to be a way out of here.

No one took our phones and I quickly realize why. There's no signal and the screens have frozen, the time recording the moment we arrived.

Dad. Mum. The twins.

We just disappeared. They probably think I'm sulking at Sam's but by tomorrow, when they still can't get through and Lucrezia hasn't seen us, they'll panic. Mitch can tell them what happened, but they'll be up against a world they've no idea exists. And Meryem made it very clear she didn't want Mitch to know where we're hidden.

They won't find us.

If we live through this, I'll come clean about everything – the ghosts, the wraiths, everything.

Is Mitch all right? Does it hurt, will he … will he still be himself after this? And Leonie… she could die. They're only involved because they're my mates who got mixed up in my world.

Exhaustion and bile make the cell spin. I want to slam my head back against the stone wall because everything is too much and my feelings don't fit inside me any more.

I feel time stretch, years becoming decades. Alone.

They promised; they lied.

The sadness tightens my lungs, making everything feel distant and behind it all is the bitter burn of resentment. But that's not how *I* feel.

Who lied? The Hand? Who did they lie to?

I sit forward sharply, startling Sam. I motion behind us, wanting to say, "There's someone in the walls," but knowing how weird that sounds. And it's not right, not really. I bet it's a theorem. The Hand probably magicked this place to make us feel like shit – take our sadness and fear and despair, amplify it and spit it right back. Wear us down. Wear us out until we'll confess to conjuring the wraiths.

Except the same thing happened when I was on the floorboards upstairs. Have they spelled the whole building? And where are we anyway? Still in York, I reckon, but I've no idea where.

Sam chews on his lip. The circles under his eyes are heavy and his hair is a rumpled mess. Suddenly I see him in his dad's lab, the multiloop cracking behind him, his face covered in blood and bright blazing eyes turning from me as he walked to his death. That feeling of desperate frustration and fear and the panic of losing him comes searing back.

I wanted him to turn back, a final goodbye, but he never did.

There's been a space there ever since – filled with the dead and their demands, Sam's grief, my anxiety, my fear at fucking this up, because I will. I already am. I'm not enough for him; I know I'm not.

Something changes in his eyes.

"Can I touch you?" he whispers, and it feels like a safety rope thrown to a lad hanging off the edge of a cliff.

I lean closer. *Please*. His hands slide either side of my jaw, fingers on the back of my neck. He kisses me softly, like he's sorry for something, and I don't care about anything else. This moment, with him, is perfect because we're together. We're both terrified, exhausted and in pain. But we have each other.

"I can't lose you," Sam whispers when we break apart. "I won't survive that. Without you … I don't know what to hold on to."

"Hey, listen. If they're going to take you from me, they'd better bring a whole fucking army." I put my hands over his and grip tight. He's breathing hard. So am I. "Sam, I'm never letting go."

"But…" A tear drifts down his cheek. "What if you don't have a choice?"

I float along corridor and stairwell. Books stretch ahead in a maze of shelves. One is in my hand, slim in weight. I'm pleased with progress, the cleaning is going well, even if Terrance doesn't pull his weight and financing is tight. The ladder creaks as I climb to the top shelf. I've never been fond of heights but it's a requirement of the job. As I slide the book into place the ladder shifts. My shoe slips. Heart leaping, a scream caught in my throat, the flagstone jumps to meet me—

A book in my hand.

I climb the ladder.

My foot slips.

A book in my hand.

Two women, one barely out of girlhood, tell me that I'm

dead. Who will supervise the collection if I'm gone? The library's fine, they reassure me, well managed and thriving.

"You've been dead for forty years."

They call it a necromic cycle, an endless loop of my final moments. An accident, a senseless, tragic accident. Somehow, that's harder to accept. The elegant woman in the silk dress asks me to be part of something bigger. I can leave, become a spirit, or I can stay and have my memories of the Minster library preserved into a haven for their people. This aperture will be mine. I will be its seed soul and keeper. They have an archive of books they need help cataloguing. I will have a place with them.

Her name is Meryem, and I accept. Above all, I need to be helpful.

The girl ... I know her from somewhere ... I know her face...

The days are happy: cooking for thirty, discovering interesting manuscripts. So many wonderful discussions with Vi and Tempest by the fire in the evenings. Vi reads our fortunes with her knucklebones. The clatter of bones on tables becomes a rhythm I know well.

I can't leave. There are spells keeping me here because if I ever exit the aperture, by accident or by force, the magic collapses and the archive will be destroyed. Worse, the ruh tasi will break, freeing their prisoners. I understand the precaution, and I am not concerned. I've all I need here – companions and purpose.

Vi's gone. Dead. Torn apart by a shade. Meryem is

heartbroken. York holds too many memories so she moves The Hand to Jaipur for a time, but she needs me here, to mind the Spicer Archives and the Obsidian Gallery where the ruh tasi are shelved. The Old Place is their prison and I their jailer.

I won't be forgotten, she promises.

Weeks become months. Tempest and Sweets come back to shelve more captured shades. They stay longer than they're permitted but eventually they're needed in Dublin.

"Aren't you lonely, old chap, here all on your own?"

I smile, rueful. "One can never be alone in a library."

For a while, the books are enough. Visits from The Hand become less and less frequent. I start wandering the Obsidian Gallery, taking ruh tasi from shelves to gaze at the shades within – dangerous, corrupted ghosts gleaned from cities around the world. I want to see the places they've come from. Outside this aperture I'd not be able to touch anything; I'd be a ghost, invisible and unremarkable, but I don't care any more.

I too am a prisoner.

Endless days. I read books on magic never meant for my eyes. I play cricket in the long gallery. I open a ruh tasi from eighty years ago, expecting to see another shade. Instead I find the face of a young woman, barely out of her teens. A girl who was once my friend.

Viola's colourless face stares up at me from inside the dark glass.

"She killed me, Charlie."

Sweating, I lurch upright, startling Sam and scraping my back on the stone wall I'm pressed up against.

"Hey, hey, breathe." He shifts around, turning my sweaty face towards him, and makes me look into his steady eyes.

"Just a dream, but it felt…" *Real.* Like a memory. I gulp the cool, stagnant air. "Viola was here, trapped in those double mirrors like Heather and Villiers."

Ruh tasi.

Is that what they're called? How can I possibly know that? I close my eyes, but the filaments of the dream are already fraying.

By now Ollie will have told Viola what happened to us. Viola knows so much about The Hand: maybe she has some idea where we're being kept. Maybe she can free us.

Leaning back against the wall again, a sudden wave of anguish washes over me, mixed with anger and regret. It really feels like a memory, like the kind I used to have from falling into deathloops, but that doesn't make sense. Wherever we are, we're not in a deathloop.

I wince. "The stone's cold."

"Here, swap," says Sam. "I'll be big spoon."

We settle back down but I don't close my eyes. I stare at the stripy shadows cast by the cell's bars and remember the sadness seeping through the floorboards, Viola's face in the polished obsidian and the clatter of knucklebones on wood.

25

WRITTEN IN INK

When I wake up on the hard pallet bed, my side is one solid ache. The sticky coat on my tongue and my sandpaper throat tell me I've been sleeping a while, but my phone is still frozen so I've no idea what time it is. Sam's arm is tucked over me, his nose against the curve of my neck. With him at my back, I didn't have any more dreams.

I ease him off, careful not to wake him.

There's a bit of drinking water left. There'd be more but I used a lot of it to clean the inside of my liners and my stumps before we slept. Dirt means possible infections, which means not being able to use my prostheses. I have to maintain them as best I can.

Footsteps on stone and the scrape of a door. Movement outside the cell. I rouse Sam and whisper, "Someone's coming."

His eyes fly open, but he sits up slowly.

It's the pale-eyed man from the stairs, the one with ink stains on his cuffs.

"It's Victor, right?" I ask. I rattle off questions about Leonie, if we can see her, where we are and when we're getting out, what Meryem's plans are to take on the wraiths and if they've found where Claire Cole is hiding yet.

Silent, Victor's long, fine hands flick open a shutter on the far side of the cell and slide through a tray. Two bowls of some kind of stew, crusty bread and more bottled water.

Not a ghost, then, if he can touch things. No, wait, the rules are different here. Ghosts are as good as living when inside an aperture – I've no idea *how* I know that, or what an aperture is and how I know that word … but it's familiar.

Victor is probably dead, though. A ghost.

He nods once at us, and then, wordlessly, heads back the way he came.

"What? No butter on the bread?" I holler after him. "This will be reflected in my Tripadvisor rating!"

"It could be poisoned or drugged," says Sam. "We shouldn't."

True. But using prostheses takes a lot of energy and the food smells so good. They already have us locked up, what would be the point of drugging us?

"Let's not risk the stew," I say, ignoring the rumble in my belly. "Bread with no butter?"

Picking up the plate to offer Sam a slice, I spot something hidden underneath. Three pages torn from a notebook, crudely folded and weighed down.

We exchange a surprised, excited look. We've not found any cameras in here, but we have to assume listening spells or spying theorems are a thing. If someone has taken the risk to send this note, then they must think it's safe for us to read in here.

Putting our backs to the bars, just in case, Sam unfolds the papers. I glance behind us. The little bit of the passage we can see is clear, no one about.

Words are crammed into the paper in blue ink that's so faded it's a pain to read. The handwriting's loopy too.

Sam holds it steady. It's a letter, or maybe a diary entry, that's been torn from a notebook. Once I work out that the lower-case r and n look basically the same, it reads easier.

—an experiment only, for Victor says he's content as he is. I rather doubt I shall ever put such a theorem into practice, but the possibilities are exciting. I long to charge ahead but I must be cautious. Meryem would never approve of me designing such things because she rather intends her prisoners to stay where she puts them. You would like her; she has travelled all over the world to many of the places we always talked about visiting. When I find you again—

The next few pages detail a theorem, complete with workings out and crossing off and paragraphs of theory. In the margins, the entries keep going and we turn the paper sideways to read even more writing crammed in vertically.

—The Old Place's stability is reliant upon its seed soul having constant presence, without which the collapse of the aperture is expected, expelling souls—

—becoming a prisoner of what is a mere extension of their necromic cycle ... the binding Meryem and I placed in the forging of this place—

—Edie, I figured it out! You will be proud of me—

I blink. Edie? I *know* that name. I know some of these other words too – words I shouldn't.

The word "binding" is circled and starred. The note attached to it reads: *used similar mechanism as the root of binding on holding cells – countermeasure to unlock and link, so that unlocking the cells will unlock the aperture allowing Victor to leave.*

"A necromic cycle?" Sam wonders aloud.

"Yeah, it means deathloop."

His brow goes up at my confidence.

"I…" My dream. The man who fell and broke his neck, he called it that. Yeah, it's feeling less and less like a dream, and more like I somehow slipped into a memory. But that kind of closeness to a ghost's mind only happens if I'm in a deathloop.

Grabbing the pages, I read over some of the notes again – *becoming a prisoner* – that's what the man felt. He was happy to be a part of something at first, but when The Hand left he was on his own for too long. He feels abandoned, forgotten.

And I *feel* that too, but only when I'm in solid contact with the building. I put both palms to the stone floor. Sam asks what I'm up to.

"Give me a sec." I wait.

It comes softly at first – sadness that makes me want to curl up and cry, then resentment crashes into me like a wave. It's dragging me under as if I'm falling into a loop, out of control.

Snatching my hands up I look at Sam, shocked. "Right, this is going to sound … weird, but … I think we're … *inside* a deathloop right now."

Sam looks around the cell. "What?"

"Not just this room, the whole building. I can feel things through the floor and walls – memories, like, like a ghost's memories. That dream I had last night, I don't reckon it was just a dream."

"A flashback then, like you used to get?"

"Yeah."

He squeezes my hand, worried. "I'm not doubting you, but this … doesn't seem anything like a deathloop."

He's right, and it's not. Not quite. Closing my eyes again, I sink into the fragments of memory, trying to tease some sense out of them.

Seed soul.

Memories preserved into a haven.

Aperture.

"There *was* a deathloop," I say. "But it's been changed by magic into something else … an aperture."

"Liska called the multiloop that, didn't he?" Sam looks scared.

"Yeah, I don't think it's the same thing, more built on the same idea. Remember how far we walked when we were in the multiloop, but we never left the lab? I think it's sort of a pocket universe."

Deep down, I've been hoping for rescue, but if we were tucked away in some kind of magical pocket of space and time then Ollie, Viola, Mr Broomwood and the rest could be right next to us and never know it. No one's coming; we have to find our own way out.

To my surprise Sam sits up straighter. "This makes sense." He gestures to the wall. "If this aperture we're in is made from a deathloop, then it's no wonder you're getting flashback dreams. You're so much more empathic than I am, Charlie. You lose yourself in loops, taking on the feelings and fears of the ghosts inside."

And their memories.

The writer of these papers is the same lass who offered the man a choice. Not any man, I realize. "It's Victor. Meryem and—"

I stumble, not trusting the third face I saw in the dream. It was a memory, yeah, but it was also happening in my head.

Viola knew The Hand, she knew Meryem, but she wasn't ever one of them. Viola's face appeared in one of the obsidian-mirror traps, a ruh tasi, and she said my name. That can't have happened so the dream must be a blend of Victor's memories and my mind.

So how do I know this aperture thing is true? It *feels* it, but I could be wrong. One way to find out.

I turn back to the letter, tapping the pages where "binding" is circled. "I think this theorem is a way out."

"Of the cell, or the aperture?"

I hand the pages over. "Both."

Sam blows out his breath, squinting as he angles the papers closer to the light. "Magic doesn't work in here, though." But he keeps reading. He has such expressive eyebrows. They lift in surprise, then hope as he flicks thumb and forefinger on a paragraph. "Well, shit. You're right, this really might work, but can we trust Victor? Why would he help us?"

I remember the pent-up resentment I feel whenever I touch the walls.

"Because he wants out of here and he'll do anything to get it," I say. "Including helping us. I'm also pretty sure if Victor ever leaves, this place collapses."

"Killing everyone inside?" asks Sam, shocked.

If I ever do leave the aperture, by accident or by force, the magic collapses and the archive will be destroyed.

"Nah, it expels the souls, but I think material stuff is crushed. Either way, The Hand lose their little sanctuary, so they put this spell on it to stop him wandering off. Now he wants out."

"And you … *feel* that?" Sam taps the floor.

Loud and clear. "Somehow the way this cell is secured is linked to the magic binding Victor here. We escape, so does he. He helps us, we help him."

"Fine." Sam clambers up and offers me his hand. "There's an active element to the theorem here, a glyph." He gestures to the pages. "But it also relies on an instinctual link with the aperture's origins as a deathloop to convince the door of the cell to open."

"Convince?" I replay everything he just said. We're

supposed to connect to the voice I feel in the walls, appeal to it, or something.

"You do that bit, you're better at it." Sam picks at the cut on his hand, coaxing blood to the surface. "I'll cover the active theorem. It has to be done at the same time."

I read over the instructions again. Somewhere in this building, Heather and Villiers are trapped. *Shelved.* We're getting them out, and then we're finding wherever they're holding Leonie and getting her to a proper hospital. If she stays here, she'll either die, or be sealed like Mitch.

I couldn't stop it happening to him, but I'm going to bloody save her if it kills me.

"OK, let's try it."

There probably should be words to say, something impressive-sounding that I can barely pronounce, but the notes don't reveal a structured theorem; it's more haphazard than that. Experimental.

Papers in one hand, Sam traces the glyph on the floor in front of the barred door. The mark shimmers, bold and clear. A hooking sensation runs through my body. Yup, that's working.

"My turn," I say.

Intention is important, so I try to focus on what I want – *the door to open.* I wrap my hand around one of the bars and try to sink into that place where I connect with a soul in a deathloop.

"Open," I whisper, putting command behind it, more desperation than confidence that this has to work. *Open, please. We need to help our friends.*

Tentatively, I push. The door swings with the deep groan of little used hinges. As it does, just before I let go, I feel something else rooted far deeper in the aperture release too.

Stairs. Always bloody stairs.

Sam goes first, inching along. There're no guards anywhere. Either Victor took care of them, or there never were any.

Folded small, Sam stuffed the note pages in his pocket. We need to get rid of them somewhere. If we're caught, it won't take much to work out who it came from and then Victor will get a bollocking, maybe even be locked up himself.

We need all the allies that we can get.

Back on the ground floor, I take a moment to lay my palms against the wall. In my dream I knew this place as well as Victor did, all its twists and turns and hidden rooms. But dreams fade, and the harder I grasp at it the quicker it slips away.

C'mon, Victor mate, tell us where to go.

All at once I can feel the silent rooms, furniture covered with white sheets and the layers of dust. It's the emptiness, like the heart of this place is lonely, remembering a time when the kitchens were busy, the libraries full of readers and the practice rooms packed with recruits learning to control new abilities.

There are people here now, a bustle of souls. I feel them all like pulses under my skin, fifty at least.

It won't last. They'll catch their occultist, and then they'll leave.

I need directions to where Heather and Villiers are locked up, but all I get is a wave of annoyance.

"We're on our own," I whisper to Sam, feeling like I've let him down.

Keeping low, we hurry along the corridor, passing closed doors with voices behind them. This aperture used to be empty, now it's bursting at the seams. We're not going to get far without getting caught.

But we have to try.

The walls are honey stone above light wood panelling. There are benches, and alcoves draped with dusty cloths. Some are empty but others are filled with marble busts under dust sheets. The air feels full of static.

Opposite, through the grimy track marks on the rain-streaked windows I can make out a pale bulk propped up by green. The Minster. I know that view.

"We're somewhere in Dean's Park," I whisper. Trying to think of the grounds and how they're laid out. I've not spent much time around the Minster, but I know we can't be too far from Grays Court Hotel, though we might as well be a world away.

"You're right, this is the Minster library," says Sam, looking around. "Just a different version of it."

"Oh my God, The Old Place, that's what they call this aperture; it's a play on The Old *Palace*, the other name for the library." It's daft how long it took me to work that out.

Nothing outside the window is moving, not even the rain. It's like a photo-real, painted backdrop. Just a memory. It hits me that even if we can free our friends, there's no easy way out of this aperture, not without Victor's help.

A door along the way opens, spilling voices and footsteps. "Why would she want her own team *dead*?"

Sam crushes me backwards, pulling one of the heavy drapes aside and squeezing us both into the shallow alcove behind. The curtain settles with just a slit to spy through. I brace myself. Whoever's out there must have seen the curtain move. I think about the semi-invisibility theorem we know, but there's no time or room to cast it here.

"She wouldn't, she relied on them." Ariadne's cool, detached tone comes closer. "Some had been working the con for years."

Sam's leg is between mine, our bodies pressed close, his hair tickling my nose. He's looking at the rise and fall of my Adam's apple as I swallow. Slowly, he presses a finger to his lips and holds it there.

"Then Ms Cole had no motivation to summon a shade?" I don't recognize the mellow voice, but it sounds like a lass.

"None. We have no evidence that she was enhancing her performance with theorems. It's possible she's not aware of phantomological power."

Wait. The summoner *isn't* Claire Cole?

Sam looks as shocked as I feel. I saw the bone impresa around her neck and the lines of dark electricity that connected her to the wraiths as they tore people apart and drank their souls dry.

"It doesn't mean the boys were lying, merely naive." The third voice – male – is familiar.

"You sound like Cassie," groans Ariadne. "She thinks we can trust them."

"We can't," says the second female voice. "They've been playing with some powerful mathemagics."

"And perhaps someone is playing with *them*," says the man.

Light moves in the corridor. The trio have stopped a couple of metres away, partly blocking the window. I was right, it's Ariadne and the redhead lass Gage gave Leonie to when we arrived. The bloke with them is the budget *Bridgerton* duke, a faded yellow cravat wound about his collar.

Me and Sam lean deeper into the alcove, but there's nowhere to go.

"Cassie's perfectly capable of being her own judge of people," snaps the duke. "Meryem keeps her on too short a leash."

"Can you blame her?" asks the redhead. "This is her first time back after Viola was killed by a shade. Imagine losing your mirror like that. No wonder Meryem avoided returning for so long, and Cassie is so young."

Viola.

Meryem's mirror? What? No, that's… Wait.

Viola knew Meryem, she told me that herself. I can't remember exactly what she said now but there is no way she mentioned she was *part* of The Hand, that she was Meryem's *mirror*. They wanted to recruit her, yeah, but…

That *would* explain how she knows so much about them and their magic.

A shade killed Meryem's mirror and, if what this lot are saying is true, that mirror was supposedly Viola. And Meryem mourned her so much she left York for the better part of a century? That doesn't make sense. Viola told me Meryem murdered her because she got too close to occultists and didn't want to play by The Hand's strict rules.

Or did that all happen after she joined?

Silence. The quiet stretches. Finally, Ariadne says, "You must miss Viola, Tempest."

Sweat slides down my neck. Tempest. The duke's name is Tempest Lawson. *Sitting in a fireside armchair, Viola laughing at something Tempest said.* He, Viola and Victor were friends.

How many more of Victor's memories am I holding on to?

"I do." Tempest sighs. "Does Meryem have a new suspect? Is that why she called a meeting?"

Ariadne flicks her brow and smiles, as if answering their questions is a cheeky favour. "She's certain it's a young occultist called Jory Chambers. The prisoners mentioned her, but seem to think she's innocent. She's not."

Sam's hand squeezes my wrist. My mind scrambles to make sense of it all.

If that's true, Sadie wasn't afraid *for* Jory the night she went to Cumberland House with a bag of bones. She was afraid *of* her. She wasn't there handing over stolen bones to the summoner to be forged into bone impresa, she was betraying

255

her girlfriend, taking someone else the finished impresa to try and stop any more wraiths being summoned.

Who was she meeting?

Sophie and Tomas. It had to be. Maybe they were on to Jory anyway, or maybe Sadie gave her girlfriend up. Either way, Jory had to stop word getting back to the rest of The Hand so after she executed Sadie, she sent the wraith after Tomas and Sophie.

But … the wraith tried to kill Jory. It almost got her.

Almost.

At her house it was slow and sloppy in its attack. *It missed her on purpose.*

Somehow, when we showed up at her door, Jory already knew who we were and that we suspected her. That bone necklace she wears, the one she claimed is for protection – ha! I almost choke. Sam flashes me a warning look. I'd bet anything it controls one of the wraiths.

Jory called on a wraith to pretend to attack her. After that, we went out of the way to protect her, salt circle and all, as she fed us more lies.

"How confident are we that it's Chambers?" asks Tempest. "I'm not saying the muses don't do their work well, but we suspected four teenagers only yesterday."

"Firstly, motivation. When Ms Chambers was fourteen, her brother died in a car accident," says Ariadne. "Naturally, the family was devastated and, in their grief, they turned to an up-and-coming medium for support."

"Claire Cole?" asks the redhead.

Ariadne snaps her fingers. "The very same, though she went by Clarissa Vizgirda back then. Jory's parents paid for private sessions to speak to their dead son. They became obsessed, so convinced by the con that they re-mortgaged the family home and lost it to the bank. Mr Chambers' printing business folded and, three years later, he disappeared, presumed dead. A body was never found so the insurance company refused to pay out and the family's court case against Clarissa Vizgirda fell apart when she vanished."

Wow. If all that's true, I'd say Jory has *every* reason to want revenge on Claire Cole.

"Secondly, the means," Ariadne goes on. "Dressler and Lin tested the magical trace at Ms Chambers' home, the one she'd supposedly been kidnapped from. It matches the missing signature from the theatre. She might not have been there in person, but she'd planted a syphon on Ms Cole, who became the unwitting soul source for the wraith's transformation."

I'm pissed we were so easily tricked. We slept on the floor and on a cot bed to protect Jory and she was setting us up. She sent us to the theatre the night of the attack. Was she hoping to kill us, get us off her back?

"Is Ms Cole dead?" asks Tempest.

"Not yet," comes a gravelly voice from down the corridor. Through the narrow gap at the edge of the curtain I see a bulky shape join the trio. Gage, Ariadne's mirror. "She's still the wraith's soul source. It won't be long till it drains her dry."

It's coming together now. No wonder Claire was popping

all those vitamins and supplements. She probably thought she was just working too hard when really her soul was being sapped to the dregs.

Somehow Jory or Sadie tricked Claire into wearing the bone necklace. A gift from a fan. Really, it's the key to syphoning Claire's soul to fuel the very wraiths that were killing off the people who'd helped her con Jory's family all those years ago.

But why the overkill at the theatre? Why stage a big public attack that drew international attention if she killed two of The Hand to keep herself a secret?

"Why does Jory even need the wraiths any more?" asks the redhead lass. "She's got her revenge."

"Oh, she's not done yet." Ariadne opens her hand and white ribbons twist absently around her fingers. "There's clearly someone else at play here."

"Who?" asks Tempest.

"Too soon to tell, but it won't stop us locating Ms Chambers and sealing her. Once that link is broken, any connection she has to active theorems will disintegrate and we can contain these wraiths. We just need to find where she's hiding."

"The theatre and Ms Chambers' house are clear," says Gage. "Dressler and Lin are searching Ms Cole's hotel right now. If Jory Chambers is using osteomagi to summon an ancient shade as obscure and destructive as a wraith, she'll be cloaking her power."

"She didn't before," drawls Tempest. "What's changed?"

"We did." I can hear the sneer in Gage's voice. They don't

like each other much. "Jory's no longer facing a lone pair. Meryem brought an army."

As if remembering they've got a meeting to be at, the group starts to move off down the corridor.

"These wraiths are faster and stronger than most shades," says Ariadne.

"Ruh tasi will take care of them," the redhead replies.

"No spirit can escape obsidian." Gage's gravelly voice is made quiet by distance. Fading footsteps on stone, a door slams and then silence.

Sam's breathing is heavy. We stay hidden for a moment longer, sweating and scared. When there's been nothing but silence for a full two minutes, I risk whispering. "How wrong could we be?"

Perhaps someone is playing with them.

Yeah, Jory, but also Viola. There's so much she kept from us.

"Viola always did love an experimental theorem."

Sam makes the connection, taking the folded papers out of his pocket. "She wrote this," he gasps.

I see the word, *Edie*. I remember where I know it from. The lost girlfriend Viola mentioned when we were in the cemetery. "Yeah."

The curtain pulls back. Watery light floods the alcove and Sam spins so fast he trips over my foot. I catch him. We look at the man standing in front of us wearing a mustard cravat and a sly smile.

"I thought I saw the curtain move," says Tempest.

26

☦HROUGH A GLASS, DARKLY

☦empest raises both hands as if we're the threat to him. My breath catches at the top of my chest, mind spinning as I try to think through the surge of adrenaline. Are we about to get locked up again or will Tempest drag us straight to Meryem to seal us, or execute us or worse? What would happen to Heather and Villiers then? Nothing good.

One of us needs to get away.

If I go one way and Sam the other, Tempest will have to pick a target. He can't chase us both, so to make sure Tempest chases *me* I shove into his chest, pushing him back. It's like trying to move a brick wall, but then he steps away, straightens his waistcoat and says, "If I wanted you caught, you'd already be locked up. I just want to talk, follow me."

We don't move.

He's a ghost; no living person dresses like that unless

they're into cosplay. And he knew Viola, so he's been dead a while. No silver eyes, though. He's not mirrored which means although he's strong, he's not super-villain strong.

"Or by all means stand here and get caught." Tempest strides off.

Sam glances at me at the same time I look at him. I'm sure I look just as confused and wary.

Fuck.

We follow, because what choice do we have? Around the next corner, Tempest pushes open a door and we're unceremoniously shoved into a small, dark space. Green light flares close to my face. Wincing, I lurch back, smacking my shoulder into the shelving.

Sam yelps. "What the—"

I squint at Tempest. He's holding a torch as long as his forearm made from a tied and tapered bundle of rough fibres. I can't help thinking about The Hand's symbol emblazoned in the stained glass.

"I was a moon curser in London. A link boy," Tempest clarifies when he sees our bemused expressions. I've still no idea what the hell he's on about. "Before public lighting I'd light the way home for wealthy people. The Uber of the eighteenth century. Guiding people is kind of my thing."

So what, he thinks we're just going to trust him? We don't. I don't see a good reason why he'd help us. He was standing right up there all chummy with Meryem.

We're crammed into some kind of broom closet. It's dusty and stinks of mildew and the bite of old vinegar. Tempest's torch doesn't kick out smoke and there's no heat, just a steady, pale green glow. It makes us all look sickly and drawn.

OK. Tempest obviously wants something from us or he'd have turned us in. Listen, stall for time, learn what we can.

"How'd you get out of your cell?" he asks.

Neither of us answers, but Tempest snatches Sam's hand and lifts it to the light to show the shining cut there. He curses.

"Do you think you're immune because you're death-touched?" he snaps, letting go of Sam's wrist. "Of all the reckless, foolish... Your friend is fighting for her life and you're *still* casting. The holding area is heavily protected, I don't know what theorem you used but—"

"We're *fine*," I say.

Tempest blinks, looking from me to Sam and back again. "It's not what it does *now*, it's a long drain. You're eating into your life. Oh, lord have mercy, who *trained* you? I know occultists can be a ruthless bunch but to teach you complex mathemagics without boundaries or containment is a death sentence."

A death sentence? Sam sucks in his cheeks, hands to his face as if he's been slapped.

"Do you not know this?" asks Tempest.

No, we didn't.

The small room is spinning. I grip the shelf hard, thinking about the feeling of working a theorem.

"All active magic has a *price*," Tempest emphasizes. "Occultists steal souls either from bottled ghosts or they syphon from the living. Augurers syphon their own souls. They die young, that is why we seal anyone using mathemagics, even if they haven't committed the crime of draining another soul. Being sealed is a hard way to live, but it protects them from killing themselves or turning to occult practice in an attempt to save their lives later."

"We're … killing ourselves?" Sam chokes. "I thought we recovered? A day of rest and—"

"For small magics, yes, but the more you use and the more complex the theorem the more it costs. You don't feel it at first, but it builds up and in a few years you have to pay the toll."

"What about Leonie?" I ask.

"She's pushed way too far. I don't know what experimental magic she's been playing with, but *if* she lives, she'll have a couple of decades at most."

My head swims; I blink back tears. My guilt is overwhelming. Without me, Leonie wouldn't know about souls and magic and occultists. She'd not have the cryptolenses to see the parts of the world she was missing. She'd be hard at work at her A-Levels, getting amazing grades, heading off to some proper posh uni and then who knows; curing cancer, sending the first manned mission to Mars, winning a Nobel prize for some invention that solves the global energy crisis and halting climate change in its tracks.

Now, thanks to me, her time is cut short.

Bottled ghosts are finite resources. They can be used up and burned out of existence. It makes sense that living souls are the same. Viola got well upset whenever Leonie pushed herself, or tried things that were too difficult for her, but I didn't think she was worried we were burning through our *souls*.

I lean against the shelving, trying to process everything, a low anger sparking in my belly, rising through me like a wave of heat.

Viola kinda warned us, but at the same time she *didn't*. She should have spelled it out for us instead. And why would she encourage Leonie to practise experimental theorems without warning her of the cost? Viola also lied about being part of The Hand, and how close she once was to Meryem. They were *mirrored*, for fuck's sake. What else is she hiding? And why?

There's sweat on Sam's top lip. "But The Hand all use magic."

"Mirrored death-touched do, yes," says Tempest. "Because two souls sealed in a mirror bond are mutually supporting."

Seer flesh and blood is special, a link between life and death. It can stabilize the restoration theorem. It can support a bond between souls.

I've not used lots of magic, but Sam has. Not as much as Leonie, but a fair bit. All of the wards, the shield, invisibility theorems—

What have we done? Why were there no warnings in any of the books we read? Is this just so basic to mathemagics it's common knowledge? Probably. And we've been hurting ourselves this whole time. It feels like a trick, a nasty, vicious trick. I let loose a string of curses. Sam says my name and I let him pull me into him, my forehead to his temple.

I won't let him die.

"There is one way to get back what you've lost," says Tempest.

I look up, hopeful.

"Why would you help us?" Sam asks, face flushed.

264

"I'm not, I'm making a deal. You heard everything Ariadne said." It's not a question. Tempest knew we were listening; he could have exposed us but he didn't. Now he's playing some kind of game and I don't think we're going to like it. "We need you. There've never been enough death-touched. This past century Meryem has located more than ever, but still, there are never enough to go around. You're both assets The Hand hope to acquire."

I remember the concern Tempest showed me when we were being questioned, and what the suited man sneered at him. "You want to mirror with one of us?" I ask.

"I do," he says, matter of fact.

My cheeks feel like they're on fire and Sam's looking at me weirdly so I stare at the cobwebs trailing over the old cleaning products on the shelves. All those daydreams about what it might be like to mirror, to be fast and strong and capable of amazing things. Now the offer's on the table I want to be physically sick. I always imagined teaming up with Heather, or another mate. I don't want to be tied to someone I don't know for the rest of my life, and definitely not to someone in The Hand.

But the power Tempest is offering is unrivalled. Would being tied to someone I barely know matter when I can actually protect the people I care about? If I'm going to help deal with these wraiths, then I'll need to be mirrored.

"What's in it for us?" asks Sam, bold as anything.

"The symbiotic syphoning reverses whatever you've stripped off your soul, restoring your full capacity for a long and healthy life, so long as you don't get killed by a shade. What we do is dangerous, but it is worthwhile."

Tempest is trying to manipulate us, of course he is. He wants this badly. He wouldn't be risking pissing Meryem off by helping us if the gamble wasn't worth it for him.

"Yes, it's agreed," Sam promises before I can. "One of us" – glances at me and he's impossible to read – "will be your mirror, *if* Meryem doesn't have us killed for our supposed crimes."

"She won't. Not if you agree to join us."

Sam sounds proper sincere. Does he mean it? Or is he trying to play Tempest at his own game? When we talked about mirroring, Sam dismissed the idea as too dangerous or unpredictable; he didn't want to mess with something that might make him anything like Caleb Gates. And he said the idea of someone else riding shotgun in his body when he's going through his transition is too much. Which makes total sense.

Now he's just agreeing to this? Maybe he should be the one to do it, he's used more magic than I have. He needs to heal that damage. Ultimately, that means he'll have to mirror one day, but I don't want him to be pushed into this now. He deserves better than that.

I'll mirror with Tempest; I want to anyway and Sam won't have to compromise.

Will Sam still like me after? What if he thinks I'm too much like Gates?

Don't think on it now. We need to get moving or we're going to get caught in a closet.

"There's one more thing we want," I say.

Tempest nods. "Name it."

"Our friends. You help us free them. Right now."

"The augurer I can do nothing for." He holds up a hand when we start to protest. "Cassie might be a child, but she's Meryem's mirror and casts some of the strongest healing charms I've seen. If anyone can save your friend, it's her. As for your other companions, I know where they are. I'll help you, but only in exchange for some information."

He pauses, waiting for us to agree before we even learn what he wants to know. He has the power here. One word from him and we'll be right back in our cell with no hope of escape. But he needs us now too.

Curious, I fold my arms. "What do you want to know?"

"Two of our members, friends of mine, came to York on the trail of an occultist. Their notes were … incomplete. They don't mention either of you but I have to know. Did you meet Dusan and Jan?"

I chew on the inside of my lip. I don't know if Jan Liska's body was ever officially identified when it was pulled from the rubble of the Harrow house, but with the resources The Hand have, they've got to know he's dead.

"We only met a couple of times."

"But you were there when Jan died?"

I nod, nervous.

"What happened to his soul and where is Dusan?" As a ghost, Tempest doesn't need to breathe, but he looks like he's holding his breath anyway. This matters to him, more than anything, maybe more than being mirrored.

"They're dissolved, if that's what you call it. This bloke, the occultist they were tailing, Caleb Gates—"

Tempest nods, he knows the name. I expect everyone in The Hand does.

"Liska and Dusan fought him and … after Liska died they didn't stop fighting. I don't know how they did it, and they had help from other ghosts, but they killed Gates and tore his soul apart, exhausting themselves doing it. Heather said they'd come back one day but not for a long time."

Tempest backs up against a cluster of brooms hung behind the door, face a still mask. "Thank you for being honest." He stares at nothing for a long moment, then clears his throat. "A deal is a deal."

He twists his wrist, and the torch light goes out.

I don't know how we manage to get from the closet to the main library without being spotted. Luck. A miracle. Or at least Tempest's knowledge of the layout of The Old Place and some quickly gestured hand signals.

In the library, beams break through heavy drapes, streaking a high-ceilinged room rammed full of bookcases packed with heavy bound volumes. A fireplace in heavy stone blazes with cheery flames.

"The Spicer Archive, confiscated from a local occultist in the late 1930s when this aperture was established," says Tempest softly as he leads us through the stacks, passing little desks with those posh green table lamps.

Specks of light drift at the edge of my sight. When I try and look at them, they're gone. I cast an eye over the titles on the shelves as we go – *Materia Osteologica, Restless Dead: Encounters Between Death-touched and Ancient Shades*, and *Mathemagical Discussions Vol 5.*

"Are they all books on magic?" I whisper, excited. I wonder if I could slip a small one in my hoody pocket. Yeah, not the best way to get The Hand to trust us.

"It's currently the second largest collection of esoteric works in The Hand's possession, the first being hidden in an aperture in Istanbul," Tempest replies quietly. "The Eastern Archive has scrolls and tablets from as far back as the library of Pergamum, but it would be irresponsible of me to tell you that, so I didn't."

For a second, I want to grab a book off the shelf, find the infirmary and wave it under Leonie's nose. If anything is going to wake her from a coma it's the knowledge that there's a whole magical library to explore.

Tempest places his palm to a low wooden door at the back of the room. It clicks and creaks open. I slip in after Sam, Tempest behind us. The door closes and we're plunged into a dim chamber.

It's the room from my dream – from Victor's memories. The Obsidian Gallery is a mirror of the library on the other side of the wall, vast and echoing but darker and cold. There is no smell, but there's a tingling in the air that promises danger.

The shelves are full of ruh taśi – all bound in cloth or leather to look like books. Some are round instead of square or rectangular. There are different sizes and bindings but they all work the same way. Thousands of shades and spirits are locked up here.

"How do these work?" asks Sam.

Tempest hesitates, then teaches us the name ruh tasi – soul glass. I pretend that it hasn't been echoing inside my mind since last night when Victor's confused memories became mine.

"Souls can't see themselves in any other kind of mirror," Tempest explains, "but with the right spells and two obsidian mirrors set at an angle, a ghost's reflection appears. Seeing their likeness can draw in and contain most ghosts and shades."

All I feel is disgust. "How are you any better than soul catchers?"

"Catcher traps mimic deathloops to amplify phantasmic essence and make a stronger battery." Taking a ruh tasi from the shelf, Tempest clicks the latch and opens it. "These do no such thing. No loop, no cycle, no amplification. It's like … stasis. The souls inside don't suffer."

Within the open ruh tasi is a face, human – just. Fleshy, distended skin sliding off bone, no eyes, mouth frozen in a terrifying grimace.

"My god," whispers Sam.

"This shade murdered three children in Wisconsin before we contained it. Trust me, the world is a safer place with *this* locked away." Tempest snaps the trap shut and reshelves it. "That is the work we do."

I look along the rows. There must be *thousands* of ruh tasi here. Not all of them contain shades, but still, there are a lot here. Plenty of traps to check. How are we supposed to find Heather and Villiers? It'll take hours to search each one, and I doubt we have long before someone clocks our escape from the cells.

Please let them be all right. Please. Please.

The remembered dream wraps around me, soft on my eyelids and sleepy on my tongue. Victor, wandering the Obsidian Gallery looking at the shades and spirits for the barest hint of company. I walk his path, fingers trailing the shelf until my nail snags on a ruh tasi. It's square, covered in worn fabric that's fraying on one corner.

They murdered me, Charlie.

In my dream I opened this case and saw Viola. She was never trapped here, why would she be? I open it. There's just my pathetic and pallid reflection in the dark glass.

"Why are some of them empty?" I ask.

Tempest frowns. "They're not. Unoccupied ruh tasi aren't kept here."

"Well, this one must have got mixed up." I show him the inside. "There's nothing."

Tempest flicks his wrist and his torch appears in his hand, bursting into flame. He holds it up, using the light to peer into the layers of shelves. "Or something was released that shouldn't have been…"

We freeze, on edge as our skin prickles. Is there a shade in here with us? We wait, time ticking a tattoo on the inside of my brain. Every minute of freedom wasted is another minute we're not helping our friends. But I don't want to be slaughtered by an escaped shade either.

After another long moment, Tempest signals us to continue, but to be quiet and watchful.

Around the corner is the stretch of gallery where they keep regular souls that they consider dangerous to seers or other ghosts, but who aren't corrupted by magic. We start our search for Heather and Villiers there, ignoring shelves covered in dust and clearly undisturbed for decades.

We search and find nothing. I tamp down panic. What if we *never* find them? I can't think like that. Keep going, one trap at a time – an old white man, whip-thin and gristle faced; an East Asian woman in a blazer with an enamel pin on her lapel; a Black woman with twists and a lip piercing; a monk in a brown cassock; a slender woman with hungry eyes; a white woman in her late twenties, the dark etchings from the wraith's claws on her cheeks and forehead, messy plait, flyaway strands around her face, freckles and slightly wonky front tooth—

Heather.

"Oh, thank god," I gasp.

She looks like one of those trippy 3D pictures. "How do I get her out?"

"Top right corner, press the symbol," says Tempest. "Or smash the whole thing, but that would draw more attention than we'd like."

I can't press my thumb to the frame fast enough. Nothing clicks or catches but there's a feeling of *release*, like a quiet exhale, and when I blink Heather's standing next to me.

Oh, thank you, thank you, thank you.

"Hey," I breathe. "H-how d'you feel?"

She frowns, like she's trying to remember how she got here. I reach for something else to say, but there's nothing and too much all at once. Then I've thrown my arms around her and she's hugging me back. When did I get taller than her? Years ago, years and years, but in my head, she's this towering adult who can fix everything.

She's never been that, I realize; who we are to each other is more complicated. I'm so relieved to have her back.

"Found him!" comes Sam's triumphant call, and then Villiers is there, rumpled velvet, lace and pointed beard as he leans on Sam, a hand to his chest. Blinking, he pulls himself together.

"Master Harrow, I— What place is this?"

It all floods out in a rush. By the time me and Sam are done explaining what we've learned about The Hand, Claire Cole, Jory and Viola, Heather looks stressed and Villiers is proud that we broke out of our cell.

"This is Tempest," I introduce him. "He's … all right."

We don't mention Victor. As much as Tempest's helping us, I reckon he's still loyal to The Hand. If he wasn't, he'd want out, same as Victor. Instead, he's asked to pair with one of us to get back *in*.

"You know a ghost called Viola?" He's trying to hide his confusion and unease and failing. "It … it can't be the same death-touched girl I knew."

"About yay big." I hold my hand to just above my

shoulder. "Floral dress, reads fortunes with a set of human wrist bones."

"But her soul never remained earthbound. She was murdered by a shade."

"She tells it different, says Meryem killed her."

"*Never*," rasps Tempest.

"We need to get out of here." Sam's forehead shines with sweat, his face blotchy. "Tempest, come with us and ask her yourself."

My skull pulses. I'm getting a headache. The strange pressure of this room must be getting to me. "Not without Leonie."

"She's safer here," Tempest insists.

"Bollocks to that," snaps Heather. If she and Villiers are feeling any aftereffects of their incarceration, they're not showing it. She squares up to Tempest and, even though she's shorter than him, there's something in her voice when she says, "Take us to her, now," that leaves no room for argument.

Tempest raises a hand warning us to be quiet – he needs to scout the exit, make sure it's clear to leave. One last look back, and he snuffs his torch.

The darkness isn't complete. There's still soft cold light coming from somewhere. I sense the shapes and shadows of my friends and hear Sam's breathing as we wait.

OK, next steps. Get to Leonie, find Victor. I know he has the power to get us out of this aperture. It's a fact that I feel in my bones, the same way I know there's something moving in the shadows near us.

Finding Sam's hand, I squeeze twice in warning. He tenses and stops. My entire body screams, *Wraith!* But that's impossible, isn't it? I remember Tempest's warning. Not a wraith, but some*thing* that escaped from the empty ruh tasi shelved with the really scary shit. Heather backs up with Sam, putting the shelving behind them, knees bent to find a better centre of gravity. Villiers draws his rapier, the metal singing into the dark.

What darts at us isn't a shade, but people in dark coats with glowing silver eyes. Steel strikes, a sound like bone crunching. Villiers shouts curses. A sharp cry.

Sam!

Someone twists my arm up behind my back and I grit my teeth as muscles scream and stitches pull. I'm hungry, tired and done in, but I bend the other way to break the grip and trip into the sharp point of a scythe that rests against my jugular. I look up its curve to the cold, calculating snarl of the suited man. "Move and I bleed you dry, boy."

Villiers is caught in a gleaming net, Heather's trussed in Ariadne's ribbons and Gage holds Sam at axe point. Tempest is gone.

That bastard, did he set this up? But why would he?

Ariadne glares at me with callous, pathetic hatred. Then she nods at someone behind me and magic wraps around me like a cloak.

27

BONES AND ALL

Rows of seers and ghosts line the hall as we're marched in with a guard of scythe- and sword-wielding jailers at our backs.

The air smells of dust, cloth and the crackle of magic taut and waiting. Meryem's sitting in front of the table and her chair might as well be a throne. Maybe she was a queen when she was alive: commanding armies, sending soldiers out to fight and die in her honour. Long necked and elegant, she's flanked by the crusader and Bathily, the old lady.

The great stained-glass window spills flame over my face. I spot Tempest, off to the side with Victor. Why's Victor still here? If he leaves this place like he wants to then everything comes crumbling down. This whole aperture will shred, freeing us all into the real world. I thought that was his plan, what he wanted and I'm sure I felt the magic release when we opened the cell door. Why is he waiting?

A door opens down the hall. It's the cheerleader, Cassie, leading—

Leonie!

Oh, thank god. She looks tired, hollowed out and scared but she's *alive*, awake and walking on her own. Her hospital gown is gone and she's wearing simple black clothes. She doesn't look like herself, but honestly, she's never been more beautiful than she is right now. I choke her name and she says mine and Sam's when she sees us. I could honestly cry right now, but when I try to move towards her, Gage is having none of it.

"Stay," he orders, pickaxe in his meaty grip. He's not messing about.

Leonie stumbles, still weak, and Cassie lends her arm to lean on. Have they done it already, have they sealed her?

"I'll make them get you a chair if you need one," says Cassie and I catch the twang of an American accent I didn't notice before. She's a long way from home.

Leonie shakes her head and Cassie guides her between me and Sam, glaring at Gage as if daring him to argue. He doesn't. Sam pulls Leonie into a trembling hug.

"Where's Mitch?" Leonie hisses at us. "They won't tell me."

"Home, we think." I keep my voice low. "He's—" I can't say "fine" or "all right" or "OK" because there's no way he's any of those things. "He's alive."

Gage nudges me to shut me up. Cassie goes to stand behind

Meryem and there's a sudden hush, like the silence before a headman swings the axe.

"Leonie Agyemang, Charlie Frith and Sam Harrow, you are all guilty of practising mathemagics and phantomatology at the detriment of yourselves and others."

Oh, this is a trial. Bollocks to that! They know we didn't summon the wraiths and they've got plans to deal with them, so what are they playing at? Is this just because they hate occultists, augurers and magic users who aren't part of their club?

"Thou art mistaken," Villiers interrupts. "It is with great dedication and risk to their own persons that our seers, assisted by Mistress Agyemang, aided the souls of York, protecting us from catchers and others who might do us harm." Raising a hand, he sweeps into a courtly bow. "I am George Villiers, First Duke of Buckinghamshire, and the favourite of three kings. I give you my word that they art trustworthy and noble."

"Trustworthy?" The crusader's voice rings through the hall. "They destroyed an expertly cast binding on the cells to break you and your companion from a protected room. As such, they will be sealed immediately."

"Whoa, whoa!" I say, finding my voice. "Where's the trial part of this trial? Aren't we going to hear evidence? And I'm pretty sure there is supposed to be a jury."

And what about mirroring? Tempest said they needed us. We've been investigating the wraiths since the beginning. We can help.

"If we promise not to cast any more theorems, will you let us go?" asks Leonie, her voice small. "Theory only."

Meryem's gaze is level. "And when you start to die, will you remain a theorist? No, you will reach for any solution to save yourself, syphoning from other souls."

"I'd rather *die*."

"And you will, girl. You will unless you take from others. The temptation will be too great, anyone would succumb."

Meryem's acting like this is all Leonie's fault, *Ah, well, that's what you get for messing with big old powers. Bet you wish you'd left it all alone now.*

"You have broken our laws," Meryem continues. "There are consequences."

"That's bullshit," I snap. "We didn't even know there were laws to break. You're not even in York any more, you can't decide the rules for everyone."

Meryem rises in a swish of silk. She doesn't walk; one moment she's holding court and the next she's in my face, nails biting my chin as she glowers into my eyes. I'm smothered in the scent of a flower garden.

"Perhaps you cannot feel how very *alive* this city is. Souls fuel life. Death is memory, history, it is the essence of a place and people. Catchers here have only plucked a few souls, like harvesting a choice crop. This city still has its essence, its heart." She releases my chin but I can still feel the iron strength in her. She looks delicate and elegant, but she's a warrior like the rest of them. "Have you ever been to Sicily, Bucharest or Istanbul? No? You'd feel the difference.

Soul catchers came to Istanbul when I was only two decades deceased. They didn't just trap one ghost, or even a few. They took them *all*, every soul on those streets, some as old as Hagia Sophia. All of that memory, that wisdom, gone in a single week of terror. That's all it took them, a week. I alone endured."

Occultists stripped a whole city of souls in a *week*? I can't help imagining what that would be like in York. Traps on every corner, spirit sinks, splashes of red sealing wax and the panic. Thousands of ghosts just … gone. Empty streets, silent and unhaunted.

"A death-touched helped me escape the harvesting of Istanbul," says Meryem. "We founded The Hand to push back against those who treat the afterlife as fuel for the living, to protect death-touched from harm, and the living from shades and monstrosities wrought by occultists. We make the world safe. Whether you intended to or not, you have threatened that safety but, as a gesture, I offer you and Sam a choice. Join us and mirror with one of our number or … be sealed like your friend. For you, sealing means that you will also lose your ability to see and interact with deceased souls."

A cold jolt of shock. We won't be seers any more?

Younger me ached to be normal. I hated seeing the dead and being afraid all the time, having to hide from ghosts and keep the living away so they didn't think I was weird. I might have jumped at this chance once, willing to be a stranger to myself forever just to feel a little bit safe.

No more errands, I could live my life for myself. Go to

college, get a job, and forget about deathloops and wards and occultists.

And I would lose everything that really matters. Heather, Ollie, Dante, Villiers, Broomwood. Plus, that's not all the first seal does. Viola made it clear being under its influence isn't living at all. I don't want to be a zombie person, disconnected from the world and myself forever. Fuck that.

Deep-seated rage runs through every part of me and makes me feel like I'm going to explode. I see the same feeling shining in Sam's face, in the furious flex of his jaw, the square of his shoulders. Being a seer has always been right for him. He's never questioned it, just accepted it and done what he can with it.

Meryem's offer isn't a choice.

They're not giving Leonie the same deal, how can they? She's not death-touched: she has no value to them so her fate is sealed. And soon, she will be too.

I want to be mirrored; it's an easy choice for me but what about Sam?

"Meryem." He steps forward. "I request an audience with you, in private."

What? Why?

Is he going to try and make a different deal? Gage is between us so I can't reach out and whisper in his ear, try and understand what he's up to.

Turning her attention to Sam, Meryem drums her fingers on her arm, *tap tap tap,* but I can tell he's caught her interest.

"Very well."

He's escorted towards a small door cut into the panelling, locking gazes with Tempest as he passes. Meryem follows and as soon as the door closes a murmur chases through the assembly. They're wondering the same thing as me. What's he playing at?

I'll mirror with Tempest, keep our promise, and buy Sam more time so he doesn't have to mirror until he's ready. Or is there a third option? He might be trying to convince Meryem that we can help stop Jory without being mirrored, but that doesn't feel right. Nothing about this does.

They're not gone long, minutes at most, but by the time the door clicks open and Meryem emerges, giving nothing away, Sam at her heels, I feel like I've run a sodding marathon twice over.

Sam's face is flushed, he's supporting his sore arm, still in its brace, fingers fiddling with the Velcro. *Look up, look at me.* But he doesn't.

I've got a nasty feeling about this.

Meryem takes her place at the front of the hall. "Miss Agyemang, I revoke your sentence. Mr Frith, you are also free to leave, as are your spectral companions."

I blink, confused. A moment ago she was raining down brimstone and punishment and now we can just … go? I don't want to argue, but—

Sam.

I look to him again but he keeps his eyes on the floor. What's going on?

"Mr Harrow has elected to join us. He will mirror with

Tempest Lawson and assist in bringing the occultist Jory Chambers to justice."

A shocked rumble travels through the assembled Hand. Tempest looks pleased as fucking punch. There's a nasty, angry hollow in my guts.

Heather shouts, "Sam, what the hell?"

Yeah, Sam, what the hell?

"Your freedom is contingent on Sam's position in The Hand." Meryem nods at someone behind us. "Get them out of here."

The reality of what's happening clicks and I yell, "Sam? Sam!"

He won't look at me. I kick and fight Ariadne's ribbons tangling around me, locking my limbs, biting into the stitches in my arm until it's agony, but I don't give a shit. He won't look at me.

I think of the way he kissed me in our cell, hand on my face and tears in his eyes. Was that goodbye? Had he already decided then?

Why didn't he talk to me about this? Why didn't I tell him how I really feel about mirroring?

This isn't how it ends. This isn't how I lose him.

I almost shout out that I'll mirror in his place but stop. That makes way more sense, for a start, I actually *want* to mirror. But Sam doesn't know that because I was too scared to be honest with him about it, and now he's made a deal and we're actually being released – Heather, Villiers, Leonie, me. He's traded himself for all of us. How did he even convince Meryem to do that? I know he can be a charming bastard but—

Fuck.

He has a plan, he has to have a plan. *Trust him*.

But then why won't he look at me?

No, I can't mess this up. I have to walk away for Leonie's sake, and to make sure Heather and Villiers are safe. They deserve a better future than an eternity trapped in a magical mirror prison just for sticking up for us.

Victor watches us, silent and serious. I want him to do something, but what? I felt the magic in the aperture, the locks keeping him bound here are gone, so why doesn't he walk out of the front door with us and stick two fingers up at the lot of them as their precious books and bullshit are crushed to pulp and they're spat out one by one?

Whatever game he's playing, I'm starting to think we were only ever pawns. Now it's too late.

28

REUNION

Breathe. Keep breathing, and don't look back because if I do I'll break and I can't right now. Not yet. Dean's Park is filled with stretched shadows streaking away from the up-lit Minster. The trees shiver, spilling leaves, and I flinch, thinking the movement is a wraith darting from the dark to drag one of us away.

Heather on one side, Villiers behind me, Leonie holding my hand and it's the only way I keep walking. She falls into me crying. I hug her close and say sorry over and over.

"Are they here?" she asks, voice breaking.

She means Villiers and Heather. Outside of the aperture and without her cryptolenses, she can't see them any more. "Yeah, they're here and they're really happy you're alive."

"I've got twenty years, tops." Leonie rubs her arms against the chill, blinking at the world like she's seeing it for the first time. "*If* I never use another theorem. Cassie warned me the next spell I do could be my last."

I apologize again. I'll never stop saying sorry. My mess, my problems, yet it's my friends who pay the price.

The oversized black shirt and dark trousers Leonie's got on are thin, not enough against the October night. My hoody is pretty gross, but I peel it off and pass it to her.

"You'll freeze," she protests.

The cold bites through my sweat-stained T-shirt. "I'll live, and you almost died."

Will die. Sooner than you should.

Sniffing, she pulls my hoody on, tucking her hands into the sleeves. It's way too long for her. "It's really … over?"

I look back. The Old Place is just the Minster library. The lights are all off. The gates leading to the main entrance are locked tight.

He didn't even look at me.

"It's over for *us*," I say, trying not to feel bitter. York and its ghosts are my responsibility, ours, mine and Sam's, and now Sam will mirror with Tempest while I stay home and play Mario Kart. They'll find Jory, rescue Claire, end the wraiths. It's not supposed to be *my* problem any more. Leave it to the professionals. I'm just meant to go home and go back to worrying about the wards—

Shit.

How are we going to ward the city without being able to use magic? Or will The Hand take care of that too? My head hurts. When The Hand leave York, will Sam go with them to a lifetime of hunting shades and occultists? That's bleak. He chose them, but he did it for me. For us.

It should've been me.

He saved Leonie from being sealed, sacrificed his freedom and I just stood there and let him. What the fuck is wrong with me? I could have offered to take his place, argued with him, with them. But Meryem might have changed her mind and sealed Leonie, and I couldn't let that happen.

Sam has to have a plan, this can't be *it*.

Except, he's used more magic than me so he needed to mirror to repair the damage. Is that why de did it, because he's worried about how long he's got left to live? Then why didn't he say so? I'm happy he's gonna repair his soul source, but I should be mirrored too. We're a team, me and him.

A cold wind shudders through the trees. I feel numb.

"Let us get clear of this heinous place," says Villiers.

We walk south towards the park's main gate. My phone unfreezes, the clock jumping to 10:30 p.m. and – damn, we were in The Old Place for *two* days. A flurry of notifications fill my screen – from my parents and from the friends they reached out to in their search for us.

I go to call our landline.

"Don't," says Heather, closing her hand over mine. "I'm sorry, but we need to work out a cohesive, believable story before you contact anyone. Sam is still technically missing."

My heart sinks. She's right. How can we explain where we've been and how we disappeared from the hospital? We were kidnapped, but they used magic so there won't be any security footage to back up our story. Maybe we can play the amnesia card and say we just showed up in Dean's Park, missing time.

Would they buy it? The police might … at a stretch, but my folks won't. They already know there's something going on with me. Telling the truth won't make a difference. The rozzers would storm the Minster library and find nothing.

I relay what Heather said for Leonie.

"Message Mitch," she begs. "I need to know he's all right. We might be able to go to his for a bit if his dad's not there or … the bookshop. I know the alarm code, but I don't have a key. Can you pick the lock?"

"Yeah … no, I don't have my picks."

Thinking of the bookshop reminds me of Viola and what she didn't tell us.

"Viola was one of The Hand," I tell Leonie.

She stops walking, silent.

"She knew," whispers Heather.

Un-fucking-believable. Tears sting the corner of my eyes. I can't deal with this on top of everything. Shivering in the chilly air, I keep walking, wanting to be moving, to be out of the cold wind.

"She *was*, past tense." Leonie catches my bare arm and makes me face her. "The story of the last seer of York, the one Ollie tells, that's her. Sister Agnes *ate* her and Meryem did nothing to stop it."

"Why?" I ask. "Why wouldn't Meryem save the person she was mirrored to?"

For all of their faults, The Hand have each other's backs. I saw it in Tempest's face when I told him what happened to Dusan and Liska.

"Because they're fucked up power-hungry bastards who want everything on their own terms," snaps Leonie. "And Viola didn't *tell* me. She was teaching me the three seals and I realized there was no way she could know all that and not have been one of them. The Hand guard their secrets well."

"Viola taught you the seals?" A bubble of hysterical laughter bursts out of me as I motion back towards The Old Place. "Shite, Leonie. What if they'd found out you were using them?"

"I wasn't *using* them. Theory only."

"Like that makes *any* difference to them," says Heather.

I could scream just to get this pressure out of my head, an outlet for the anger. But Leonie's like that, always wanting to understand how and why the world works, recklessly pursuing knowledge no matter what it costs her. Yelling at her won't change who she is and it won't help anything.

We're at the fork in the path, the wrought-iron gates to Minster's Yard up ahead. As tall as me and topped with spikes, they're firmly locked this time of night. We're going to have to find a way over the top. My body aches at the idea of it.

"I'm *sorry*," says Leonie. "Vi made me promise not to tell anyone, not even Mitch. She thought if you knew, you wouldn't trust her."

"She is not mistaken," says Villiers coolly.

Fucking right.

"And do *you* still trust her?" I ask Leonie. "Did she bother to mention that syphoning our own souls as a source is *killing* us? No, didn't think so. She pretended to give a shite about you and your magical education when she was letting you throw away decades of your life. We can't trust her; we never should have in the first place. Something's not right with her and deep down you know it too, all the *lies*—"

Leonie hiccups a cry, clapping a hand over her mouth and turning away. Shit. I pull her back to me but she slaps me away.

"I'm sorry," I say. "I'm not pissed at you. You're one of my oldest mates, and you almost *died* and she could have stopped that happening and she didn't and I just—"

Leonie fits under my chin. I close my eyes and hold her as she cries.

"We'll get Sam back," she says, voice croaky.

Her words strike deep in my chest. They hurt because I want to trust him and I hope so much that she's right. But what if secretly he wanted to mirror this whole time and never told me. He would have, right? But I never told him how I really feel about mirroring. *About him.* "The second seal, the one that will mirror Sam and Tempest, can it be undone?"

She shakes her head. "None of them can. They're for life."

We can't unseal Mitch.

"Then Sam's made his choice." I don't mean to sound so cold. That's not how I feel but I'm too tired and numb to process everything.

Don't think about Sam.

I'm shivering. Time to get out of here.

Oh, crap, we have to climb the gate.

"I shalt give thee a boost," says Villiers, seeing my exhaustion. I'm more worried about getting Leonie over. When she hugged me I could feel how weak she was after being unconscious for the best part of three days.

She gasps. Something has Villiers' and Heather's attention too. There's a figure near the Minster heading this way. No, five people – two smaller, three taller. Shit, is it security?

A sharp, excited bark. A shape near the group's feet breaks away and comes racing over the cobbles, moving through the solid iron gate as if the barrier's not there. "Dante!"

He licks my palms, leaping up in excitement.

A shout goes up. "It's them!"

Two more ghosts run through the barrier. Ollie cheers, calling my name. I ruffle his hair. He hugs my waist and tells me I stink, which I do. Reid has Villiers in his arms and they're kissing like it's the end of the world. Ollie hugs Heather. "Good to see you, old man," she says, voice catching.

Mitch rattles the bars of the gate, then heads a couple of metres towards the Minster where the fence is lower and vaults over, iron spikes be damned. My heart races at the sight of him.

He's wearing Leonie's cryptolenses. The left lens is cracked but they survived. "How did you get out? What did they do? Are you OK?"

Leonie folds into him as he kisses her, lifting her up and burying his face into her neck.

I realize who the two other people with Mitch are. Al,

wrapped up in a warm coat and Mr Agyemang. He has a wrap of bold geometric colour bunched tight around his fist. I recognize it as one of Leonie's favourite scarves. Did they use Dante to sniff out her scent? That's genius, but that also means—

He knows. Shit, Mitch must have told him everything.

"Stand back." Mr Agyemang's at the gate, his other hand raised. He makes a shape in the air. It takes a soft flare of light and the soft click of the lock before I realize what he's just done.

Magic.

Mr Agyemang is an augurer, or an occultist.

My brain short circuits for a second because that *doesn't make sense.* Before I can question it, they're all around us, arms, elbows, cheeks pressed to mine. Mr Agyemang cups Leonie's face, as if to make sure she's real and then he's crying and she's crying again and Al has his arms around them both and Mitch is sliding his jacket over me.

I pull down the neckline of his hoody to run a finger over the pale raised flesh on his sternum in the shape of the first seal. "Mate, I'm sorry—"

"Don't." His smile wavers and he slides his hand over mine. "I'm … I'm … there was nothing you could have done."

"What's it feel like?"

He just shakes his head. I slip my arms around him, relief caught up with guilt. The seals can't be broken, well, I'll find a way. If it's not his dad being a dick or trouble at the restaurant, Mitch is always being punished for just being himself. Especially for helping me and being a better mate than I deserve.

"They dumped me in the street way south of here," he tells me when we break apart. "Ollie and Reid found me but I didn't know they were with me until I got to Leonie's and got her cryptolenses. Her dad— We've been following the compass for hours, hoping to find you."

What compass?

Leonie's staring at her dad's hand and the stain on the scarf, mostly hidden by the night-time shadows and twisted and discoloured by the Minster's uplighters.

Blood.

They didn't get Dante to trace Leonie's scent, they used a theorem. A magical compass.

"Dad, stop." There's fear in Leonie's eyes. "You're burning your soul. Stop, please."

He drops the scarf as he catches her up and hugs her again, tears on his cheeks. "I can't believe it worked; it's been almost two decades since I—"

He knows about magic and the price of using it. Surely, he'd have stopped Leonie over tapping her soul source. Instead, he just stayed silent. Like Viola.

No way would he do that. So he didn't know we were messing about with mathemagics. We were careful, kept our chats about the dead low key, and Leonie keeps her notes hidden. Surely, he would have recognized the cryptolenses, but then Jory didn't know what they were. She uses an obsidian mirror to see souls.

"Not gonna lie," says Ollie, "it shocked the hell out of me too."

I've always liked Mr Agyemang's voice. It's deep and rich and reassuring, but now it's tinged with fear as he breaks out of his daughter's hold. "We have a lot to talk about," he says. "But not here."

Mitch sweeps in a circle. "Wait … where's Sam?"

There's a cardboard box on the coffee table in Leonie's living room filled with notebooks, crystals and a pair of obsidian mirrors, not ruh tasi but two separate, identical disks with a protruding nodule on each fixed with a simple leather strap. The oldest way of seeing the dead.

Mr Agyemang uses one of them to reflect the room. I'm not at the right angle to see the reflection, but he nods, obviously noting Heather, Ollie, Reid and Villiers. Dante's on the rug, his interest fixated on my half-eaten sandwich. I'm ravenous but struggling to eat. My stomach feels like lead, the upset of what I've lost weighing on me.

"Charlie, you're death-touched?" He lowers the mirror, then nods to himself. "Of course, your meningitis, that makes sense. And … Sam?"

"He drowned," I say past the lump in my throat.

Leonie closes the notebook filled with mathemagical notations and smooths a hand over the cover. "Explain."

Her dad nods a few times, as if steeling himself. Slowly, he puts down the mirror, maybe addressing fewer people is easier, and steeples his fingers. "I wasn't ever skilled in mathemagics. Your mum was the one with the talent." He looks at his children, Leonie on the couch with Al, his older sons Terry and Joe standing behind them. "We ran with some experimental magicians at university; she wanted to help people. It was only later, when it was already too late, that we realized the damage we were inflicting on ourselves. I used so little, maybe I've lost a handful of years but Effia…"

Joe clears his throat. "Her sickness?"

My Agyemang's expression says it all.

I remember what Mitch said at the hospital – *they think it's the same thing her mum had.*

I'm livid at Viola all over again. She was part of The Hand; she *knew*. We should've worked it out but why didn't she just *tell* us? How much of my lifetime have I burned? How much has Sam used? At least when Sam mirrors with Tempest, he'll heal that damage. But why did we ever trust Viola?

She was friendly and helpful when we needed it most and that was enough. I hate myself for it, and what's worse is I can't work out *why* she'd do any of this to us. What does she want?

"Friends told us to syphon from the dead," Leonie's dad says slowly. "Your mum refused to save herself at the cost of other people, said she made her mistakes and she'd live with them." He pauses, gathering the strength to go on. "When she got pregnant with you, Joe, she burned most of her books and notebooks, packed up a few precious tools and totems into this little box and locked it away. But I need you to know that she didn't whittle down her years with us for trifles and glamours. She helped people, saved more lives than I can count and understood the balance had to be paid against her own."

In the silence that follows, Leonie admits that she only has twenty years to live now, at most. Terry curses. Joe and Mr Agyemang start to cry and I can't be there any more. Mitch is part of this family, has been for years. I feel like an intruder into their grief.

"I should have told you the dangers sooner," I hear Mr Agyemang say as I slide off the couch. "You're so logical, so focused on the sciences, I … I just never thought you'd encounter *true* magic."

Closing the adjoining door as quietly as I can, I limp across the kitchen towards the small nook near the back door where there's an oversized armchair. My stumps are weightbearing, but tile is hard and I've been wearing dirty liners and socks for two days. Now I'm paying the price.

By the time I've settled into the chair, my ghosts are all around me. I wanted to be alone, but as Heather sits on the chair arm, and Villiers and Reid curl up, backs against the side of the chair, Reid leaning into Villiers, I realize they've not come to talk things through. They've come to just be with me.

My family.

I sleep. Fuck knows how, but I do, the air rattling in my lungs. Cooking smells and the rumble of the washing machine chase away the mildew scent of The Old Place.

A sound drags me from sleep – hours later, or maybe minutes – the door opens and there's a soft shuffle of slippers on the tile. Mr Agyemang's hand gently presses my shoulder.

"Charlie, call your parents."

29

WE NEED TO TALK ABOUT CHARLIE

Lucrezia is elegant and dramatic in her worry, speaking so fast in high-pitched accented English that I struggle to pick out individual words. She questions me and I gulp the answers.

Yes, Sam is alive.

Yes, I know where.

No, we can't get to him. They have magic we can't rival. He made a choice but I trust that he has a plan. Unless he didn't and his deal was only ever meant to save us. Sam would do that.

Mr Agyemang ushers her to the kitchen for a coffee, allowing me to take up a tense vigil at the front window. Mitch is with me, running a finger over the raised white scar below his collarbone.

"Does it hurt?" I ask.

He shakes his head. "Hurt's the wrong word, it's like … everything feels distant. I can't feel heat or cold, can't smell or taste anything. A chef who can't taste his own food, I don't know how that's going to work."

"I'm so sor—"

"Don't you fucking start." Mitch sounds so tired. "Me and Leonie both chose to be here, and not just for you and Sam, though that's part of it. For ourselves too. Leonie lives for mystery, of course she's gonna want to learn everything she can about magic."

"Do you really like seeing the dead?" I say. "You don't wear lenses all the time, even when we had two pairs."

Mitch isn't wearing cryptolenses any more, having given Leonie her pair back. "It doesn't mean I don't want in. I'm not always comfortable; some of this shit is scary … and I'm going to be … was going to be a pastry chef for a living, but I'm glad I know, and I'm glad to be a part of it."

"Even now?"

Mitch's lips ruck in a charming half-smile. "Yeah. Even now."

Dad's taxi pulls up, too fast, almost hitting some bins. My nerves fire, heart speeding and I barely have time to think. My folks don't lock the car, just charge up the short driveway, Broomwood ghosting after them at a jog. I've never seen him move faster than a disapproving stride so it's a momentous occasion.

I distantly wonder who's looking after my sisters. Probably Aunt Chrissie. This is it. I'm going to tell them. I have to tell them. It's getting harder and harder to hide the truth. They deserve to know.

The front doors open. Footsteps in the hall. I get down from the chair. Dad is in the doorway. Going on his knees so we're the same height, he wraps me in a hug so powerful I hiss in pain. He eases off, checking me over for more hurt. When he sees I've no new injuries, he starts shouting.

He doesn't shout often, my old man, but when he does the ground fucking trembles.

"*Paul.*" Mum's crying. She smells like fabric softener and home. When we break apart she asks, "Where *were* you? What happened—?"

"I'll tell you everything," I promise. "But … you might want to sit down."

I can't meet their eyes.

"Sit down, why, what's going on?" asks Dad, red in the face.

The folding doors to the kitchen open, and Mr Agyemang's standing there like a patient teacher waiting for the class to settle. He has a measured kind of stillness that rubs off on folks.

"Please sit down," I tell my parents.

"I'll put the kettle on," Mr Agyemang offers.

Mum doesn't so much sit as perch, forehead lined by worry. Dad slides his palm into hers, pulling her hand into his lap. Mr Agyemang brings in some coffee.

I stay standing because I'm way too restless and I need to pace a little. The carpet's soft enough.

"It's going to be hard to believe," I warn. "I need you to just … listen, right? Listen and then I'll prove it to you."

Deep down, I don't want to do this. My parents don't belong in *this* world with the dead. Leonie's dad is already part of it. Sam's mum is a law unto herself. My mum and dad are just regular folks, honest, salt of the earth people.

I shoot a glance at Heather. The nod she gives me is tiny, but there's strength in it. Ollie winks encouragement at me.

God, this feels like coming out again.

"So, um … I can, I…"

I can't say it. I just can't. But they have to know the truth. It's not fair to keep them in the dark any more.

"Do it, lad," says Broomwood. "It's the right thing."

Villiers and Reid are near the edge of the TV. Their blood families are long gone, stolen by the centuries. Mine is right in front of me and I can't be honest with them about who I am. Broomwood's right, that has to change. I need my parents to know the real me; no more lies.

"Mum, Dad. I see and speak to the dead – to ghosts – and I have been able to since I got sick. It was the coming back from the dead that did it, and now I help take care of the ghosts of York."

Dad blinks. Whatever he expected me to say, that wasn't it. "Ghosts?"

He doesn't believe me. Dad only deals with what's here and real. He likes a problem he can tackle head on, so what's he supposed to do with a problem he can't even see?

"I know it sounds daft," I say. "Impossible, like, but it's true. I see them, and so does Sam."

Breathe.

"It's true, Paul," says Mr Agyemang.

"All the cuts and scratches I come home with." I force more words out. "I'm not getting into fights, well … not with the living. The dead can be dangerous and they can rough me up a bit, but not all of them are like that," I add quickly. "Most of them are good, and some of them are mates of mine."

Maybe sensing I'm nervous, Dante pads over and sits beside me, whining. I give his head a quick scratch. Mum tracks the movement, paling like she has so many times before when she's caught me smiling at Ollie or Heather. "You're friends with … dead people?"

She's a sensitive, I realize. Like my sisters. Like Neelam.

"You've felt things at home that you can't explain, haven't you?"

Mum shifts on the couch, uneasy. "I…"

"It might be easier just to show you," I say. "But you have to promise not to scream, or like generally panic."

"O…K?" Mum separates the word out, turning it into a question.

Mr Agyemang hands my parents an obsidian mirror each. "You need to be touching one of these to hear the dead as well as see them."

My palms are sweating. "They're spelled obsidian that let regular people sort of see and hear what me and Sam can. Try it out."

"Or you can try my cryptolenses," blurts Leonie. "But the dead look more unsettling … you know what, one thing at a time."

302

Silence as my parents angle the mirrors to reflect the room. I can feel how restless the ghosts are, the sudden awareness that they'll be seen by two of the living, neither of which are guaranteed to take the experience well. Only Ollie seems keen, and I know it's because he's waiting to rock the finger guns and make a joke out of all this if it goes badly.

The couch groans as Dad flinches. He turns the mirror away. "Wha—"

"They won't hurt you, I promise."

He angles the mirror back, taking in the ghosts. "This is a … trick."

"It is no trick," says Lucrezia. "Our sons have a gift."

I almost roll my eyes. I don't think my folks will think of this as a "gift" any more than I do. I just want them to accept me exactly as I am, that's all.

Mum angles the mirror. "Mr Broomwood?"

"Lovely to see you again, Joyce. You have an exceptional lad, I hope you know that."

"Th-thank you." She touches her hair, then her earring. "I can *hear* him, Paul."

Broomwood smiles. "He's taken good care of my roses, and that counts for something, so don't be too hard on him, eh?"

"I am George Villiers." Villiers bows with a flourish. "First Duke of Buckinghamshire, former Lord Admiral of the king's fleet, Knight of the Royal Garter, and the favourite of *three* kings, at your service, and this is my lover James Reid."

Reid touches his hand to his heart. "It's an honour to meet the parents of such an exceptional son."

Dad reaches out.

"Ah, alas, we cannot touch, sir," says Villiers. "For I am but made of memory and dreams."

"Yeah, that's not what we're made of," Ollie chimes in. He raises a hand. "Hey, I'm Ollie, sickly Victorian waif – not contagious – I mostly live in Charlie's bedroom with Dante, that daft mutt there." At the sound of his name, Dante cocks his head, his tongue lolling. "I like ancient history, reading, and Marvel, which is good because my best mate is basically a superhero." He jerks a thumb at me and grins.

"Charlie's invisible friends?" Mum whispers. "Goodness, they don't watch me pee, do they?"

"Madam, I assure you we have never, nor will ever, watch you pass water." Villiers says it with a straight face and everything.

She giggles and the giggle turns kind of tearful.

"You all right?" I ask my parents.

"It's … a lot," says Mum.

Mr Agyemang sips his coffee. "I'm afraid there's more."

I sit in an armchair, missing Sam as Mr Agyemang lays all our secrets bare – the wraiths, The Hand, where Sam is. He's just gone through all this with Lucrezia, but she jumps in with details like she's been privy since the beginning, which pisses me off. I don't say anything; it's best to let the adults hash it out.

When it's all been covered, Dad's face is red. Mum is silent.

I wait, a sinking feeling in my stomach. Dad looks at me and says, "We're leaving."

My folks are silent on the drive home, Mum staring out of the window as the city gives way to suburbs. I sit in the back seat, missing Sam with a fierce pain that churns my insides, or maybe that's also regret. I shouldn't have told my folks the truth. They're not taking it well; I should have waited until there was less going on. Or just never said anything.

We pull into our driveway. The porch light is on. Coloured flashes from the TV flicker through the half open curtains. *Here we are again.*

The police are waiting for us. When four teens connected to a string of mysterious deaths vanish from a hospital, folks pay attention, which is a pain in the arse. We were going to lie and say we hitched down south and that Sam's still there with a mate but there are no phone records or train tickets to prove it and they'll want to talk to Sam.

We're *not* going to say a mysterious magical organization kidnapped us. Even if they wore masks and we didn't see their faces, or we went with them because they threatened Leonie it doesn't add up. So... yeah, we're claiming amnesia.

Dad angles the obsidian mirror Mr Agyemang lent him so that he can see it's still just the three of us in the car. "If this Hand cult is as dangerous as Abam suggests, then let him and his occult people handle getting Sam back."

Mr Agyemang is set on calling round a bunch of his old uni mates. The Hand has a reputation, mostly hearsay, but he reckons they'll help if they can. I made it clear that if they do come to York, they're not to bottle any ghosts. Mr Agyemang agreed but I don't get how he can make promises for folks he hasn't seen in two decades.

"I know you're worried about Sam," says Mum. "We are too, love, but your dad's right, you need to leave this wraith thing alone. You've handled a lot, more than most kids ever have to, but this isn't your responsibility."

I believed that once. And then a stubborn southern lad with dimples and a waxed jacket exploded into my life and changed everything.

I'm not ready to give up on Sam.

Mum fixes her gaze on me in the rear-view mirror, taking in my bruised, tired face. "This stops now. No ghosts. No magic."

I don't bother arguing.

30

†HE MEMORY BOX

"They probably took it with them, lad." Broomwood watches me rifle through my parents' dresser.

I'm grounded for the first time in my life, which is bullshit. My folks confiscated my phone and have stashed it somewhere. I've got to find it before they get home from Lidl with my sisters. Broomwood, Ollie, Reid and Villiers are helping me, but they're not much use. If I was mirrored, one of them would be able to open drawers and have a proper rummage. As it is, they just boss me about.

My folks tried to ban ghosts from our house but there's nothing they can do about Dante who refuses to leave my side. Mum says that as he doesn't shed on the couch, it's not such a big deal. She sounded a bit hysterical when she said it, so I'm not going to tell her that as soon as they go out, the ghosts come flooding back inside anyway.

I knew telling my folks the truth wouldn't go well. No one shares their darkest secret and has someone say, *Is that all?* like it's no big deal.

Deep down I think I hoped it would bring us closer, tear down the barriers I've built. Instead the lies count against me. Every time me and my folks talk, even if it's just about what to have for tea, the air between us is taut with tension.

I'm not saying I was expecting them to start making extra coffee for Heather or put in a doggie door for Dante. But they're pretending *none* of it's real, even though they've seen the evidence— No, not just seen, they've had a *conversation* with the evidence. Just like I predicted, they think it's too dangerous and they want me to stop.

As if being a seer is something I can switch on and off.

I need my phone. When he's mirrored with Tempest, Sam might go with The Hand to hunt the wraiths. If he leaves The Old Place then he should get signal back and I can get a message to him.

Maybe I'll just shout at him for being a prick and not talking to me about any of this. The idea of that makes me feel sick. Unless that's the envy. I hate that it's there, but it is. He has what I want, the chance to mirror and he doesn't even *want* it.

I should have told him the truth. I can't blame him when he didn't know what I was thinking and feeling. And I didn't ask him again, I didn't push to talk about mirroring because it wasn't something I thought might *actually* happen. And because it's a hard chat to have. Even more reason to have that conversation.

I just want to know if he's all right. Mirroring sounds intense; magic tattooed into half the rib cage, then being bound to another person for the rest of your life. And it's not even someone Sam *chose*.

Being a trans guy, he's got so little control. He knows who he is, but he has to constantly prove it. Therapists, doctors, clinics, paperwork, so many barriers and delays. If he doesn't perform *their* idea of manhood well enough, they can make it even harder. It's bollocks, and unfair. Now another group of people have control of his body and his future.

Don't cry. Don't think. If I pause for even a second, I'll scream. I *need* that phone. I've torn this room apart and it's not here, not in the kitchen either. They wouldn't hide it in my sisters' room...

"Up there." Ollie points to three old shoeboxes on top of the wardrobe.

Memory boxes. Mum has one for each of us. It's worth a look.

I have to put on my prostheses and push a chair over to reach. When I take the lid off my box, my phone is on top, a trickle of battery remaining. Thank fuck for that. I need my charger, but that's easy enough.

"Ollie, you're a bloody genius."

He mimes brushing his non-existent lapels. "Obviously."

There's a bunch of messages on the Team Spectre group chat from earlier today; Leonie's also grounded but she's allowed to go to work, because she insisted it would help her feel "normal" after everything she's been through. Really she wants to check in with Viola and ask why she lied to us and hid her past as one of The Hand. Was it just something she was ashamed of? I get that, but she's done more harm by keeping secrets.

> **Leonie:** She's not here.

Yeah, why would Viola hang around now her secrets – and lies – are coming out the woodwork? She's involved in all this somehow, or why would she keep so much from us? Maybe she's just following what the bones tell her to do – God, why did we ever listen to her?

I scroll through Mitch and Miri's replies and then:

> **Leonie:** The book Sam ordered came in! A whole chapter on the Lake Assynt story. Will read it behind the till this afternoon.

I almost ask why she's bothering. The Hand know how to put an end to the wraiths, they're literally professional shade hunters. While they're busy tracking down Jory, we can try and save Sam. I don't know if he even wants to be saved, but I don't want him to be forced into mirroring against his will. But this is Leonie, she has to *know* stuff.

Before I put the memory box away, I sit on the bed and sift through the things Mum thought were worth saving: photos of me, Mitch and Leonie as kids in a blow-up swimming pool in someone's back garden, my old Scout necktie, drawings from preschool, small fingerprints in primary colours, Toad – the stuffed toy I dragged everywhere until he fell apart. Mum's kept him, though he has no stuffing and only one eye. Here are scraps from an old favourite T-shirt and the pyjamas my folks got me when I went into hospital for follow-up surgery. There's more recent stuff too: a pair of silver hoops from my failed attempt to get my ears pierced last year, and the gold paper crown I wore at Christmas.

My life reduced to a box.

Well, half of it.

There's nothing of the dead here. No memories of Heather, Ollie or Dante. I know that's not fair, there's no way to preserve that anyway, no photos or mementos. But I don't want one life without the other. I'm made of both – every challenge, failure and triumph, every nightmare, every dream.

If Sam mirrors with Tempest they'll be tied together for the rest of Sam's life, a plus one who muscles in where he's not wanted.

I'm not going to let Sam go without a fight.

"Charlie?" Heather's in the doorway, wringing her hands. "Can … can I have a word?"

I know it's bad before she starts talking because she makes everyone else leave. Heather paces, opening her mouth and closing it, fiddling with the end of her messy plait. I sit on the end of my parents' bed. Honestly, I just want to be here for her the way she's always been here for me.

"So … about my tether…" She hesitates.

Oh.

Neelam – the way Heather looks at her, the way Neelam reacts when she's around. It's like they're in each other's orbit, two souls drawn together by gravity.

"It's Neelam," I say, half-hoping Heather will frown and ask what I'm on about. When she freezes, I know my instinct is spot on.

"You … you know?"

Not until right this second. I would have figured it out sooner if it wasn't for all this wraith business, if I hadn't lost Sam—

I can't deal with that and this at the same time. Heather was my first ghost; she brought me back from the dead and made me a seer, she's one of my best mates. She's like the big sister I never had. I need her.

"How far?" I ask.

"I can be a few miles from her; within York is usually fine but any further than that…"

All those times Heather disappeared for a week or two, and once for a whole month. I thought she'd vanished because the Mouldy Oldies had drained her as punishment for standing up for me. I'd worried for her, blamed myself. All this time she was probably being dragged off to wherever Neelam was going on holiday.

Neelam's moving to Manchester.

My vision contracts. Blink. Breathe. "Were you even planning on saying goodbye?"

That's what this is.

"Of course! I kept thinking she'd change her mind. Neelam loves this city so much, she always said she'd never leave but—"

"We can break your tether," I say, blossoming hope. It's all about emotions and attachment, solving a riddle about her past and then she can let Neelam go and stay here.

A soft shake of her head and I understand what Heather's telling me. She doesn't *want* to break her tether. She's not ready to let go. All this time I thought I was Heather's connection to the living but it was always Neelam.

Always her.

I think of the moment by the window at Grays Court. Heather did try to tell me. She did. But she's had seven years to have this conversation.

I'm going to lose her. No matter what I do, she's going to leave. Why make it harder than it needs to be?

Suddenly, I feel bloody exhausted.

"When does Neelam go?" I ask, wondering how long we have.

A contracted breath.

"How long?" I demand.

"The car's packed. Tomorrow." Heather pauses. "It's bad timing."

My laugh is hollow. "No shit."

Grow the fuck up, I snap at myself. She's already given me seven years of her afterlife, and that's after giving up her life for me. I'm not a kid any more. And I'm not alone, I have Leonie and Mitch, Ollie, Villiers and Reid.

Sam. Sam. Sam.

"Will you stay with me until—"

You're dragged away.

Numbness. I don't feel anything now, just a cold, calm acceptance because if I tell her I can't do this without her that's just emotional blackmail that she doesn't deserve. But at the same time, I can't fucking handle this.

The bed is a mess of photos and memories. I finish packing them away, needing to do something with my hands, and eyes, giving me an excuse not to look at her.

"Charlie?"

The last photo – me holding my newborn baby sisters, beaming and proud to be a big brother.

"Charlie?"

I look at her, because it's cowardly not to.

"Being your friend has been the greatest privilege of my afterlife." She ruffles my hair. "I'll stay with you for as long as I can. That's a promise."

My phone starts to vibrate. It's Leonie. She'll have to wait. I cancel the call. Three seconds later a message comes through.

Answer your phone, you dick.

Then:

We have to stop The Hand sealing Jory.

As I place a call to Leonie, I wrench open my parents' door and almost walk into the cluster of ghosts eavesdropping outside. Ollie looks wretched and I realize he didn't know about Heather's tether either.

"Charlie!" Leonie's breathless and half-muffled, like she's cupping the phone. "Thank god, listen—"

"Two secs, got to plug in." The ghosts follow me to my room where I grope between bed and nightstand for my charger, connecting it just in time. "What's this about stopping The Hand? Let them deal with Jory – while they're distracted fighting the wraiths we can try and get to Sam."

"Just *listen*, OK," says Leonie in a rush. "There's no doubt that Jory and Sadie used this book to work out how to make wraiths. In the context of osteomagi and the historical use of bone impresa, there's enough detail in the storytelling to instruct someone in the know how to build a wraith with a bit of trial and error."

Trial and error.

Yeah, that's what they did. The first three victims didn't die and their souls were unconsumed. Jory must have remixed the recipe and tried again. This time, sending the wraith after her own girlfriend when Sadie betrayed her to The Hand. But it didn't work like she wanted. A remnant of Sadie's soul was enough to form that short-lived deathloop. So, Jory tried it again, this time attacking Tomas and Sophie before they could stop her getting to Claire Cole. Her wraith shattered Tomas and consumed his and Sophie's souls completely.

Perfection achieved. Jory was ready for the final show.

"The author also details what happened *after* the massacre," says Leonie.

"Didn't it disappear into the loch or something?"

"Sort of."

"What's she saying?" Ollie hisses. The ghosts press closer, trying to hear the conversation. Dante props his chin on my knee and whines.

"Leonie, let me put you on speaker a sec." Taking my phone from my ear I switch it over and put it on the nightstand. "OK, Heather's here, and Ollie, Villiers, Reid and Broomwood. We're listening."

"After the rival family was slaughtered and her revenge enacted, the witch tried to send her son to eternal rest by destroying the bone impresa and ending the theorem. But she *couldn't*. Listen to this…" A pause as Leonie finds the right paragraph and starts to read. "And she mourned, for although the curse-marked bone crumbled to ash and was no more, her son's twisted soul could never find rest, condemned to rage and feed for all eternity."

"They're not going to destroy the impresa though, are they?" I say. "They're going to seal Jory. Me and Sam overheard some of them talking and the wraiths will disintegrate or something."

"No they won't," says Leonie, frustrated. "Maybe that's what will happen to a different kind of shade, but as this book details, wraiths are unique. The Hand might not realize it, but sealing will sever Jory's control over them and if that happens—" I can hear the sting of panic over the sound of her pacing; boots on wood floor followed by the crisp rustle of turning paper.

"*What* happens?" I ask.

The ghosts look on, nervous and unsettled, as Leonie starts reading again. "Released from the witch's control, the wraith's hunger was overwhelming. It fed first on those who could see its unearthly form, next on those who could sense its anger, before turning upon the people until the waters of the loch ran red with blood."

A shiver chases over my skin.

"'Those who could see it' means seers," says Ollie. "Death-touched, like The Hand. Like you."

And when we're dead, the wraiths will turn on "those who can sense its anger". That means sensitives. Hands trembling, I clutch my belly, as if that can settle the dread that creeps over me.

"The children," gasps Reid, meaning my sisters.

Mum too. Neelam.

And Sam.

31

SMALL MAGICS

"Charlie?" Leonie's voice echoes into the empty ring of my stunned silence. The ghosts are all talking at once, asking questions, expressing fears and all I can think is: *I need to warn Sam.*

The Hand are walking into a trap. Jory planned this – The Hand seal occultists, that's what they do. Predictable. Their arrogance is going to get a lot of people killed.

"We have to stop this," I say, determined.

"They're never going to listen to us," says Leonie.

She's right. To them we're criminals and outcasts. But Meryem might listen to one of their own, even if they're a new member. "I'm gonna call Sam. I don't know if he'll have access to his phone, but it's worth a try."

"Wasn't Mr Agyemang calling in reinforcements, old friends?" asks Heather.

I relay the question to Leonie.

"Yeah, some said they won't tangle with The Hand, but a few are definitely coming. I don't know when they'll get here, or what they're capable of. If they intend to use bottled souls then I won't have anything to do with them." There's steel in her voice. "That's not an option; I don't care how desperate we are."

What Meryem said really got to her.

Broomwood shakes his head. "We still need a proper plan, lad. Sam might not get your message and the occultist lot might be useless, for all we know."

"We can't just waltz up to The Old Place, knock on the door and ask to chat," says Ollie. "They'll ignore us or detain us."

"Agreed," says Villiers.

"Then we go direct to Jory." I unplug my phone. There's not much charge, but it will have to do. "We find her first, before The Hand do, go from there."

"Where would she be, though?" asks Heather.

"Not at her place," I say, remembering The Hand and the police have checked her house.

Think. If I was a murderous occultist hell bent on revenge against a scam medium whom I kidnapped to syphon her soul and fuel nightmare creatures, where would I hole up?

"She needs a sheltered place," I say, pacing in front of my bed. "Somewhere she can keep Claire. She blames her for scamming her parents and bankrupting them..." I snap my fingers. "The house her family lost to the bank, is it in York?"

"Yeah," says Leonie. "Miri's got us the address already,

but someone lives there so she probably won't go back. What about the factory?"

"What factory?" I ask.

"Her dad's printing business. It went bust just before he disappeared."

OK, yeah, I remember Ariadne saying something about that when I was crammed behind the curtain with Sam.

"I'll find out where." Leonie sounds better for having a task to do.

"You still at the bookshop?" I ask.

"Yeah. Mitch will be with me in five. I've told Jasper I need to go home sick."

"OK, send me the factory address as soon as you have it. We'll meet there."

The voicemail I leave Sam is a minute long, starts with, "I hope you get this", and ends with, "Call me back if you can". I pause, wanting to add, "I love you", but I can't say it for the first time on a message he might not get.

Hanging up, I press the top of my phone to my lips and plead with the universe that the message gets through. My background is a photo of Sam, propped up in bed drawing me as I take his pic, his smile caught and frozen.

I love you.

Tears sting my eyes. I brush them away, snapping myself back to reality.

Coat, keys, wallet, phone, gloves – it's cold out. I stuff my charger in my pocket with my screwdriver and some spare socks, hoping I'll get a chance to top up my phone battery at the bookshop.

I can't just disappear without leaving a note for my parents. Taking an old envelope from a pile of post, I'm rummaging for a working pen in the kitchen junk drawer when I hear a key in the front door.

"They're home," warns Broomwood.

Ollie glances around the door frame. "We'd better go out the back."

I'm halfway to the back door when I change my mind. If I'm not honest with my family now, I never will be again and that kind of thing festers.

If we fail—

I need to get them out of York. It might not be enough, but it's better than staying in the city with the wraiths so close.

Mum hangs her coat up in the front hall as Dad herds my little sisters in from the car and gets the shopping out of the boot. She takes one look at me in puffer jacket and prostheses and shakes her head. "You're grounded."

"I have to go."

There must be something in the quiet way I say it, because she stops and really looks at me, stony faced and concerned.

"What's going on?" asks Dad, coming in behind her with two bags full of shopping.

Poppy waddles in carrying a huge bottle of milk. "Are you going to fight monsters?"

I swallow. "Yeah."

Mum's shaking. "No, no those Hand people will take care of it—"

"That's kind of the problem."

I don't have the time to explain, but I've got to try. I gloss over the magical background, cutting it down to The Hand not knowing everything even though they think they do. I explain Leonie found the book Jory used to make the wraiths and if we don't stop The Hand from sealing her, a lot of people are going to die. Including me. "I've left a message with Sam but I've no idea if he'll get it. I've got to stop this."

Dad puts the shopping down. "I'm calling Abam."

"His mates won't get here in time and…" I shake my head. "There might not be much they can do against wraiths."

"But you can?"

No. I can't even use magic; I've no defence except throwing salt and legging it, which is why we've got to stop The Hand while there's still time. But I don't want to leave on an argument, not when there's a chance I won't come back.

"You could get hurt." Mum's chin quivers. "*You* could die."

"I already did, once."

She flinches, tears welling.

I step closer. "And that made me … *me*, Mum. I'm tired of lying to you, so I won't promise it's all gonna be all right. It's dangerous and I'm scared. But this is who I am and what I do. It's not something I can change about myself or my life and, honestly, I wouldn't want to, not now. If I stay here and do nothing, Sam will die, the wraiths will come for me too, and for you and for the girls."

Poppy starts to cry and I bend down to give her a hug. "I'm not gonna let that happen, Pops."

"You can't do this alone, lad," Dad says.

Standing, I ask him if he has the obsidian mirror. He fishes it out the big pocket of his coat. "Look at me in that."

Turning, they do. Mum's reflection is next to Dad's. I'm between them and behind me are my undead family. Dante at my feet. Heather and Ollie on my right, Villiers, Reid, Broomwood on my left and behind me, all sombre and serious.

"I'm not alone," I say, keeping my head high.

Handing the mirror to Mum, Dad turns to look at me, *just* me. "All right, I'm not going to fight you on this any more."

"Paul?" says Mum.

"We can't lock the kid up, can we?"

Mum looks like she wants to actually, yeah.

"Charlie's got enough battles to face, he doesn't need to be fighting us too." Dad pulls me into a hug. I could cry with relief. He pulls back, looking right in my eyes like a sports coach before the most important game of the season. "What can I do to help?"

"Dad—"

"I don't care if it's homophobic bullies or these wraith things, you're my lad and I've got your back."

"Pack some stuff and get Mum and the girls out of York."

"For how long?"

"I'll call when it's safe and if" – I swallow – "if you don't hear from me, call Leonie's dad."

Dad looks like he wants to argue, but he doesn't. His jaw is clenched. Sniffing, he pulls me into another half hug, then

323

pats my uninjured arm. "I said I wouldn't fight you, so I won't. You'll need your phone."

"I've got it, low battery, though."

"Take mine." He reaches into his pocket.

"No, you'll need—"

"Mum's got hers." He slides his handset into the front pocket of my hoody. "Password's 1306."

My birthday.

As I hug my sisters one last time, I take a deep breath, committing the smells of home to memory – laundry detergent, toast, lemon cleaner. Mum's crying softly. Her hug is the most crushing of all.

"Oh, also." Rifling through the shopping bags, Dad pulls out two big plastic pots of salt and gives them to me.

"Thanks."

"Time to go," says Heather softly.

She's right, and looking at her, I realize there's something else I have to do. "What's Neelam's address?"

She gives my parents the side-eye, surprised. I get it, this whole not having to hide thing is very new. "Why?" she asks, suspicious.

"Because she isn't safe either."

"She's leaving tomorrow."

"It needs to be today. *Now.* And you know it."

We don't say anything, because there's too much to feel and words aren't enough. Somehow, all the years, the fights, the laughs, the lessons learned pass between us anyway. *There's never enough time.*

"Dad, Heather's staying with you. She'll give you an address and contact for Doctor Neelam Iyer, who doesn't know about ghosts or what's going on, but she'll believe you when you tell her. Show her Heather in the mirror, explain you're my folks, that I see the dead. Tell her I'm sorry I lied to her at the hospital." I smile sadly at Heather. "My Heather is her Heather. She'll know what you mean."

"Charlie, I—" Heather hugs me and I squeeze her back.

"I'll see you again," I whisper. I'll love her every day for as long as I live, and then every day after. I'm glad my two families have finally had a chance to connect.

When we separate, Heather says her goodbyes to Ollie and the other ghosts, scratching Dante behind the ears. "Take care of our lad."

The collie yips his agreement.

On the road, I look back at the squat brick bungalow with its boxy porch. Toys in the front garden, a bit of brick chipped off the low wall at the edge of the driveway where Aunt Chrissie clipped it with her car, my sisters leaning against Mum and Dad at the door, waving. Heather stands beside them, hand on her heart.

Whether I make it home or not, nothing will ever be the same.

32

SIGNED, SEALED, DELIVERED

The industrial estate down Fulford is a mix of modern factories with large flat roofs, corrugated sides and solar panels but most are older, built in red brick and slate. The Uber drops us off. Mitch and Leonie aren't here. My phone's long dead but I've added important numbers to Dad's and messaged the group chat.

His phone rings. It's Mitch.

"Fuck, we just— Oh fuck." He sounds like he's running. "All these Roman soldiers, the ones who like marching around, yeah? Well, they all just turned into wraiths."

"What?" I didn't hear that right. A voice in my head begs over and over that Mitch is wrong and that it's impossible. My heart drops as I think of the missing bones stolen from different remains, mostly Roman digs, gladiators and soldiers. Octavian and Lucius go missing and then two new wraiths show up at the theatre. Not a coincidence. We are in serious bloody trouble.

Throat thick, I ask, "How many?"

"Thirty or more, maybe, I don't know. I've got Mr Agyemang's obsidian mirror but I didn't see them all turn. Leonie did, she's … um, throwing up. It was messy."

Thirty or more.

"Where are they now?" I ask. "Is anyone hurt?"

"They've not attacked, just changed and started heading south. Towards you. We're still central, getting a taxi is gonna be hard tonight, being Halloween."

With everything going on, I'd forgotten the date.

"Stay put," I say.

"But—"

"Call an emergency moot. We might need back-up from the dead."

"How?" comes Mitch's choked response. "They won't listen to *me*."

"I'll sort it," says Broomwood. "Ollie, lad, I'll need your help."

"But the wraiths—" Ollie looks at me, worried.

"I shall ensure his safety," promises Villiers.

In the end, Reid goes too. He has friends who will fight. Clasping Villiers' hand, he vanishes a second after Ollie and Broomwood.

"Help's on the way," I tell Mitch. "Keep yourselves safe."

Villiers points to the rooftops and a dark shape silhouetted against curdled clouds. And another, and another. The wraiths leap over the road and into the industrial estate. Trying to keep track of them is like focusing through a strobe light.

I take out the heavy pots of salt Dad gave me, flicking the lids open, ready to strike. It's not much of a defence, but it will have to do. Out in the open I feel how exposed we are. Villiers' rapier is barely enough against just one wraith, let alone an army of them.

We stick to the shadows as much as we can. A few factories still have lights on and cars parked up, but most are closed for the day.

Dante's ears flatten. He growls, fixated on something up ahead.

Villiers gently pats my arm. I follow the point of his rapier to a roof further down the way. Wraiths line the slate, keeping low against the gables. There are more behind us, all fixated on a single factory. It's one of the Victorian buildings attached to a bigger, more modern warehouse. The to-let sign is rusting and there are weeds growing over the parking spaces out front. We slip behind the bins.

"Why aren't they attacking?" I whisper.

Villiers shifts his weight, thinking. "Perchance they await instructions."

He's right.

What happened at the theatre never made sense to me. It was bound to bring The Hand back to York, especially with two of their own already missing. It was like Jory wanted to make the news.

Because she *did*.

It makes sense that The Hand would keep an eye on newsfeeds from all over the world to help them find shades, occultists and other death-touched. Caleb Gates was a dangerous occultist developing a weapon that could have destroyed the city and The Hand only sent *one* mirrored pair to deal with him.

To lure as many of them here as she could, Jory had to slaughter innocents and create terror. Yeah, she wants revenge on Claire, but ultimately, this has *always* been a trap for The Hand. But *why*? What connection does Jory have to them?

We have to get in there.

There's a door on the side of the building. No one about. Are The Hand here already hidden behind magic?

No choice but to go for the door. We don't get more than twenty metres across open ground before the illusion breaks. Dark SUVs with tinted windows line up in the forecourt and figures materialize at the door, which is now open and spilling light.

One of The Hand – the guy in the plaid shirt and manbun – heads towards one of the cars carrying something wrapped in a dirty tarp. A body. The tarp shifts and an arm slips into view – age spotted skin enveloped in dirty black chiffon.

Claire.

Drained and dead, probably when half the legion were turned not long ago. She was a terrible person: a con artist, thief and a liar. She ruined people's lives. I'm not going to mourn her but I still feel sick and uneasy. Jory's just getting started.

"What are *you* doing here?" asks the silver-eyed ghost on the door. He's a scrawny bloke, twitchy and on edge.

"We need to talk to Meryem."

"Not going to happen," says the seer beside him. It's the redhead lass we overheard talking to Ariadne and Tempest back in The Old Place. She sticks her freckled face in mine. "Get out of here. She won't give you a second chance."

"Listen, if Jory's sealed, a lot of people are going to die." I go to push inside but the scrawny bloke catches my wrist.

"That makes no sense."

"Trust us," says Villiers.

The redhead lass manifests a sword and presses the tip to Villiers' throat. "We don't."

I'm sweating, my nerves screaming that we don't have time for this. Any minute now the wraiths will come flooding down from the rooftops and tear into everyone here.

"You're surrounded," I hiss. "Look up, at the roofs."

They look, drawing weapons and shaping theorems as they clock the danger and realize we're surrounded. Dante darts for the open door. Villiers shoves his weight into the scrawny bloke and I pull free. Don't look back, just go. One foot in front of the other. Someone shouts after me but I'm through the door and into a small foyer with stained carpet and shoddy walls. There's a lingering smell of resin and glue, stacks of mouldering paper and a fallen old sign that reads, *Chambers: Printing Specialists.*

It's cold, the electric light unsettling. Voices echo up ahead. Dante sticks close, leading me through another door.

The main warehouse is a shell. Holes for extractor fans and scrapes on the floor from machinery are now criss-crossed with lines of salt and magic that hold back three wraiths. They're fixed on members of The Hand standing in front of them, all holding an open ruh tasi. Held, but not captured. The wraiths haven't disappeared into the obsidian the way Heather and Villiers did when they were trapped.

I don't see Meryem, but her inner circle is here. Ariadne and Gage, pacing and restless. Nearby is the suited man and salt-lashed woman talking to the old lady – Bathily. Her eyes are glowing silver, which means she's already merged with the crusader, sword and shield in withered arms made strong by the mirror bond. When possessed, The Hand are unnaturally tough.

The next person I spot is Tempest.

My heart climbs up my throat at the sight of his silver eyes. *It's too late.* He steps aside and there's Sam, dressed all in black, the clothes serious and simple. It's a daft thought to have but he doesn't look like himself, he looks like one of *them*. He needs his lucky cravat, a tweed jacket and some grandpa shoes.

"We need to augment." One of The Hand holding the wraiths back adjusts their grip on the ruh tasi. "They're not secure."

Someone starts to laugh. Jory, immobilized in a glowing net of magic, drips with bone impresa. Finger bones, ribs and femurs, pieces of spine and skull, all wired together cover her like armour. She looks like some dark goddess from the underworld come up here to claw out hearts.

"No ruh tasi can contain a wraith," says Jory with a sick grin. "Why do you think we chose them?"

We? Does she mean her and Sadie?

Cassie walks towards her. There's something different about the way she's moving – of course, Cassie is Meryem's mirror and the ancient ghost is *wearing* her. I shouldn't think about Cassie like she's some kind of coat that Meryem can put on, but watching them I don't see much of the young lass. No nervous excited bobbing walk or kind smile. She's smooth and confident. Her head tilt and the way she's holding her arms, it's all Meryem.

They don't make sense as a pair. They're so different; Cassie's a healer, she seems to care about people – even prisoners – and she's just a *kid*. Maybe Meryem likes to mirror with someone young so she has more time with them until she has to find a new mirror, who knows.

"Do it," Jory spits the challenge. "Go on, seal me."

Cassie's hand shapes a mark in the air, enclosing it in a circle. Meryem's power flares. Jory gasps, her wild smile stretching wide. There's blood on her teeth.

"Stop!" I yell. Cassie jumps and spins, silver eyes flashing Meryem's wrath. "If you dare—"

Bathily motions and a magic chain locks my limbs, snapping my hands to my sides and pinning my tongue. No! I didn't get this far just to watch them condemn all of us.

Tempest tries to hold Sam back, but he shrugs him off and runs my way. My boyfriend doesn't look happy to see me, he looks livid, cheeks red, fear sparking in his eyes. Dante barks and barks.

Someone yells, "Shut that damn dog up!"

The wraiths stir.

"It has to be now!" shouts the suited man.

"Let him go," Sam snaps at Bathily. "Charlie, why are you here? You can't be here!"

I try to speak but the sound is squeezed. My frustration is hot. I blink away desperate tears and look at Sam, begging him to somehow understand. His irritation mellows to fear as he sees in my face that something's very wrong.

"Wait, I think we should listen to—"

Too late. As one, Cassie and Meryem complete the first seal, pushing it into Jory's chest. The magic snaps into place and the occultist screams.

It's a cry of triumph.

33

DUS† †O DUS†

The impresa on Jory's arms and shoulders crumble, flaking into dust that pours from her like sand as she falls to her knees. The manifested net trapping her evaporates and she stares up at Meryem in Cassie's skin. Her mouth cracks into a bloody smile.

"Remember, you did this. You sealed me, you sealed your own fate."

Outside, a sudden sharp scream is cut off.

A surge of movement. The three wraiths held at bay by magic and salt snap out of whatever bind is on them and dive past lines they shouldn't be able to cross. There's a sickening crunch. Ruh tasi smash as The Hand go down, shrieks replaced by choked gurgles and the steady drip of blood.

Tempest curses, shouting to Bathily to free me. A wraith drops from the ceiling in a mass of tangled limbs and billows of oil slick smoke. It falls on the old woman, levering the shield off her arm. I want to look away, but I can't. Frozen, all I can feel is the strangling panic that steals my breath and roots me where I stand.

The crusader knight falls from the breaking body of his mirror to strike at the wraith, but it's too late. His sword flickers and fades. The theorem binding me shatters and I slump against Sam, in control of my body again.

I still can't look away. Bathily's face is streaked with blood, eyes roving the room as she fights to cling to life. The crusader vanishes into nothing as the old woman crumples to the floor, her eyes unfocused, their silver light extinguished.

At the moment of death, her soul should rise from her body, but there's nothing left. She's just a shell.

The shadows part and the wraiths turn away, looking for their next meal.

Us.

"Retreat!" I don't know who shouts it, but suddenly everything is moving at once.

Like frenzied piranhas the wraiths tear into the nearest members of The Hand. The seer's mirrored souls fight to save them, but it's a losing battle. The wraiths are faster and deadlier than when they were under Jory's control and there are more of them oozing in smoky billows through the walls. Meryem bellows orders through Cassie, who looks petrified but focused. Ariadne's ribbons snake and weave, catching on corrupted souls and tearing them aside to let people escape. Gage keeps the wraiths off her back with his double pickaxes.

"Sam?" Tempest barely waits for his nod before he steps into his skin. Something shifts in Sam, a new awareness as Tempest's form settles in the bones of his face, living behind eyes that tip from brown to silver. With a smooth motion he – they – twist their good arm down, flick their wrist and a tapered torch appears in their hand. It blazes, casting pale green across the walls.

I quash a pang of jealousy.

"Stay within the light," they tell me. I can hear Tempest in Sam's voice, deepening it. It's Sam but it's also not.

Cassie, Ariadne and Gage hurry closer, their faces washed pale and sickly by the torch light. Meryem glowers at me, as if this is my fault, like I didn't try to warn her.

I focus on putting one foot in front of the other. Get out. Magic flies through the air and the screams of wraiths echo in our ears. They pour through every wall as Tempest urges us forward in Sam's voice, Dante charging ahead.

"We have to get to The Old Place," shouts Meryem. "No shade can enter an aperture uninvited."

But the Minster library is *miles* away.

Outside, fresh bodies steam in the cold. Three survivors have wrenched apart a skip and are using the heavy panels as a partial shield. The wraith's claws slide through their makeshift defence, savaging one of them across the chest. Others are fighting in the open or trying to make it to the line of SUVs parked on the forecourt. Several cars have already driven off. Only three left.

Meryem and Cassie throw their hands up and a shimmering wall materializes between wraiths and the struggling Hand. Not a wall, it's manifested silk, the fabric twisting around the shades as they attack, tangling them up. Gage and Ariadne work together, her ribbons and his pickaxes.

Villiers battles with a wraith, trying to help protect someone who's fallen behind. It's Manbun, a nasty gash in his shoulder bleeding through his plaid.

"Ariadne, Gage, cover Dressler, Cricket and Ralph. Everyone else, get to the cars," Cassie bellows in Meryem's voice. "Move."

They break from our huddle to obey the orders. My trainers slip and I'm about to go down into a pool of blood, but Sam grabs me, stopping my fall. His hold feels stronger, more solid now Tempest is possessing him. The red-haired seer is dead, her body eviscerated. I choke back vomit, as my belly rolls in protest at the stink and the gore.

Don't look, just keep going. I find my balance but I'm still unsteady.

"Boys!" Villiers cries as he spots us. A wraith takes him down, claws flashing. Dante leaps, teeth bared, and latches on to the smoky mass, which bucks and snarls.

"Dante!" Sam's shout cracks through Tempest's possession. As the green light of his torch strikes the wraith it hisses, retreating from the glow.

Cassie hauls Manbun to his feet, shaping a glyph into his

shoulder. A soft wash of light flares and the pain on his face eases a little.

I help Villiers up. He clings to me, his sword arm a mess of torn velvet and black gore. A wraith appears to our left, wailing fury as it attacks. My action is pure instinct, twisting around to shield Villiers as I draw his rapier.

They can't touch the light. Tempest's torch is some kind of shield. What job did he say he did when he was alive? A moon something who guided people safely home through dangerous unlit streets.

Rapier in hand, I let him lead us forward. The metres to the nearest SUV feel like a mile. Cassie wrenches the door open and Sam shoves me inside the vehicle. Manbun and a guy who looks like a Victorian boxer push in after me as does Villiers, his arm oozing black tar.

"Dante!" Leaning over Manbun I see a flash of white fur as the brave collie goes for another wraith. The front door opens and Cassie climbs inside. Sam and Tempest slide into the passenger seat as one, the torch still blazing.

Behind us, headlights flash.

"We can't leave Dante."

"We have to," snaps Tempest through Sam. I refuse to believe Sam would say that.

"Can you even drive?" I ask Cassie as she turns the key.

But I'm forgetting there's an eight-hundred-year-old soul sharing her skin. Without a word, they shift the stick and send the car squealing forward, throwing us back against the seats.

Villiers groans in pain. Ghosts can hurt each other by

draining each other's phantasmic essence, but it's never like *this*. Is he going to get sick? Can ghosts get sick? Heather's face healed from the wraith's claws, but not entirely. Will she and Villiers carry scars for the rest of their afterlives?

Smoke churns around the car, claws sliding through the roof and hooking in. Sam and Tempest shove the torch upwards and the wraiths recoil. I look back, but I can't see the other SUVs.

I'm slammed into the side door as we swerve through traffic. Horns blare as we mount the pavement. I should be wearing a seatbelt, but we're packed too tight for me to sort it out.

"Traffic lights," Cassie warns. "Tempest!"

Tearing Sam's arm from its brace, they shape something in the air, spit a word and *push*. The truck ahead of us shunts to the left, as does the next car, and the next. We plunge through the gap, taking the red light at sixty or more. I hear metal crunch as a car and a minivan swerve to avoid us and hit each other.

We cross the bridge and charge over the roundabout, veering to avoid crashing into the war memorial in the middle of it. We lurch into the warren of the city centre. Cassie – well, probably Meryem – is making liberal use of the horn.

"Doth they pursue us still?" asks Villiers.

The wraiths are on the buildings either side of us, matching our speed. Their shadows thicken, making it harder to see where we're going. We're forced to slow.

Manbun groans, clutching his shoulder. He's slick with

blood. Taking off his gloves, the boxer puts pressure on the wound. "Cassie, he's going to need something to help him clot, it's bad."

"Not far now," she promises.

We charge up Duncolm, sending a pack of trick or treaters scattering as we head straight over the broad pavement, passing the steaming mess of another SUV. Its bonnet is crumpled into the tree it smashed into, wraiths swarming the wreck.

We don't slow down.

The gates to Dean's Park are locked. A word burns from Sam's tongue, a flick of his fingers and the iron springs open just as the front of our car hits it, sending us storming inside. We skid to a stop mere metres from the Minster library. Clambering out, I help Villiers and Manbun, hearing the roar of a third SUV across the park.

Meryem slips out of Cassie's body. The girl sways slightly, holding on to the open car door for support.

"My brother's really into NASCAR," she says, like that explains anything.

Meryem adjusts her silk overgown. "Tempest, you're with me."

She's going back to help who she can. She won't abandon her people. Fine. Bare minimum in my book. That doesn't make me like or respect her.

"What's going on?" A security guard hurries over. Where did she come from? In a minute she'll tell us we can't park here.

A wraith clambers down from one of the scraggly trees. It's all right, it probably won't hurt her until all the seers and sensitives are dead. She backs up anyway, seeing the fear on our faces, unless—

"Run!" I scream my warning too late. The wraith dives on the guard, sliding into her mouth. Her limbs bend and buckle as her ribs fracture outwards and her heart implodes.

I gag in horror. Is she a sensitive? The wraith is going after them before all us seers are dead. Or maybe no one is safe.

Tempest steps from Sam's skin, taking the torch. "Get Charlie inside, Meryem and I need to guide as many as we can."

"But—" Sam goes to argue.

"Go!"

The boxer and Manbun have already disappeared inside The Old Place. Cassie snaps into action, helping Villiers as more wraiths scuttle towards us, their forms strobing with dark light.

Sam puts his arm around me, flashing his palm at the heavy wooden door beneath the giant stained-glass window. A pale symbol shines against his tan skin, not a tattoo, a charm. Slamming his hand down, he calls Victor's name.

Light flares, glyphs dance and we fall forward into the aperture.

34

†HE MIRRORED WAY

Lying on the flagstone, I cling to the warm scent of Sam, sinking in the softness of his hair. He's breathing heavily into my collar.

"Anything dislocated?" I whisper.

His whole body is shaking, skin sallow with shock. "Just sore."

I feel a wash of emotion – relief, and a kind of glee, not quite believing that we both made it. I hope my family got out of York with Neelam all right. I need them to be safe.

Leonie and Mitch?

God, they're still out there with the wraiths. I reach for Dad's phone, then remember that it's frozen here. I can't even check in.

Victor.

I've got some questions, if I can get him alone. He's

directing anyone who can walk up the stairs. Of those that made it back before us, some are in one piece, others struggling to hold on. Cassie kneels by the side of a seer missing their lower arm, flesh raw below the makeshift tourniquet. They're pale with shock and blood loss.

"I need a stretcher!" she shouts.

Me and Sam pick each other up. He puts his arm back in its brace, brushing off the worst of the mud and dust.

I want someone to look at Villiers but he's more upset about the state of his doublet, "The second one in a week!" and is too tired to manifest something new.

"Where's Meryem?" someone asks.

"Getting the last of us back alive," Sam tells them.

Us. Like he's one of them now.

More survivors come tumbling through the door, shattered and shell-shocked. A gash to Ariadne's scalp has her blinking through a veil of blood. Either the pain hasn't hit her yet or she's so distracted by the lass in her arms she doesn't care.

The girl, not much older than Sam, is making horrifying noises. She's alive, but barely, her mouth scratched to shit and there's something wrong with the shape of her rib cage. A wraith got *in*, and somehow they pulled it out of her.

"Aesop's gone," Gage mutters to Victor. I guess that was the lass's mirrored ghost – consumed by a wraith while she clung to life. Someone brings a stretcher for her and for the seer who lost an arm.

Sam's beside me, but he feels a thousand miles away. I don't know if my friends and family are safe. So many people

343

are dead and it's far from over. I'm close to falling apart but I can't, not here, not surrounded by The Hand with death outside the door. Keep busy. I imagine a ghost bottle of all things, feeding it my panic and nausea and sealing it with wax. Heal the hurts. Focus on anything except my shaking hands and how wrecked I feel.

The girl dies on the floor of the vestibule.

Biting back tears, I tell myself I don't care.

We take as many people as we can to the infirmary. It's a bright green and white room full of metal-framed beds with thin mattresses. There's a British flag hanging on the wall. Everything looks like it's out of a wartime TV show.

"A hospital in a library?" ask Sam, settling Villiers on one of the free beds.

"We needed one," says the ghost of a nurse in a vintage-style uniform. "This room was added from Victor's memory of the Royal Infirmary. Don't attempt to make the layout make sense, you'll hurt yourself."

No one asks why I'm there or treats me and Villiers like we're prisoners. Everyone's either focused on the next patient, or their own troubles.

Someone puts a bowl of water in my hands. I sponge off Manbun's shoulder wound. It's deep, down to the bone. I don't ask his name and he doesn't offer it. When they learn that I know how to stitch a wound, I'm set up with gloves, a needle and thread, and pliers to tidy up a deep gash in a lass's thigh while Cassie keeps back the worst of the pain with a clever charm.

"Magic doesn't truly heal," she explains. "It can strengthen, disinfect and help take away pain, but the body must heal itself. We do our best." She turns away to help Sam tie a bandage.

What am I going to say to him when we have some time alone? I can't forget what I saw in his eyes when I arrived at the factory. He didn't want me there. Was he just worried for me, or does he not want to be with me any more?

I'm never letting go.

I made that promise and I meant it.

But Sam has Tempest now. Not like *that*, but still, someone to be a team with, a soul to walk through life beside. It hurts so much. I just want to scream at Sam that I love him so why does this have to be so complicated and hard.

Yeah, that won't help anything.

I wonder how many of us are left. I count fifteen injured here, not including ghosts. Like Villiers, several of The Hand's souls sport deep black gashes and we learn that damage inflicted by shades on other spirts is slow to heal.

Eventually, the ghost nurse barks at me and Sam to wash up. Someone hands us a mug of soup each. The hot tomato burns my throat as I take a big gulp. Sam sips his. We sit together on a spare cot, old springs sagging beneath us.

The ache in my chest is too much. I grip the mug to disguise how much I'm shaking. I can't look at him.

"Why did you come back?" he asks suddenly, staring at the small croutons in his mug. He still sounds pissed off.

I could say it was to save everyone. That wouldn't be a lie, but it's not the whole important truth. I'm afraid to say it, but too exhausted not to. I need him to know. My breath hitches. "For you, Sam. I came back for you."

He turns his body closer, eyes catching on my chin, my lips, settling his plain brown gaze on mine, and the room suddenly feels too small.

I wipe dirt and blood from his cheek with the side of my hand, feeling the ghost bottle inside me crack, spilling my emotions into something bigger and more tangled than before. "Why'd you agree to mirror?"

"To give you a chance."

The sob catches in my throat. Sam puts his good arm around me as I shake. I was right, he pledged to The Hand because he thought he was saving me when I've been desperate to mirror all along. Right from the beginning, when he hardly knew me, he was already ready to risk everything. He's the most insufferable, confusing, perfect bastard in this world.

"I fucking hate them," I hiss. "Mirroring is supposed to be consensual and considered and you didn't get that."

"I did, Charlie."

Leaning back, I look at him, confused. He swallows, nervous. Underneath his exhaustion and the shock of everything that's happened, he's different now and … it suits him. He looks surer of himself.

"After you all left, Tempest asked me if this was what I really wanted," explains Sam. "He said his selfish desire to be mirrored again overtook his good sense and he'd never want me to be stuck with him. If there was someone else I'd rather be linked to, he'd step aside, and if this wasn't what I wanted at all, he said he'd talk to Meryem for me."

Sam had a chance to walk away and he *didn't*?

"But … I, you said you didn't want this. When I asked you—"

"I didn't think I did, and it was just an abstract idea. We had no way of making it a reality, but then… I'm not OK, you know that and you've stuck with me through it all. This past year's been the hardest of my life and the idea of losing you, us, our friends, I couldn't deal with that. This was the only way I could think of to keep you safe."

I pull away from him because fuck I'm crying. My heart is breaking. Yeah, he consented to mirroring, but not because he really wanted to, not deep down. He's as desperate as I am to do what's right. I could have saved him this.

"Charlie? I'm sorry, I didn't mean to—"

"Nah, this isn't your fault." I swipe away tears, swallow my fear and tell him the truth. "I really want to mirror. Not be part of The Hand or anything, but the power you have now I-I wanted that to protect *you*, and our friends, and I should have told you how I felt but you were so against it, and I didn't want you to hate me or think I was anything like Gates—"

Sam swears and pulls me into him, tucking my head into his neck. We just hold each other for a while, our soup forgotten.

"What's it like?" I ask when I draw back.

"Different." He eases his sore shoulder, grimacing a little. "Weird, but not bad weird, just very new. Tempest's in my head: I know how he feels, I always know where he is, and there are memories sometimes. I know this wasn't part of the plan but I think it's going to be all right. He's a decent man, complicated certainly and messed up in a similar way to me... We're ... actually a good match."

Yeah, that just makes me hate the guy more. But Tempest is part of Sam's life now, maybe for longer than I will be. Sam can break up with me, move on, find a lad who understands modern art and likes the opera and all that posh bollocks. Tempest and him are tied together for as long as Sam lives.

Them being mirrored shouldn't change anything between us, but it already has. I know we can't be everything to each other, that's not healthy, but I don't like how Tempest forced his way into our lives for his own ends. Even if he did admit to being selfish and supposedly gave Sam a way out if he wanted it.

"I want a complete inventory of our supplies," says a familiar voice behind us. Meryem. She's at the door, talking to Tempest, Victor and the nurse. "How long can we last before we run out of food and water and medicine?"

Victor picks nervously at his cuffs. "Approximately three days, longer if we are frugal."

"Then we have three days to find a way to kill these fiends."

Three *days*? We can't wait that long. My half empty soup mug spills on the floor as I head for them. Sam scrabbles after me.

"Oi, what about the sensitives out there?" I snap, gesturing to the windows. "If the wraiths can't get to us, they'll go after

348

innocent people." I think of the security guard's torch falling to the gravel as her bloodcurdling scream echoed across the park. "They already *are*. We have to do something, now."

Conversations stop, heads turn, as the infirmary settles and everyone listens.

"And what would you have me do?" Meryem draws herself up to her full height. She just about reaches my shoulder, but I'm the one made to feel small because that's the kind of person she is. "We have no way to destroy or contain these entities yet. Our numbers are depleted. To go forth now would mean certain annihilation and I will *not* take that risk until we have a chance of success."

"You said The Hand protects folks from shades and occultists. That's what you do."

There's a dangerous flash in Meryem's eyes. "We are not *gods*, boy. We have limits." Sam tugs on my arm but I ignore him. If I'm not careful Meryem'll hex me or kick me out to be wraith food, but I'm bristling and exhausted and pissed off.

"Yeah, like *listening*," I snap. "I came to warn you what sealing Jory would do, but you zipped my trap shut without letting me speak. You're so fucking high and mighty, thinking you know what's right for everyone but you don't. Now your own people are dying and that's on *you*."

Where's Jory? She got away, I realize. The Hand had to run from the wraiths so I doubt there was anything to stop her walking away from the chaos she's created. Sure, she's sealed now and she has to live with that, but it's hardly punishment for murdering so many people.

Maybe the wraiths got her. But she wouldn't be their first target.

"You know, Leonie went back to the source material and figured it out," I tell Meryem. "Yeah, the girl you wanted to seal up tight and not let her anywhere near magic found something your researchers missed."

I never realized silence could be so loud. It rings with shock and I know I've gone too far. Never question a leader in front of their people. Big mistake.

"We just assumed they were like other shades," someone whimpers behind me. Someone else shushes them.

Tempest goes to say something, maybe in my defence, maybe to condemn me, but Meryem's hand snaps out and he clams up. Her kohl-lined eyes narrow as she assesses me.

"We have archives here to rival any great library," she says eventually. "Clearly, we have not used them well. Perhaps somewhere in those books is a method to destroy the wraiths. If you have such strong opinions on how this should be done, you will help us find that solution, implement and plan and dispatch the threat. Did Miss Agyemang discover anything else that might aid us?"

She's not going to argue or throw me back in a cell?

"I ... I don't think so, no." I wrack my memory, but everything is hinged on not severing the link between Jory and the wraiths, not what to do if it happened. "She said there's no way to destroy the wraiths, or turn the souls back."

"Containment, then." Meryem addresses Victor. "Find out how many empty ruh tasi we have. They will need to be modified. At present they catch a wraith's attention and hold it, but the entity itself can't be imprisoned. We'll need a solution."

"On it." He hurries off.

And when we have that solution, what then? I can't stay in here safe while Sam and Tempest are out there fighting wraiths, but the shades will cut through me like butter. If I'm going to be truly useful, I need the advantage of speed and strength and to be able to do theorems without killing myself.

Excitement and fear play out inside me as I say, "I'll mirror then."

Meryem's painted lips quirk into a smug smile.

"But not with one of yours," I add quickly. Yeah, Tempest might have turned out to be all right, according to Sam, but I'm not letting Meryem pick who I spend the rest of my life symbiotically tied to.

She seems to accept this. "Who, then?"

Villiers rises from the cot he's sitting on. His arm is a tattered mess but he places it to his chest and bows low to me. "Master Frith, it would be my sincerest honour to be your champion and mirror. My sword and soul are yours."

I clear my throat, and clap him on his uninjured arm. "Thanks, mate, likewise." I turn to Meryem. "We'll mirror, but we're not joining The Hand."

"Only those within our organization can walk the Mirrored Way," says Meryem.

"Bullshit. The Mirrored Way is sacred to the death-touched," I argue, remembering something Jan Liska said once. "Which *I* am. Being part of The Hand, that's different and I don't like the way you work."

"Sometimes the best way to change something is from the inside," offers Tempest.

"Yeah, *if* that change is welcome."

"Let us neutralize this threat, and then we'll talk at greater length about your future." Meryem twists her wrist and a silver spike forms in her palm. "Are you both ready?"

"Right now?" I ask, eyeing the spike. No, spike is the wrong word, it's twice the length of her hand, smooth and tapered, like a quill made from metal instead of feather. A very sharp pen.

"It will give you some hours to get used to your new situation. Mirroring is not without its challenges."

Cassie scrunches up her face. "It was the most painful experience of my life, and I was internally decapitated when a cheer pyramid collapsed."

"Let's not put anyone off or anything," mutters Tempest.

Cassie crosses her arms. "He has a right to know what's going to happen."

Sam's brow is furrowed in concern. There's a shadow in his eyes, the memory of pain. Yeah, it's bad.

Meryem spins the manifested pen in her hands. "I've performed this theorem hundreds of times. It will be as quick as I can make it, but once it's begun, it *must* be completed. There is no changing your mind, Charlie. The formula I mark into your ribs cannot be undone and to live with it incomplete will burn through your soul source and you will die."

Oh, yeah, I forgot the theorem needs to be *etched* into my ribs.

Once we start, we can't stop.

"Do you understand?" Meryem asks.

Part of me can't believe it's happening. Soon, I'll be powerful enough to properly keep my promise to the ghosts of York. I think of Villiers teaching me how to pick locks and training me in fencing. He's a proper mate, as good a match as I'm likely to find.

So why don't I feel excited and relieved?

I want this. Mirrored I stand a chance at surviving, but it feels too sudden. An uncomfortable prickle of regret chases over my skin. This wasn't how I thought it would happen, and I don't trust The Hand. But if I want to live through this, I don't have a choice.

Before I lose my nerve, I fix Meryem with the steadiest gaze I can. "Let's get this over with."

35

†WELVE BONES

H alf my rib cage. Twelve bones in total.

We could do this in the infirmary, it's as good a place as any for a magi-medical procedure, but there's general agreement that my screams of agony will disturb the recovering patients. Which is why I'm stretched out on the table underneath the gleaming stained-glass window in the domed hall.

It's cold in here. My skin pricked by gooseflesh, the heat of my fear isn't warming me up. I'm no stranger to pain, but the anticipation is torture. Being shirtless in front of strangers is weird – Meryem and Cassie, I understand, but why do Ariadne and Gage need to be here? I hope they gave Sam more privacy than this.

"How bad was it?" I ask him quietly.

Sam's expression is grim. He laces his fingers through mine. "I'll be here the whole time."

Not what I asked, but I get that he might not want to talk about it.

I can't have any drugs or help from Cassie either. Any charms that could soften the pain might interfere with the primary theorem and we only get one shot at this.

I look up at the ceiling. Sam squeezes my hand, Villiers says something poetic about bravery and asks Cassie if afterwards there will be leeches to prevent fever.

God, I hope there are no leeches.

Because regular ghosts can't practise magic, only fuel it, I thought Meryem would have to possess Cassie to do this, but apparently not. A flutter of anticipation makes me regret eating the soup.

Mirroring really has so many advantages. A list will help. Make a list.

One: I'll be a hell of a lot tougher, super strong and fast.

Meryem lifts my arm so she has full access to my chest and presses the tip of the silver stylus to the skin just under my collarbone. Adrenaline sings through me, charging my heart. I expect her to say, "You'll feel a sharp scratch", like a doctor would.

Two: Villiers will be able to draw strength from me and interact with the physical world again.

Intense, cold pressure explodes into searing agony. My heart speeds. Eyes closed, I grit my teeth. The pain moves lower, widening, opening.

Three: when this is over I might be able to manifest a rapier, or something else.

I can feel all twelve bones and they're on fire but the flame isn't hot or sharp it's—

Four: I'll be good enough ... stronger... I'll be better than I can ever be on my own.

Pain, shit, the pain. It's white and endless. There is nothing else.

I want this, I want this, I want this.

I open my eyes – when did I close them? I'm in a cage of lightning; white, yellow, blue, it riddles the air, tracking along cartilage to find bone and pierce it. It's like staring into the sun.

"Charlie, keep breathing," Sam's voice echoes, distant.

Keep breathing.

The magic carves deep, sinking through muscle into bone. I fight to calm my heartbeat. Breathe. Focus on something real. Sam beside me. The wood of the table. The smell of the air – like ozone and salt and burning hair. The pain lessens and I gasp.

"You need to sit up," says Meryem.

Hands on me, making me move. Sam has me. I lean into him, head on his shoulder. Is it over?

A shock in my back, searing and sharp. Twelve ribs, that includes the two floating ones at the back. I forgot those. I trace my thumb over the flutter of Sam's pulse, following the green-blue vein in his wrist. Strong and steady.

I'm sweating, forehead slick, beads streaking my neck and chest. When I think I can't stand it any more, the hot press lifts.

"It is done, Master Frith." Villiers beams with pride. "Thou hath endured."

Cassie pats me on the shoulder. "You did good. Most of us faint at least once."

I look down at my chest. The theorem is made up of strands of complicated glyphs tattooed along each rib; white haloed by puffy flesh, as if I'm having an allergic reaction. I can feel the magic singing deeper, settling into my bones, the fire dulling to a wash of heat.

It *feels* incomplete, like I've breathed in and I can't breathe out yet.

"They'll be invisible within the hour. When they disappear, you're ready for the second seal," Cassie explains. "That bit doesn't hurt."

"You can put your shirt on," says Meryem. "The second seal works through cloth and skin, through everything."

Sam helps me ease my T-shirt over my head. The cotton feels rough on my sore skin. I wince as the stitches in my arm ache.

When I gather the strength to stand, I realize Ariadne's looking at me with a weird expression on her face, like the piece of crap on the bottom of her shoe just showed potential.

"You were made for this, Charlie Frith." She sounds pretty pissed about it, then she inclines her head and adds, "I hope you will reconsider joining us when this is over."

"Well, that *would* be a shame," comes a lilting drawl from the top of the stairs. "I rather think he's a better judge of character than I ever was."

A young woman stands bathed in speckled light from the stained glass, rolling a fistful of knucklebones in her palm, picture pretty in her tea dress.

Tempest breaks the silence first. "Viola?"

It feels like some kind of sick joke. We've not seen her for *days* and now she shows up here. From the shock in Meryem's eyes, her taut shoulders and trembling hands, I don't think Viola's welcome. It's hard to believe that they were mirrored once. When Viola died, Meryem was supposedly so heartbroken she fled York.

But I remember Viola's words in the cemetery: They murdered me, Charlie. Whatever they used to be to each other, there's nothing but loathing left.

"Hello, my mirror." Viola's completely calm, but there's an edge to her too, sharp and eager. "Miss me?"

Meryem says nothing, but her jaw is tight and tense.

The bones clack in Viola's palm, spinning round and round. "No, I don't suppose you would."

"Vi, is it really you?" whispers Tempest, his eyes shining.

I want to flourish my hand at Viola and say, "See? Same person." Viola, formerly of The Hand, now our sometimes mathemagics teacher who fucking lied to us and then ghosted us, *literally*. I can't say I'm thrilled to see her, frankly. What is she even doing here, why would she—?

My brain clicks puzzle pieces into place. Jory wasn't

working alone. Viola loathes The Hand. The wraiths were a trap for them and for Meryem who she blames for her death.

She did this.

Viola couldn't summon the wraiths herself. But Jory could. She wanted to see Claire Cole punished, and Viola offered her a way to do that. In return she had to submit to being sealed when The Hand came calling. The attack at the theatre was over the top because they wanted to bring as many of The Hand to York as they could. They needed Meryem to respond to the threat in person.

It was always Viola. She and Jory have been in this together from the beginning. Shit.

"But … you were killed by a shade," says Gage, confused. "Your soul didn't stay, how—?"

"Is that what she told you?" Viola's sudden laugh is cutting. "I've been here, locked in a ruh tasi so that I couldn't spill *her* secrets." She points at Meryem. "I wondered if, when she finally came back to York, she'd rush to the Obsidian Gallery to make sure I was still exactly as she'd left me. Apparently not, or you'd have known this storm was coming."

My dream comes back in flashes, Viola's face in the dark obsidian mirror. I doubted if it was real, but now I know it was all a memory.

The empty ruh tasi I found. *Something was released that shouldn't have been.* It wasn't a shade like Tempest thought. In his loneliness, Victor would take a peek inside the obsidian traps, look at the prisoners, make conversation, pretend he had company. One day, he opened a ruh tasi and saw the impossible – someone he'd known and cared about. Viola. Confused, there was no reason for her to be locked up, he'd freed her.

And she told him the terrible truth.

"You let her die." Sam's accusation at Meryem is breathy and emotional, like he's in awe. I realize he's shaking. So is Tempest, their feelings blending between them.

I know how he feels, I always know where he is.

"I tried to *save* her," protests Meryem.

"Liar," Viola spits. "You heard my call for help through our mirror bond and you kept your distance so you wouldn't have to hear my screams when Sister Agnes tore me apart." Her eyes gloss with tears. "And when I was dead you trapped me and left York to protect your dirty secret."

"What secret?" asks Ariadne.

Turning, Viola gestures to someone hidden in the stairwell. It's a teenage girl, gap-toothed and round-faced, dressed in a red and white cheer costume that clashes with her auburn ponytail.

Cassie lets out a cry and flings herself down the hall at the lass. "You passed over; I thought you'd gone. H-how are you here?"

"It wasn't an accident, Cas," says the girl. "Someone kicked my knee, that's why I fell."

"A lot of *accidents* happen when Meryem's in town," Viola says calmly. "There aren't enough death-touched in the world, such specific circumstances are needed. She makes sure to create … opportunities."

"That is some accusation," warns Gage.

It's plenty cold in here already but I swear the temperature just dropped. My heartbeat is a slow, washed-out pulse at the back of my skull as I struggle to absorb what this means.

Meryem's been killing people, or at least, setting up situations where a seer could be created. I shiver. For every seer, there's a second soul who sacrificed everything to bring them back. Two people die at the same time in the same place. One is fated to live, the other to die and the soul fated to live can choose to return to life, or sacrifice themselves for the other soul. It's a pure, selfless act and Meryem's been trying to create the right circumstances for it to happen.

Cassie clings to her dead friend, staring at Meryem with horror and disbelief. "You wouldn't."

But Meryem doesn't deny it. Instead she gathers herself. "We are failing. There has been a resurgence of occultists. Practitioners can exchange theorems online in seconds, young people with no notion of the powers they're dabbling with conjure shades or unknowingly burn their souls on petty glamours. We have never been stretched so thin."

"You thought you'd take things into your own hands?" spits Tempest, cheeks flushed with fury.

"We are all that stands against humankind and the—"

"You told me Laura didn't stay earthbound!" Cassie's crying. "It … the pyramid collapse wasn't an accident. You killed her, you killed *me*."

Meryem reaches for her, but she flinches away, keeping a tight hold of her friend.

"I found Laura trapped in a ruh tasi like me," says Viola. "A prison supposedly reserved for dangerous shades used to hold a helpless teenager."

Tempest glances at me and Villiers and snaps his fingers. "Of course, it would not do for a new recruit to choose someone outside of The Hand with whom to mirror, and what is more natural than pairing with someone they know and love? You removed the option." He glowers at Meryem.

The horror of it settles over all of us. Meryem created accidents in the hope of making more seers. If it didn't work, she moved on, tried again. If it did and the ghost of the person who'd sacrificed themselves lingered, she'd trap them and say they'd moved on, and then convince the newly born seer that The Hand was the best way to do good in the world.

That's fucked up.

"Jan and Dusan knew, didn't they?" Tempest's voice is dangerously soft, his disgust written in Sam's features. "I always wondered why you sent them alone against an occultist as determined as Caleb Gates rather than face him yourself. I thought, perhaps, you were sending a message that Gates meant nothing, despite the threat he posed and the secrets he'd gleaned. But you didn't expect my friends to return, didn't you?" His lip curls as he takes a step forward. Meryem doesn't flinch. "I should have listened when they shared their concerns with me."

"You told me soul catchers bottled Edie, but it was you," says Viola, clenching her fists. "She's still down in the Obsidian Gallery, trapped with countless other innocent souls. Well, not for much longer. I'm going to give her an afterlife without *you*."

"How many innocent souls are locked up in ruh tasi?" whispers Ariadne. Gage pulls her away, talking in low, swift tones.

I wonder who else in The Hand lost a parent, friend or partner in the supposed accident that killed them, and how many of those ghosts are still trapped here, left to rot.

"You turned me against my friends," says Viola. "Manipulated me into joining The Hand and then threw me away when I found out the truth. You destroyed me, Meryem, but now you face eradication."

Hate something or someone enough and you'll risk it all to tear them down.

The wraiths are not just spirits of revenge, they're the perfect weapon against a mirrored pair. Killing and consuming the seer also destroys the soul they're paired with. "You knew you couldn't destroy Meryem yourself so you found an obscure shade who could." Ariadne's voice shakes with anger.

"Oh, the wraiths are a gift to all of you. The only way to make the world safe for Edie is if your corrupt organization is in ruins. By sunrise it will be, and just to make *extra* certain," says Viola with a nasty, gleeful smile, "I had Jory make a *lot* of them."

She's unhinged, seriously. What she's been through is beyond rough, but what she's doing in revenge is proper messed up. We thought she was our mate, she hung out with us and taught us magic. *And lied.*

"What did me and Sam do to deserve death by wraith

then?" I spit. "Because your pets are killing more than just The Hand. They're going for all seers, sensitives too."

"Nothing," Viola admits with a sigh. "I'd hoped you might be allies, but there isn't enough hate in your hearts. Still, the bones told me I'd need you to break the wards on The Old Place and serve as a distraction."

The bones told her a lot more than that. Maybe it was all bollocks, just a way to string us along to get what she needed out of us.

"Vi, please," Sam begs. "Call off the wraiths, stop this."

"As soon as Meryem sealed Jory she chose all of your fates. *I* can neither command the wraiths, nor stop them." Her gaze fixes on me shaking against the table, angry and afraid.

"We didn't know what she was doing, yet you would punish us all?" says Tempest. He looks heartbroken, his grief spun with the sting of betrayal. I get exactly how he feels. I might not have known Viola as long, but I trusted her and confided in her.

"Bathily knew, as did Fenrick and others."

"But the new members whose loved ones are likely shelved? Would you punish them for being as easily led as you were?" Tempest's shaking. "You were my friend. I *mourned* you and now I don't recognize the monster you've become."

"This is why you're going to lose." Viola's smile is soft, almost sweet. How can she be this cold? She was so warm and friendly, so convincing. She tricked us all. "You're so fixated on *me*. What you should really be asking yourself is who else Meryem used and threw away. And where, oh, where, is Victor?"

36

✝HE CIRCLE

Something creaks deep in the building. Dust rains from the high roof.

"That's not good," Tempest confirms.

A wheezing sound, like an old pair of bellows drawing in. I'm not even touching the walls but I feel the exhale coming, a rough wind stirring in the depths of the aperture and a whisper of release.

Victor has left the building.

That's what Viola needed me and Sam for, to get captured and locked up so Victor could slip us the theorem that would let us out of our cell, but also break down the spells keeping him trapped here.

An aperture can't exist without its seed soul. He waited until The Hand were beaten and bloody to destroy their sanctuary and throw them to the wraiths.

The floor trembles, drawing back, floorboards rattling. The Old Place is pulled inwards, panels rippling, floors groaning, mortar slipping from blocks of stone.

"Sa—" My shout is cut short. A force sends me toppling *outwards*. Sam's startled face. Villiers' cry. Ariadne flings open her hands, ribbons streaming around my limbs, cocooning me as the ragged window flies closer and we spiral into a wall of light.

White bursts behind my eyes. Cold air. Phantasmic threads squeeze my sore chest, dragging the air from my lungs as they hold my weight, softening my fall, but I wheeze for breath as the ribbons snap taut.

The impact is brutal. A whip crack of pain. Noise. Flashing lights. Gravel against my cheek. My palms sting on rough tarmac. My broken pinkie finger throbs and I'm pretty sure the damp pain on my arm means I've ripped my stitches.

The magic around me eases, vanishing. I roll over and gasp Sam's name. Ariadne's nearby, nursing what is definitely a broken arm, Gage at her side, having just saved me from breaking my neck. I'd say thanks, but it takes all I have to keep breathing.

Dean's Park is a battlefield blur of light and sound; blue and red lights pulse from ambulances lining the road. I smell petrol, blood and grass. Body bags are being lifted on to stretchers by official personnel as nosy spectators mill beyond the cordoned-off area, and crime scene investigators set up tents.

How many of The Hand have the wraiths torn apart? Most of them were probably victims themselves, with friends or family locked in ruh tasi. Viola slaughtered them without a thought.

Villiers moves to my left, picking himself up from where he was thrown clear. Other people move in the grass. A couple hit the road and are still. Cassie and Meryem are on their feet, seemingly uninjured, helping others.

Meryem barks orders. "Defensive formation, don't let them get at our backs."

The sight of Sam a few metres away forces me to move, groaning. The fall really wrenched something. He mouths my name, relief softening his brows. A nasty cut in his hairline tracks blood over his forehead. Wiping it on his sleeve, he crawls over to me.

"I've got you, can you walk?" he asks.

My trackies are torn and my trainers scuffed to shite. I need to check my prostheses before I can risk getting up. Sticking my fingers through a big hole in the fabric over my left prosthesis, I rip all the way around and pull the remnants off. Sam hands me a sharp pen knife. I cut the tattered fabric off my lower right leg. By some miracle, both pin and locks are secure and the bushings have made it through untwisted. It's just me that's bruised to shit.

My thumb brushes the worn smiley face my sisters drew on the right-hand cover. "Yeah, but I'll need a hand up."

"The wraiths," warns Villiers. "They're close."

Tensing my stomach, Sam helps haul me upright. I suck breath in as my weight settles into my sockets and my stumps protest.

There's a clicking, bone clawing on wood and stone, the stink of earth and ash and rotten things. Wraiths skitter through the trees and snake down the side of the Minster library, sensing their prey has come out of hiding.

We fall back into Meryem's circle, Villiers trying to shield me as I work to stay on my feet. I don't want to side with her, but what choice do we have right now? Alone, we're dead.

Tempest steps into Sam, their forms merging as they raise their torch. It's not a strong enough light to protect more than a few people. Other shields go up in washes of cool silver.

The injured have been dragged into the circle to some measure of protection. There are people too, uninjured and looking confused and worried. Who are they?

No time to worry on that now. I need to find Viola. I know she said she can't, or won't stop this, but I will fucking make her listen. The original wraith must have been defeated or it would have steadily made its way through the country by now. There *must* be a way to stop them, we just need to work it out.

Sam curses and points. The things stalking towards us aren't just wraiths. I need to chuck up because what the fuck is *that* — eyes and too many teeth. One has a wide grin and pulsating flesh, another a festering black hole where its face should be, a third has elongated limbs, scuttling backwards on all fours.

"*Stranger Things* wants its monsters back," says a trembling voice to my left. Manbun guy, battered and bruised but determined. His mirror – the Victorian boxer – possesses him and they raise their fists as boxing gloves materialize on their hands.

"Where did those ... things come from?" I ask in a choked whisper.

"The ruh tasi." Gage and Ariadne have joined us, one of

their arms held tight to their chest. Ariadne's face is grey with pain, her hair a tangled mess of sweat and blood. "A collapsing aperture expels every soul it contains and crushes material things. The ruh tasi were destroyed and anything they held, be it soul or shade, was expelled."

There's a tone in their voice that says, *We're fucked.*

The police and ambulance people have finally clocked that twenty or so oddly dressed folks with glowing silver eyes, some of them gravely injured, have materialized in the middle of a crime scene and are brandishing a bunch of weapons. They yell into radios, the police hurrying forward with their batons and tasers, shouting warnings.

Springboarding off an approaching officer, a wraith launches itself at the nearest seer. The officer falls with a cry, his chest carved open by sharp claws.

Our defensive circle doesn't so much break as shatter.

I bite my lip so hard I taste iron. Ringing in my ears, sweat in my eyes – or is it blood? Screams in the night and the crack of a baton on flesh, bone and blood. All I can think, as I focus on breathing through the pain and balancing, sheltered by Tempest's light and held up by Sam, is where Leonie and Mitch are. Last I heard they were near here, but that was hours ago. There's no time to try and call them.

The sound of a piper carves the night. I squint beyond the bare trees to the warm, up-lit facade of the Minster and the wave of people pouring through its walls.

The ghosts of York.

At their head is Reid, bagpipes under an arm, playing as

if his afterlife depends on it. There's a drummer, a young soldier lad I've never spoken to. He's matching Reid's rhythm. Ollie pumps his fist in the air, shouting something as the dead charge across the open ground. Hollering defiance, they leap on the shades and wraiths, pulling them down and giving the living a chance to escape.

Dante, his fur matted with dark tar, snarls and tears into a shade that's pinning a screaming paramedic to the grass. Roderick and Mrs Tulliver throw themselves at a creature with boiled flesh that's trying to claw an injured man out of an ambulance. Ollie and Broomwood are using Broomwood's dressing gown cord to tangle a wraith's claws as it swipes at one of The Hand.

I gasp, relieved and surprised and grateful all in one. Sam and Tempest cheer. My eyes blur. A shout sounds up ahead and Mitch sprints across the park, Leonie right behind him. I can't help grinning. The sight of them and our ghost mates gives me a new burst of energy as I hobble to meet them, half carried by Sam. Tempest's possession gifts him so much strength.

"Fuck, Sam, your *eyes*," says Mitch. "Are you… Is there someone else in there with you?" He's carrying an obsidian mirror. I get why occultists developed cryptolenses because he's got to angle himself awkwardly to see the dead either side or behind him.

"Tempest Lawson," says Tempest through Sam, giving Mitch a curt nod. "Sam and I are mirrored."

"Have you seen Viola?" A different question hovers behind the cracked glass of Leonie's cryptolenses.

Sam motions to the chaos. "It was her; she worked with Jory to summon the wraiths."

Mitch swears.

Leonie sniffs. "I should have worked it out sooner."

"She played all of us." I catch my breath. "She doesn't give a shit who dies to take down The Hand, including us."

"Masters, what is your pl—" Villiers is cut off as a hooked claw drags him back and he goes flying outside of the safety of Tempest's torch. Leonie's scream is smothered by a bellow behind us. We swivel.

Ariadne, a wraith hot on her heels, unfurls her manifestation but the wraith moves too fast, slicing through her defences to catch her throat. I can feel its hunger. It was probably a ghost I knew. A legionary, maybe someone who went to Lady Faith's poetry evenings and took part in marches around the Treasurer's House. I can't save them from what they've become and that feels like another failure.

Gage slips from Ariadne's skin, leaping over the wraith's head to slam his dual axes into its smoking back. Drawing back its head, the creature screeches and bucks, then plunges down Ariadne's throat.

"NO!" Tempest shouts, cracking Sam's voice into shards of panic.

Mitch takes my weight as Sam lets me go, taken over by Tempest.

I figured they'd need time to get to know each other, work out how to move together and work as one. Nope. They dart to the side, the action slick like they've been mirrored for years. *A good match.* Yeah, Sam wasn't kidding, he looks ... focused, settled. For all his reservations, being mirrored is right for him. He doesn't regret his choice, and I don't resent it.

Green fire ripples through the dark, catching the wraith as it moves to attack again. The glow is a shield, Sam is safe.

But I'm not.

The feeding wraith has disappeared inside Ariadne. I can smell the tang of blood and hear her ribs cracking. Gage has her in his arms, desperate and panicked, cursing as he fades, cut out of existence, his soul swallowed and consumed.

Gone.

Ariadne's corpse falls into the grass. The wraith erupts with a roar of triumph and sniffs the air, then whips around to face me, Mitch and Leonie. Mitch has his obsidian mirror up, but the angle is wrong and he can't see it coming.

"Defend!" Villiers bellows, raising his rapier as he races back towards us. I blink and the wraith is gone. No, it's beside us. Villiers cries out as he falls, deep gouges in his back bubbling with black tar. The sound of pipes cuts out.

I sway and stumble, pain lancing my legs, but I stay upright, desperately searching the dark grass for Villiers' rapier against the shining wet.

A clicking sound nearby. A second wraith stalks towards me.

Ah, shit.

Sam's name tears from my throat.

The wraiths rush in, one either side, and I know that this is how it ends.

37

BAIT

The first time I died, I didn't feel anything. This time it's like falling into a deathloop, and somehow not like that at all. Half a second tops but in that moment there's a choking mass of smoke and I smell leather and horses and sweat and—

I'm marching, the beat of the song in my bones. There's an afternoon to go before we reach Eboracum and I'm starting to feel the weight of my pack. No worries, I trained for this. I can go longer. Sunlight glints off metal—

—The packed wooden arena echoes the cheering crowd. I don't look at the beast's cooling corpse, or pay much attention to the sting where it clawed me before I stabbed my gladius into its chest. The governors meant for me to die. Instead, the adoring crowd cheer my victory. The sun is in my eyes. I squint against the glare as it turns green—

—I'm on all fours, hands in wet grass. Sam pushes sweaty hair off my forehead to look into my face. "Oh god, Charlie, are you—" he chokes. "You're all right, you're... I thought they had you."

They *definitely* had me. Two wraiths. A soldier. A gladiator.

How am I not a broken corpse?

"W-what happened?" I stammer.

"They passed *through* you." Sam's voice is his and his alone. Tempest isn't sharing his skin any more, he's beside Mitch and Leonie holding the torch.

"You're still unsealed," Tempest says. "As such, the theorem in your ribs makes your form permeable to ghosts."

Reaching down, Tempest moves to put a hand on my forearm, but his fingers pass through my flesh as if I'm the ghost. It feels cold, making me shiver. No dead soul can touch me right now. Fuck, that's weird.

Villiers!

Wincing, I turn to find him propped against Reid. Dante nudges at them whining. Villiers strokes the collie's head. I think it's the sight of that dog, badly injured but still trying to wag his tail, that makes it all too much. I gasp back a sob. When Villiers and me finally mirror and I learn to manifest something, I'm making sticks to throw for Dante for as long as he wants to play.

The police are rallying, trying to arrest people. They've called in reinforcements. Riot vans pull up to the Minster library. I spot Mr Agyemang with a weathered bloke in an old band shirt and jeans. They're brandishing some serious magic. Some of the occultists are using cryptolenses, others are angling obsidian mirrors to see and target the shades. If they could bottle or trap a few, I'd be very grateful.

Wraiths rise from broken bodies and skitter towards us. A whirl of shadow cuts off my view of the battle. Tempest winces as more and more wraiths slam into the dome of light around us.

"They're drawn to you," he confirms. "Until you're sealed, you're the brightest beacon in York, and we can only keep them off you for so long. They can't kill you, or force possession on you, but so many of them would be overwhelming all the same."

I can sense their desperate hunger and a deep need for what so many souls want – to *live* again. That's what they've been trying to do with everyone they've killed, inhabit them, wear them like a skin, but people are too breakable.

What Tempest just said sinks in properly.

I place a hand to my still sore ribs, feeling the thrum of magic under my palm like a promise. Time slows, my head pounds, the sharp shock of my fear is mellowed by the fact the wraiths can't kill me, just knock me about with visions of who they were when they were alive.

The brightest beacon.

That means if I run, they'd follow. It would give Sam and the others a chance to escape, and Mr Agyemang and his friends time to tackle the shades they can trap. But then what? How long could I survive before the unfinished theorem in my ribs burns through my soul? Days? Weeks? Then the wraiths would flock to kill Sam and the others.

I slide a hand over the smiley face on my prostheses, and see the flash of Poppy and Lorna's smiles, their tinkling laughs as we played in the garden in the summer.

It ends at the river.

The way Viola looked at me when she said she couldn't control the wraiths. *She* can't. But I can lure them. I can't trust her, but what choice do I have? An idea comes to me in pieces of panic, snapping into place while the voice at the back of my mind whispers that it'll never work.

But at least I'll have tried.

Ignoring the burn in my stumps and the painful ache through my back and hips, I haul myself to standing. "We need to get to the river."

"Why the river?" Sam pulls my arm over his shoulder to help take my weight. Tempest sticks close, protecting us. We make sure to keep away from the light's edge where a wraith's claw might hook us to our deaths. They're a thick swarm around us now, striking and recoiling, angry and desperate. I try to block out their howls.

"Something Viola said to me a while back, and then I was thinking about how the witch couldn't stop the wraith she'd created," I say, hoping I'm remembering this right. "It retreated into the loch. But what if it didn't retreat, what if it was trapped there?"

"Like the river ghosts?" asks Sam, catching on.

Water does strange things to the dead. I don't know about any of that, but I do know the Ouse runs thick with souls, their edges undefined, as if the waters blend them into something else.

Mitch angles his obsidian mirror to reflect on Tempest. "Water's a phantasmic emollient, right? Viola said something about that too."

Leonie's jaw clenches at the mention of Viola, hurt and betrayal shining in her eyes.

"Even a stream can act as a natural soul trap," Tempest agrees. "But it would have to be a strong pull to drag that many wraiths down."

"The river keeps what it takes," I say. "If we can get the wraiths close enough, the ghosts there can do the rest. They're strong and there are hundreds of them."

"It's worth a try," says Sam. I hear the hope in his voice.

Reid and Villiers are spent, exhausted and bleeding. They want to come with us, but Sam convinces them to look after Dante and help other injured souls back to the Minster.

Tempest lifts his torch high. We walk in its light, ducking under barriers and hurrying down Duncombe Place away from the riot vans and chaos. The wraiths move with us, peeling from their attack to follow like rabid dogs, gnashing their teeth and growling as they throw themselves forward and retreat, stung, before surging again.

I'm not much worried about traffic but I know from the serenade of horns that traffic is worried about us. Half in the road, half skipping up on to the kerb, we press on. Pushing against each other, the wraiths block the light from the surrounding buildings, restaurants and street lamps until I feel like we're in a green lit cave with a narrow mouth giving us a glimpse of the street ahead.

Leonie and Mitch guide us. Unlike me, Sam and Tempest, they can see through the dark morass of bone claws, skulls and smoke.

The torchlight wavers. Sam's sweating.

"We'll make it," says Tempest. I can hear the strain in his voice. They might be stronger together, but even mirrored souls have a limit. It's costing them a lot to keep the torch burning this brightly.

"Keep going," urges Mitch, catching my elbow so I can lean some of my weight on him.

We reach the river after what feels like forever. Illuminated by sporadic street lamps and the light from the nearby restaurant, the ghostly hands that grasp through the surface twist and beckon. Despite the cold, the restaurant terrace is packed with diners tucked cosily beneath heat lamps. Music echoes over the waters.

I give myself three seconds to be scared, then tuck my fear deep down. This next part I have to do alone.

There's a ramp down to the bank, but it's steep and the steps are easier. I cling to the railing, getting close to the edge of the protective torchlight. Too far and the wraiths will swamp me, but I don't want Tempest, Sam or the others to get near the bank themselves.

Glowering eyes and snapping teeth and somewhere behind it all is the pounding drumbeat march of Roman soldiers on the move.

I hear Leonie say, "It's not working. They're avoiding the water, he has to get closer."

"Too close and the souls might pull *him* in," warns Sam.

As soon as he says it, it clicks.

The river, a terrible enemy, me.

The only way the wraiths are going in the river is if I do too, and I'll not come back from that. The river keeps what it takes, and what's delivered to it.

It's easy. All I have to do is inch forward until one of the river souls catches hold of me and pulls me under. Wait, no, they can't touch me right now. I have to tip forward into oblivion myself.

My mobile is dead but Dad's is going strong. I toss it on the bank so that, when it's done, Sam can call my folks.

I don't think I want them to find my body. After almost losing me so many times maybe they're prepared, somewhere deep down, for this. My ghost will become part of the river, so I'll never be far away.

I never promised to come home, I only said I'd try.

Is there any other way?

Think.

I was always shite under pressure and now so many lives are on my shoulders. The theorem in my ribs makes me feel like I'm waiting for something, endless anticipation. If I mirror to a ghost now, the wraiths would quickly consume us both. And if I don't, the magic will burn through my soul.

See. I'm dead anyway. Might as well take these bastard wraiths with me.

"Charlie?" Sam's tone is worried. "Be careful."

Doesn't he get it yet?

He says my name again, fear on his tongue. A child's face breaches the surface of the river, rolls and subsides, followed by a man, a woman, more children. Their numbers are thickening, like they can sense what I need to do. Silently, I beg for their help.

Grab every single wraith, tie them into the water, make them a part of you.

Maybe I'll be strong enough to fight the current, but I doubt it. I've never been a good swimmer. Sam drowned once. I try not to think about how cold the water will be or how my prostheses and clothes will catch on the current, dragging me under.

I can't do this.

I have to.

For my mum and my sisters. For Neelam, and for Sam. Sam, the boy who helped me back to myself when I was lost in a multiloop, who paints my portrait when I'm sleeping, who trusts me with his weaknesses, who refuses to be anything but himself, who made space for me in his life.

Love someone enough and you're capable of the worst things imaginable.

And I love Sam so much it hurts. I should tell him that at least, but will it sound like a goodbye?

Isn't that what this is?

Last spring Sam stood on the edge of the multiloop, risking everything with a raging defiance, no matter how much I screamed at him to stop. Sometimes I can still smell the ozone as electricity struck, the aperture swirled and he faced his end. I wanted him to look back one last time. He never did.

Now, I understand why.

I hope he can forgive me the same weakness.

Head high. Breathe. Don't overthink it.

I shift my weight forward. The wraiths howl, smoke licks my face. I pitch forward, gasping a last breath before the river claims me.

38

BLOOD IN THE WATER

A pressure to my back sends shock waves through my ribs as someone grips my hoody and wrenches me away from the water. I hit the stone path, hard. I smell … home. My eyes flare open.

"D-Dad?"

It's really him, arms fast around me, cheeks flushed from legging it down the bank.

"What are you doing here?" I ask, shaken.

"You really think I'd let you fight this alone?" He lets me go and sits back on his knees. "What are *you* doing trying to throw yourself in the river?"

Arms hook under my armpits and pull. Sam's got me, Mitch and Leonie too. They drag me away from the water until I'm panting against the stone slope that leads down to the lower bank.

"It's the only way to drown them." I hate how wrung out and beaten I sound, choking on my words as I sob with selfish relief. Beyond the faces of my friends and family and Tempest's dome of light, the wraiths still churn like incensed clouds.

"You're a bastard, Charlie Frith." Sam's crying. I lean my forehead into his collarbone. He draws me up and I wrap my arms around him. "You're so stubborn and so *daft* and such a fucking bastard."

"We're all making it through this." Mitch says it like a promise. I want to believe him.

Dad's clutching a phone – Mum's. There's a map up on the screen with a marker on this spot. He and Mum have a tracking app for each other, that's why he wanted me to take his phone. Dad doesn't need to understand any of this to care. No matter what, he's shown up for me. Sniffing, I blink back tears, so grateful that he's here in the end.

"Mum and the girls?" I ask.

Dad swaps the phone for his obsidian mirror, looping the cord around his wrist to keep it secure. "Far out of the city and safe. Neelam too, Heather's with them." Looking into the mirror he curses and ducks his head, glancing above him as if the wraiths he sees can swoop down and tear into us. "You didn't stop that Meryem woman, then?"

I shake my head, trembling. *It ends at the river.* That's what Viola said, so if she wasn't telling me a secret way to stop the wraiths, then … is this just another one of her tricks?

"We'll try something else," says Leonie.

Tempest shakes his head. "There is nothing— Wait."

There's a quiet filled with lapping water and the tinny music from the restaurant.

"Have you used it?" Sam asks suddenly, sliding off me.

What's he on about?

"Never," says Tempest. "But I know it."

Sam breathes out slowly. "Risks?" There's a pause. They stare at each other. Sam swears and rubs at his eyes. "We can't."

Are they talking through the mirror bond between them, thoughts no one else can hear? Like, full on telepathy?

"It buys us time," says Tempest.

"He could *die*."

"Die?" Dad barks. "Then find another way."

Tempest looks up at the wraiths still churning beyond the limits of his torch. "If he goes in the river, he'll definitely die, but we could contain the wraiths *within* him."

"Y'what?" asks Mitch.

Moving my legs carefully, I sit up a little. "How? I can't mirror with all of them; can I?" I don't want to be mirrored to a wraith, or thirty, but I'll do whatever I have to.

"Not mirroring, that will only make the wraiths stronger," says Sam. "But we use the third seal instead."

The first seal won't do anything useful. The second will give the wraiths too much freedom and make them even more powerful. But the third binds two souls into one body and the strongest takes control. It won't be a partnership of equals, that's for sure, more like I'm the prison cell and they're the prisoners.

"Can you make it work?" I ask Tempest.

He pauses, then nods. "With Sam's help, yes, but, Charlie, you need to understand, nobody is supposed to hold so many souls within themselves. You probably won't die, but … the strongest souls will win out. They could take you over completely."

Fuck.

"But they won't be able to hurt anyone?"

"They might try, but within a body we can restrain them … you."

"Charli—" Dad starts. I cut him off with a shake of my head.

Viola said she didn't know how it would happen, only that I'm the heart or crossroads or something like that.

"We can strengthen you," says Leonie. "I know a theorem—"

"*You* can't," I snap. "You work any more magic and you'll die."

Sam looks like, even though this was *his* idea, it's all gone too far. Face puffed with anguish, he fights tears. I want more time with him, I realize. I'm selfish, I want the rest of our lives to make a mess of things. I want to meet the person he's going to become in twenty years.

The truth is, I can't save him, just as he can't protect me. Shit happens, life throws impossible things at us. We're gonna bruise and hurt and somehow find the courage to keep going. Sam never needed my protection, only my support.

He presses his forehead to mine. Our breath steams in the cold air. He knows this is my choice, and he lets me make it.

Dad's eyes are bloodshot. "I didn't come here to watch you die, lad."

"Then I'll just have to survive, eh." I slap him on the shoulder and muster a grin. They help me stand. "We'd best get on with it or someone in that fancy restaurant is going to start getting suspicious."

"We can work the strengthening charm, give him the best chance." Sam's voice is raw, hopeful.

His eyes don't leave mine as Tempest possesses him. They whisper something, the magic on their tongue scenting the air around us like seawater, as they mark a charm on my forehead. Blood thrums, my heart quickens, adrenaline sings.

Suddenly, my focus is sharp and my mind is clear. I still ache all over, but it's not overwhelming any more and I can … can I see in the dark now?

"Bloody hell, that's some strengthening theorem."

Tempest and Sam don't smile. "It might not be enough. The wraiths might take over your mind and body. You get that, right?"

I nod. This way is a kind of death, just less watery. I've got to be mentally stronger than thirty odd wraiths. Not likely, but at least I can fight, try to win out over all of them.

I'll take those odds.

"And there's no going back," they warn. "Once sealed it's for life—"

"Do it," I say. No hesitation. We don't have time to doubt. The longer we stall, the more terrifying the whole idea is.

Mitch hugs me close and wishes me luck. Leonie kisses my

cheek. Tempest steps out of Sam's body and gives me a solemn nod. I want to ask them to say goodbye to Ollie, Villiers, Broomwood and Reid for me, but that's like admitting I'm not strong enough, so I don't say anything.

Dad looks scared. I hug him, not caring that I'm crushing him or if he's crushing me. He doesn't say anything; I don't reckon he can, but I know. I *know*.

I wait for Sam to say something but he doesn't. He just tilts his head, teeth against his lip, a hiccup in his throat. Fuck, he's handsome.

"I love you," I say simply, because what else is there?

He darts forward and the seal of his lips is salvation. I kiss him back, stroking his jawline, greedy and desperate, wishing I could stay in this moment forever.

No one can do this but me.

I don't know if I'll survive, or if I'll be myself at the end of it, but I'm going to damn well try.

Everyone sticks close together, taking Tempest's light with them, until I'm right on its border. The breeze changes as the green glow recedes. My fear creeps in, fresh panic, cold on my skin. I swallow it down. Yeah, I'm scared, that doesn't make me weak.

I never have been, I realize. Most people never go through even half of what me and Sam have faced. I've always been enough, just as I am. But whatever happens now, I'm about to change forever.

Your transformation is all but inevitable if we are to scourge York of this darkness.

The unavoidable storm.

As the first wraith ghosts through my chest, I wonder if this was always part of Viola's plan. Am I somehow just playing into her hands?

It's too late to back out now.

39

WHAt DOESN'+ KILL YOU

B one fingers rake my entrails and bright embers spark in my eyes as my vision streams blurred colour. Their touch is starving and desperate. I tense, bracing as I'm drawn into a tangle of memories.

An arena rich with the stink of blood, tangy on my tongue. I raise my blade towards the cheers, the metal glinting in the sunlight; dusty sandals temper packed earth; my legs are warm and heavy after a full day marching; with fragrant wine on my lips, I kiss a lass in a back alley; the thud of an arrow striking into my shield blends with a friend's scream as a second arrow whips from the dark to pierce his throat—

"Hold on, Charlie."

Sam.

River stench, a welcome relief as the real-world swims into

view. My heart trips at the sight of my boyfriend's narrowed silver eyes. Embodying Tempest, they're standing as close as they dare, waiting for the right moment to seal me and the wraiths together.

—the tiled roofs of Eboracum sprawl behind the palisade and I swell with the pride that I'm part of something mighty; a lad bears me down into linen sheets, his mouth on mine—

The press of wraiths flows through and on, tangling against my soul, momentarily caught in my ribs but unable to stick. It feels like I'm standing beneath a pounding waterfall. I've gone to my knees with the weight.

Feeling for the theorem, I find the hot, bright invitation calling to the dark. The wraiths are trying to answer but my flesh and bone is like empty air to them now, as if I was just a normal bloke, not a seer at all.

There were scratches on the mouths of the victims. That's how the wraiths get in. Throat first.

Do this, and you will become monstrous.

But everyone else will be safe.

Tipping my head back, I throw my arms wide and open my mouth. The first of them snakes past my teeth, slithering down my gullet. A second. A third. I close my eyes but I can still feel the wraiths pouring into my throat so fast I almost choke. They tighten against sinew and flesh, weaving into my muscles and pounding in my skull. I'm swamped by the taste of dates and honey, feeling cloth on my skin and the chafe of metal. Wheels on stone clatter in the distance.

My eyes fly open to heavy skies streaked with light

pollution. I can see York, *my* York with its electric light, petrol fumes and fast food.

"Now!" I gasp.

As one, Sam and Tempest hurry forward, hands shaping what I hope is the third seal because seriously, I can't hold on much longer. Power slides over my skin.

Almost...

A husky shout. Sam shoots backwards, body crumpling to the hard walkway. The magic ends, cut off as the air around us sucks and releases.

NO!

The blast catches Mitch, sending him flying into the high brick wall at the base of the restaurant terrace. Leonie falls into my dad and they hit the gravel.

The wraiths are restless, unanchored. We're going to miss our chance.

Meryem strides into view through the museum gardens, her fine silks flying around her. Cassie is with her, as is Manbun and the other surviving members of The Hand. What the hell is she doing? She's got to know this is the only way to save her and her people, to save everyone.

People move around me as angry shouts echo across the river. Sam is on his feet, bruised and bloodied. Tempest is arguing with Meryem. Any second the wraiths will break free. I'm losing them. It needs to be *now*.

A hand on my chest, magic in my ear.

Leonie.

I manage to choke, "No, you can't—" before power slams

into me, burning through my clothes, running along every rib and sinking into my heart.

Whispered Latin becomes a wall of sound wrapped in my erratic pulse as the crush of souls slithers deep, their grip on me cold and seeping and permanent. They settle into every part of me, filling the gaps, occupying me with the steady determination of an army. Voices sound through my skull, a clamour that won't stop.

One body shouldn't be able to hold so many souls. My boundaries strain as the crush of beings become *me* and I'm nothing but a guest in my own body spiralling into the dark.

Voices sound around us, distant and hard to reach as we shift inside our new flesh, taking root. Mellow tones turn sharp. "No, Sam, don't touch him. He might not be *him* any more."

"Foolish girl, how dare she forge such an abomination?"

"The wraiths are contained at least."

"She's not breathing, we need to start chest compressions."

Candles flicker in sparks of white and green. Not candles. Souls. Food.

No, a small, weak part of us argues, the disgust bitter.

Faces we don't know mill around us; survivors of the battle, ghosts freed from ruh tasi. Our flesh creaks into movement, hard to puppet at first but we remember quickly. Someone gasps, their fear a delightful burst of scent.

We find the souls we recognize. A boy slumped in pain against a wall, his glow a dull flicker. Mitch. There is another boy with wild dark hair being held back from reaching us by a ghost in a worn waistcoat. Sam and Tempest, their glows tangled, souls sealed and bonded.

There are other paired souls here – *mirrored*. Rich and strong, we hunger for them most. A sudden urge to devour, to gore and slake the ache inside.

Don't hurt them.

We need to. Feed or fade. Feed or—

Dad is crouched on the gravel. His soul is a beacon blazing beside the green-yellow burn of a newly dead soul, ripe.

Leonie.

She's not breathing.

Blood trickles from her nose and mouth and leaks from her eyes like tears, as her soul rises from the ashes of her life.

Dead.

40

ABOMINATION

I'm torn up by the root, rising through the wraiths until I surface and crack my voice at the sky. I bellow my grief and the sound is multiplied, layers of voices echoing over the rooftops of York.

No.

No.

NO!

Leonie's ghost stands beside her body, scared and confused, her future stolen.

This can't happen. It isn't supposed to be this way. She knew a last big magical working might kill her and she did it anyway. She did it for me, for our friends and family, for the ghosts she's come to love. Because of her, they're safe.

God, Leonie.

I should have stopped her, somehow. I should have saved her.

Sam gasps her name, the echo of a sob in his voice.

The wraiths swarming through my blood boil under my skin. The storm swells, slinking around the curve of my jaw, bleeding into my muscle and sinew. Directionless, they beg for focus and fury.

I give it to them.

Diving our thumbs into Meryem's arm, I grip her throat, stifling her angry gasp. I don't remember moving. One moment I was by the bank, the next I'm among the remnants of her people and she's in my grasp. Even struggling, she looks like a queen who's just ordered an execution, her chin jutted in defiance.

There's commotion over at the restaurant, people pointing and talking in hushed, shocked tones. Dully, I register hands on my flesh. I flick them away without moving my body, the action present in my mind. It sends the dregs of The Hand flying into each other. They throw magic, the sting railing the wraiths into a frenzy.

A twist of my wrist and the metal fencing around the gardens bends and warps. Concrete cracks under us, sending pain searing through my stumps but the wraiths act like a shot of morphine, fading my discomfort to a background blur.

The hollowness inside us stretches wider and I'm overwhelmed by hunger, not only for the souls that gleam around us like stars but for *revenge*. Meryem's a single spark among many, the green glow of her essence deep and old. Will she taste guilty as we strip her from the world, tearing her soul spark to scattered remnants and drinking our fill?

She's afraid.

Good.

An elated smile crosses my face. This feels as amazing as I thought mirroring would, better even. The wraiths wriggle in glee, eager to sink teeth into her. Her power will become ours, sustaining us, easing the hunger pangs. After everything she's done – sealing Mitch, taking Sam, killing Viola, trapping countless innocent others – we will have our fill.

Pressure on my arm and a voice behind us. "Charlie, *no!*"

A glinting stylus manifests in Meryem's hand, the same one she used an hour or so ago to carve magic into our ribs. She rips it into my chest, pain spidering from its tip.

We round on the soul fire that has grabbed our flesh. It's a middle-aged man with receding hair and a blocky jaw, his nose red from the cold. His grey-green eyes find mine. Dad.

The essence inside me is intoxicating and unmovable. So much greater than I ever was on my own. I was too pathetic. I couldn't even ward the city properly, now I will devour anything that threatens us. This is what I *wanted*.

But I'm not protecting the people I love, I'm scaring them. I hesitate.

That's not who I am.

I'm a tattered scout uniform, a Paralympic mug faded from too many goes through the dishwasher, a smiley face on my prostheses. I sit on the porch beside Heather, throwing sticks for Dante that he can't pick up. I hold up a stuffed three-headed dog toy and wonder if Ollie will like it. I kiss Sam in the rain, hoping that I get the chance to kiss him again and again and again.

Releasing Meryem, I back away.

"No, you don't stop!" The angry shout comes from the riverbank. Viola. "The Hand deserve none of your pity, *her* least of all. You've become what she has always feared most: a corruption of her theorem. Where Caleb Gates failed, you will succeed. End her."

Ignoring Viola, I focus on the man in front of me.

"Dad, I-I'm sorry."

He holds me tight like I'm just a kid. "You're all right, you're all right."

"No, you are *meant* for this, Charlie." Viola swoops closer, something wild in her eyes. "I saw it in the bones. This is how it ends, this is how Meryem falls."

"Y'know, most of The Hand don't even know what Meryem did." My voice cracks. "But you slaughtered them anyway. You want me to blame her but Leonie's dead because of *you*. You taught her complex theorems and encouraged her to burn through her life without warning us of the costs."

"I did," says Viola and the simplicity of it sends goosebumps chasing over my skin. "Because the bones are never wrong. She had to be the one to seal you and her death would push you over the edge to do what needs to be done. That's why I taught her just as I positioned you to become what Caleb Gates failed to be, strong enough to end Meryem's reign."

It all slips into place.

Viola never wanted a hero, she needed a villain. An executioner.

Well, fuck that.

And fuck her.

They're as bad as each other.

I could end both Meryem and Viola's afterlives right now, all I have to do is give in to the hunger and let the wraiths take control. It would feel amazing, power singing through my veins and me sinking down into the dark again. No fear, no feelings, no regrets. But it wouldn't make anything better. It won't bring Leonie back.

"You" – I point to Viola – "and *you*." I whip around to Meryem who is just behind Dad, watching warily. "Get the fuck out of my city."

"Charlie, you must let the wraiths *eat* her," Viola begs. The knucklebones are clutched in her palm. "You have to consume to survive now—"

"Vi?" There's a pretty lass in wide legged trousers and a fedora on the steps, freckled cheeks, hair in a cute bob around her earlobes. "What … what did you do?"

"Edie." Viola breathes her name like she's been suffocating for a century.

Edie walks down the steps and takes Viola's face in her hands. They kiss, sweet and light, and for a moment I see the Viola I thought I knew, standing by the river in a pretty tea gown with her sweetheart in her arms.

"I remember Meryem telling me you were meant for her, and then I was in Dean's Park and everything looks so different and people were screaming—"

"It's all going to be well, my darling," Viola soothes. "The Hand trapped you, but they won't ever again. I've made sure of that."

"You did *this*?" Edie gasps. "The dead, they were... No, the girl I fell in love with wouldn't do this to people."

"I'm not her any more." Viola takes her girlfriend's hands from her face. "You're right, I'm not the Viola you fell for. I had to become someone else. I'd do anything for you, including becoming someone you can't love if it means you being free and safe in the world."

"Vi—"

"I'm not sorry. The Hand are in tatters, Meryem is finished and you're free, your afterlife is your own now."

Hands snake up from the waters, grasping at her skirts. Edie gasps, staggering back to safety as Viola lets herself be drawn backwards. The river ghosts grip her ankles. She doesn't fight. If anything, she looks relieved.

"You weren't supposed to find me until it was over. There's no place for someone like me in your world now." Viola smiles at Edie, as if she's the last and most important thing in the universe. "Charlie, please. All will happen as it should. Finish this."

She spreads her arms wide and topples back into the water, hands dragging her beneath the surface. The last part of her to disappear is her palm full of knucklebones.

She's finished.

It's over.

"Ch-Charlie." Dad stammers my name. Meryem holds a sharp silver stylus to his throat.

41

†HE LAS† S†AND

D ad inhales in shock as a bead of blood breaks the skin and rolls down his neck. He doesn't have his obsidian mirror, so he can't see who has him. Confusion clouds his eyes. If he struggles, he'll die.

I raise my hands, trying to think of a way to buy time. Where's Sam? There, over by the restaurant wall with Mitch.

"Let my dad go," I tell Meryem.

"Not until we come to an agreement." She's got a look on her face, one I've seen on my head teacher plenty of times, it's the look that says, "You won't like this, but I'm an adult and I'm doing this for your own good".

"The third seal was never designed to be used like this, let alone to contain so many corrupted souls in one body. They will take you over and you will consume the people you love, but that doesn't have to happen. Come with us. We have

400

apertures in Istanbul, Chicago and Tokyo that can contain you. We'll make sure you never hurt anyone."

The wraiths coil around my heart, slipping heat and vengeance into my pulse. Yeah, I'm in control now, but for how long? I can feel that every day is going to be a battle. It would be easier to let The Hand lock me up.

I've kept my friends and family safe, I've made it this far. But now, what if I'm the thing they need saving from?

Meryem digs the stylus deeper into Dad's throat. "I really must insist. I would hate to have to hurt your father."

I can't go with her. She thinks I'm an abomination, a dangerous, disgusting corruption of magic that should be destroyed. Even if she keeps me alive, I'll never be free again.

Tempest hisses my name. "Do you have any idea how strong you are? Use that, make *them* work for you." There's something in his eyes he wants me to understand. I think I get it, but … how?

I just fought to find myself again, I don't want to lose that.

Loathing and love are terrible things. They seem like opposites, but they shape you the same way.

I fix back on Dad's fearful gaze. He's tense, but focused. Meryem's smaller than him, but she's faster and he can't fight her. One wrong move and she'll stab his carotid and he'll bleed out before anyone can save him.

Not tonight.

If Meryem's so afraid of me then I'll give her a reason to fear. I'm pissed as hell, and scared, but those emotions are my strength. Fuel.

Ravenous cravings chew at me. It's hard to turn away, but I do, scraping back control as I shape something I need: a sword. Dark smoky threads mass around my fingers, growing. They look more like Ariadne's ribbons and nothing like the weapon I'm trying to make.

I can work with that.

Ozone, and the electric tingle of lightning in the air. I open my fists and *push*. Street lamps along the river flicker and spark, bulbs bursting. Lights in buildings shut down in a wave that rolls out from where I stand and York is plunged into darkness.

I flick smoky tendrils like a whip and *pull* with my other hand. They slide around Meryem's stylus, smacking it from her grip as Dad flies towards me, pulled by an invisible force. Even in the dark I can see the burning glow of his soul and catch him easily. He's not even heavy.

Yeah, I'm strong, proper super-human strong. The rush is intense, like being on a roller coaster or winning at, well, *everything*.

Breathe.

It takes a lot more effort to bring the lights back on. I'm sweaty and shaky and close to tears, but Dad's safe. And surprised. He holds on to my shoulder, looking a little in awe.

Tempest stands between us and Meryem. "Charlie won't be going anywhere with you."

She scowls. "You mean us."

"No, I mean *you*. Sam will remain here with his family and friends and my place is with my mirror. My loyalty is to him."

Fine, maybe I'm warming to the guy, just a little.

"Hey, Meryem!" calls Cassie, raising something in her hands.

Meryem looks, and keeps looking. Her arms go slack by her side, face sliding into an impassive expression. Cassie has Mitch's obsidian mirror and the mirror my dad brought with him, held side by side at an angle, a new theorem glowing in them. She *made* a ruh tasi – it's a bit cobbled together, but it's working.

A hitch in her throat, Cassie speaks a final word. Meryem doesn't even look scared, she can't express anything, her mind is caught on the sight of her own reflection. Nothingness is her reward now. Gaze unfocused, jaw slack, she sways.

I blink and she is gone, disappearing inside the obsidian. Pressing the front of the two mirrors together, Cassie ties her hair bow around them. Then stands, hands shaking, the ruh tasi pressed to her chest.

A soul seal can never be broken.

"Laura and me are going back to Ohio. I want to see my family." Sniffing, she puts an arm around her friend. "I'm stuck with Meryem for as long as I live, but I don't think she'll be too much bother. We'll keep her on the mantelpiece."

I laugh, a watery hiccup of sound that's as much relief as anything. I wanted to play the hero, but in the end Cassie put things right in her own matter-of-fact way. A weight lifts, and the world feels bigger and brighter and better for a moment.

Climbing the steps to the higher part of the riverbank, Dad at my side, I face the small cluster of what remains of

Meryem's people. Manbun and the boxer are the only two I recognize.

"We'll be investigating what Meryem did," promises Manbun. "Anyone who knew about the accidents, or helped her, will be held to account, no matter how senior."

"Good. Now get out of York," I say. "Tell your people in Istanbul and Tokyo whatever you like about me, but this city and its souls, *all* of them, are protected."

"Understood." The boxer offers his hand.

I shake it, and once again his ghostly form feels solid and real.

With a last nod at the bloodied and bruised dregs of a once proud organization, I turn my back on them and hurry to Leonie.

Mitch is there, pulling his girlfriend's body into his lap. Her ghost? Where did she go? She stayed, right? Leonie wouldn't leave us, but I can't see her anywhere.

I didn't get to say goodbye, she can't just be *gone*.

Carefully wiping blood from her chin, Mitch kisses her gently, pressing his forehead to hers. His eyes are red, but he's not crying. "Babe, you need to get up."

Leonie's eyelids flutter. Her body jerks as she coughs once, twice. *What's happening?* A soft soul glow shines under her skin and her eyes open.

She's … alive! Holy shit, she's alive.

42

THE STARS HAVE NOTHING ON US

"There you are." Smiling down at Leonie, Mitch pulls her into a hug. Her arms slide around his neck and they rock softly, as if the world starts and ends with them. That's the kind of love that beats evil in the movies. It marches against armies, connects people over eons, shattering time and defeating death until it stands at the end of the universe, defiant and blazing.

I don't think I'd believe it if I hadn't just seen it happen.

"Did the seal work?" Leonie croaks.

She was dead, no soul glow. Not that I can see anyone's soul glowing any more. Maybe it's just something that happens when the wraiths are in control.

Mitch takes my hand and pulls me down with them, putting an arm around me as if he needs someone else to keep him steady.

"Yeah, it worked, the wraiths are gone. Well, not gone." I give her a small smile and lean into them both, feeling my eyes burn. Why can't I stop crying? I should laugh, because against all odds, Leonie's all right.

"She's going to need you," Mitch whispers in my ear.

Yeah, of course. I'll always be here for her, for them both.

"Do you think you can stand?" I ask her.

She nods, and a tear drips down her cheek. We both help her up. The ground is slippery and I'm unsteady too, but Mitch puts out a hand and we make it to standing.

"You all right?" I ask him. "You hit that wall pretty hard."

Slowly, he touches the back of his head, as if he's just remembering that he's injured. There's blood matted into his hair.

"Does it hurt?"

Mitch blinks, once, twice, then fixes on me. "Not any more."

Something's off.

Sam calls my name, voice heavy with sorrow. I turn to tell him it's OK, Leonie's alive, she's—

Ice crashes my veins, a wash of panic and disbelief and a voice screaming through my skull that I'm not seeing the scene laid out in front of me. Sam kneeling beside the restaurant wall, diners leaning over the railing above, hands to mouths, whispering in shock as they look down at the body propped against the brick.

Eyes blank and staring, neck at an awkward angle, blood in his blonde hair.

There's always a price.

Following my gaze, Leonie takes off her cryptolenses with shaking hands, looks back at the Mitch in front of us and implodes.

"No, no, babe, no." She hammers her clenched fists against his chest until he pulls her close. "Why did you do it? *Why*?"

"It's all right, it's all right." He strokes her hair, kisses her forehead, her cheek, her lips.

He looks so solid and calm. His hair is a perfect swoop over his forehead, his eyes are bright. I think of Heather when she told me how she made me into a seer – *the most deliberate choice I've ever made* – and I understand why Mitch said that Leonie will need me. Her world looks different now.

His smile is sad. "I can't stay."

"What? No, y-you have to," Leonie gasps.

Pulling down the neckline of his T-shirt, he shows us the first seal burning white against his chest. "Stolen time."

His phantasmic essence is already flaking apart, green-grey fragments of him drifting away. The seal cuts him off from his soul, forcing him onwards. He *can't* stay. His face blurs and I don't know if it's because he's disappearing or because I'm crying.

"Oi, Olympics." A wink and that clever smile on his lips. "See you after."

I see flashes of our lives together, a gangly blonde kid in a blow-up swimming pool; eating peanut brittle in the sunshine with Leonie; beating me in Mario Kart with a laugh on his lips; our first and last kiss on a bunk bed in a French hostel;

sweat on his forehead and spade in hand as he helps me dig manure into Broomwood's rose beds; wrinkling his nose over a pot of pungent paint; dressing up for Eurovision, painting his nails, passing the popcorn to Sam, kissing Leonie, his face full of joy.

"Until the last remnants of the last black holes," Leonie whispers, her fingers tangled in his.

He smiles at her. "The stars have nothing on us."

And then he's gone.

43

CROSSING THE LINE

The rain lets up long enough for us to bury him. A swathe of black umbrellas cluster around the grave in a sleepy corner of York Cemetery as the pallbearers lower the coffin into the ground. The vicar drones on, empty words about a lad he didn't even know. My new suit itches. It fits perfectly, proper smart, but I hate it.

I'm wearing dark glasses, even though it's gloomy out. I know I look like a prick but it's that or pretend I'm really into coloured contacts. My eyes are now a permanent, unnatural silver. It doesn't look human, and it unsettles most folk, dead and alive.

It unsettles me.

The two detectives who came to my house watch from the back of the crowd. The investigation into the mysterious deaths is ongoing. Me and Sam are still "subjects of interest" but the lawyer Sam hired says they can't prove anything.

My stomach growls loud enough for Sam to take my hand and squeeze. I squeeze back. *I'm all right.* I ate a huge breakfast at home, then a second breakfast with him and snacked on the way over.

The next rumble sends an ache rolling through my rib cage. Claws needle the inside of my skull and coil under my skin, their ugliness festering. The wraiths aren't individuals any more but a mass, like there's a river inside me that's blended them together and into me too, seeping into my soul. I bite my tongue until I taste blood.

Hold on.

Being around a lot of people is hard, especially when emotions are running high.

The wind blusters the big yews and oaks, sending leaves tumbling over the assembled crowd. My folks are here with my sisters, sorrowful and subdued. I came home, but I've changed again in new and dangerous ways. Mum avoids looking at me, like she's afraid she'll see something else in place of her son. Dad's over-attentive, asking questions and always checking in. He wants to know everything, as if this is a condition we can beat together. My sisters are scared of me. They pretend that they're not, but they don't come in my room any more.

That hurts.

Despite all that, my family still came today. They liked Mitch. Everyone did, he was that kind of lad. Half our school have come to the funeral, so have his new mates from college, teachers, chefs from the restaurant where he was doing his placement, ghosts, ghosts and more ghosts, an ocean of the dead packing the church. I didn't think many people would come down the cemetery to say a final goodbye, but almost everyone did.

Opposite me, a sour-faced woman stands next to a portly man with a mean jaw, his muscle run to fat in middle age. Mitch's mum is a shell; demure, mouth downturned, stare vacant like she's dreaming of a different life. His dad looks like he wishes he was down the pub, bored rather than sad. Dickhead.

I painted my nails Mitch's favourite colour just to piss him off.

Mitch's older brother, Luke, supports Leonie and her family, looking enough like Mitch to hurt. The brothers hadn't seen much of each other this past year, not since Luke moved in with a mate from work. He showed up at Leonie's a week after Mitch's death to ask for help planning the funeral, slipping into her family like he's always belonged there. He and Leonie talk most days now. It's helping them both.

Mitch would've liked that.

I'm sorry he didn't get a chance to reconnect himself, but I'm sorry for a lot of things these days.

We'll never play videogames until four a.m. again, or bake together, cook up stinking ward paint, or walk Dante in the rain. He won't see Europe after college with Leonie like they'd planned. He won't go to Pride next summer.

He's really *gone*.

The wraiths living in my bones hiss with grief. I feel

411

everything: a suffocating rush of agony, confusion and denial. The air tastes sweet and cloying, like something is putrefying under the earth. Decay fills my mouth and instead of disgust, hunger surges again, my cravings bleeding forward as my nerves shudder to contain them.

You will consume the people you love most.

Souls surround me. The guttering light of fragile life glows beside the deep steady burn of the dead. Their vitality smells like peace. Hunger gnaws even deeper than my belly or even my bones.

I count down from ten, breathing slowly.

Stay in control.

I am Charlie. I am Charlie.

The reality that I'm some kind of living monster that hungers for souls is impossible to settle beside the faces of my family and friends. What scares me is that sooner or later, I'll have to give in and I don't know what to do about it. I need to say something to Sam, but I'm scared. This … thing I've become, a monster, a weapon, an abomination, is so like what Caleb Gates tried to make himself that I can't ask Sam to accept me as I am.

Maybe I should just leave.

At the end of the grave Neelam stands with Heather, wearing Leonie's cryptolenses. They're all moved into their new place in Manchester. I'm not sure how it's going to work for them – they can't even touch – but they're giving themselves the space to try.

Mitch's coffin looks really far down. I wish I hadn't wasted two years of our friendship ignoring him when he deserved better. I wish I'd been the friend he needed, that we'd had more time.

His brother releases a fistful of earth on the lid. Leonie starts to cry and the cracked pieces of me shatter. Darkness escapes my skin, twisting around my fingers.

No.

Dropping Sam's hand, I push backwards through the crowd. Villiers and Reid reach for me, worried. But many among the dead scurry out of my way, as if they can sense the predators inside me. Sam says they'll get over it, just give them time, but they *should* keep their distance. Everyone should.

Low branches catch on my puffer and slick brown leaves make underfoot treacherous. Careful not to slip, I move as quickly as I can in my prostheses, cutting beneath the trees. Drizzle dusts my face. I smell heavy rain in the distance and think of Mitch again. He loved a storm.

I stagger on to the tarmac in front of the ruined chapel where a few cars are parked up, but there's no one here. Gulping lungs of cold air, I fight to quiet the rhythm in my head but all I can see is the hollow earth swallowing Mitch's remains.

It's not fair. He should have stayed. He should have lived.

But then we would have lost Leonie.

It's too much and it *hurts*.

Licks of phantasmic essence curl from my back and arms, ruffling my hair as they grow – desperate to consume and wrench and devour. Undefined, they're not anything personal like Tempest's torch, or Villier's rapier, they're just raw power.

The seal on my chest burns. A scream of rage roars from the pit of my belly – half-sob, half-bellow. Metal crunches and glass shatters. Smoky tendrils tear at the blue hoarding around the chapel, punching through the chipboard, ripping holes. The cars parked opposite the chapel are a crumpled wreck.

Someone's here.

I whip round.

Sam, his soul a soft, pale glow threaded with green. It's bad that I can see it, that means the wraiths are more in control than me. Maybe I should've let Meryem lock me up. He steps forward and I flinch away, putting a hand up in warning.

"You won't hurt me." There's so much trust in his voice I can't stand it. He's *wrong*, and he'll regret it. The cool control I found when facing down Meryem has evaporated.

I think about Viola, who'd do anything for the lass she loved, including becoming someone unlovable. I'm something Sam can't love – no, *shouldn't* love.

He needs to leave me. If he won't, I'm gonna have to go away to live in a bothy in the Highlands and get food air-dropped in. No family or friends, just me and the lonely landscape.

Fuck, that sounds boring.

I could travel then, get a van and just live on the road doing odd jobs. I'll go town to town hunting down the shades that escaped The Old Place. Mr Agyemang and his occultist friends bottled a fair few, but most are still out there. We need to deal with them and they hurt people, so maybe feeding them to the wraiths to keep me stable won't feel like murder. My chest cramps, nausea rising.

God.

Sam will live a long life with Tempest and Leonie and our friends. He'll move on, find a lad more like him.

But I want him so much. He makes all of this bearable.

Fingers under my chin, on my neck, holding my face. My shadow manifestations lick over Sam's skin, coiling in his hair and down his arms, but they don't hurt him.

Last week Sam manifested his own phantasmic object. Not a torch like Tempest, but a paintbrush. It doesn't look like much, but the boy can *paint pure magic*.

What defines me?

Wish I knew.

"There will be a lot of bad days," he says simply. "But there will be good times too. You taught me that."

I shake my head. "It's too dangerous. Meryem was right—"

"Oh, shut up, Charlie Frith," Sam snaps. "If you're going to get started on all the 'I'm not worthy of you' bullshit, then firstly, I know I'm amazing and that you're obsessed with me. Who wouldn't be, look at these dimples. Adorable. Secondly, you can't tell me what to do. I get to choose who to love. And I choose *you*, wraiths and all."

"But I'm just like Gates," I snap. "I wanted this—"

"So? He wanted power for himself. You wanted to mirror to protect everyone else, and you risked your autonomy and freedom to trap the wraiths and keep everyone safe. The power it comes with is a side effect you'll have to manage, and you *will*. You're nothing like him."

I start crying, proper gut-wrenching sobs that make me think of how Mitch cried for Leonie when she was in the hospital. Remembering him again is like a fresh knife wound to my ribs and makes me cry even harder.

Sam wraps his arms around me. At some point, I realize the smoky manifestations have stopped and I can't see his soul any more.

"Here." Sam fishes a chunky bar of fruit and nut chocolate from his pocket. "This might help take the edge off."

"Did … you bring this just in case?" Swiping my cheeks with the back of my hand, I look at the chocolate, then at him. "I really love you."

"Good." Even dressed all in black, he's radiant. He's the fucking sun. "Because I'd hate for this relationship to be one-sided unrequited pining and I rather like kissing you."

He proves it. His lips are soft, hands firm on the lapels of my suit jacket, and I am unravelling.

"Charlie?" Leonie hurries up the path, Ollie, Heather, Neelam, Villiers and Reid behind her. She spots the cars and swears. All three vehicles are smashed, windscreens cracked, bonnets and fenders bent and warped out of shape.

Yeah...

Excessive property damage is definitely more of a supervillain thing. Actually, no, scrap that. I've seen all the Marvel movies, they trash everything.

Leonie crashes into us, hugging me hard and catching Sam

up in it too. My cheeks heat with shame. She needs us, and here I was thinking of breaking my promise to Mitch so soon, like I could ever outrun what I am.

I'll do better to stand my ground and know I won't be standing alone. We're an odd trio, the seers of York, carved by grief and violence, but we're here, as we are, because of an act of selfless love.

Our ghosts are all around us. Leonie pulls Neelam into our huddle like she's one of us. I guess, now that she knows our secrets, she is.

Tempest slips from the trees, never far away and nods at me. I nod back, an understanding there. He'll do anything to protect Sam, including putting me and my wraiths down if he needs to. One day, if I can't keep control, he'll be there. I open up the circle for him, clapping him on the shoulder to let him know that I don't hate him half as much as he thinks I do.

"What now?" asks Leonie. "I don't want to go home yet."

"I um…" Sam glances at me. "I was going to tell Charlie first at the restaurant but then we didn't go and, well, I think it's about time you all know." He takes a shaky breath. "I bought us a house."

"You and your mum found a place?" I ask, enjoying the warm, happy pulse in my chest. That's what he wanted to tell me all along.

Sam blushes, as if suddenly doubting himself. "No, *us*. Team Spectre. If we're going to take care of York, we need somewhere ghosts looking for help can come and where souls we've freed from deathloops can acclimatize before they decide what to do with their afterlives. It needs a bit of renovation, but there's plenty of space for a mathemagics lab, a library, and a kitchen that Mitch would *love*. It's a home, for us all."

"I've got his favourite brownie recipe," says Leonie. "Can we…"

"When the kitchen's finished, that's the first thing we'll bake," promises Sam.

"With the calories this one needs now you'd better make at least five batches," says Ollie, jerking his thumb at me.

I lean into Sam, lowering my voice. "I think sometime, maybe soon, I'll have to … um, *eat*, to survive."

He nods, understanding that brownies won't cut it for long. "I've a theory about that, but … we'll sort it. You and me."

I feel a hook in my heart and know, no matter what the future throws at us, it will always lead me back to him.

"Masters," Villiers hisses a warning.

We all look to where he's pointing. Sister Agnes floats nearby, watching. I realize with a jolt that we're over the ghost line, way too close for comfort, but after months of threats she's not attacking. There's something in her face I've not seen before – fear.

Maybe she senses what I am now, or saw what I can do, but one thing's for sure she can't hurt us any more and she knows it. Hungry Ones like her won't ever bother us again.

"Ah, bollocks. I forgot to bring those magazines," I say. Not that she cares, but I said I would so I'll come back with Leonie's copies of *Fault* magazine and *New Scientist*, maybe comics if Ollie will part with some of his for an afternoon.

We start walking towards the cemetery gates, Villiers and Reid chatting to Heather and Neelam. Tempest follows with Leonie as Ollie whistles for Dante who's racing through the gravestones. He runs a little lopsided after the battle for York. Like the other ghosts his wounds are slow to heal, but they saved so many lives that night.

A message flashes on my phone. It's Cassie. Two weeks ago I received a postcard from Ohio with a mobile number on it. When I messaged it, I got a photo of a cornfield, an ugly oversized stone mantelpiece with Meryem's makeshift ruh tasi propped up on it, and a grinning picture of Cassie with her family. She's told them I'm a friend she made at the international boarding school she was supposedly attending.

Today, she just sends three words, a response to a question I asked her yesterday.

> I know how.

When she's ready, Cassie will help Leonie mirror with a ghost, repairing her soul and letting her use magic again. I'm not ready to share that news now. Leonie's been a seer all of three weeks, we all need time to settle.

Everything's still so uncertain. I don't know how I'm going to handle the wraiths long term, or how to deal with the strange new abilities they've given me. I glance back at the wrecked cars and splintered wood. At the moment, all I do is destroy stuff.

But maybe it won't always be like that.

I was so worried about not being enough for everyone – Sam, the ghosts, my mates, my family – and yeah, I still have no idea how to earn a living one day or if I'm even going to pass a single exam.

What defines me?

Hell if I know.

And for the first time that feels good. I don't need to have it all figured out right now. I know what I don't want to be and that's enough.

I'm enough and I always have been.

Possibilities swirl in the rain damp air and for a moment I let myself sink into the future Sam has planned. A proper home for us and our ghosts, a chance to make a real difference and keep the promise I made to the souls of York all those months ago. We can build something here.

"We've got a lot of work to do," I say.

"Yeah." Sam holds out his hand. I take it. "We do."

We're only at the start.

ACKNOWLEDGEMENTS

It turns out that the only challenge more intense and nerve-wracking than writing a first book is writing a second book, especially when it's a sequel! I couldn't have done it without an incredible and supportive team of professionals, friends and family around me.

Firstly, to my wonderful agent Maddy Belton. Thank you for saving me when I was drowning, for the WhatsApp chats, kind words of encouragement and keeping me on track when I need it most.

To my amazing editors: Yasmin Morrisey, for pushing me to do what needed to be done (if this book made you cry, blame Yas!), Leonie Lock, whose insight and care never ceases to amaze me (especially under very tight deadlines), Jenny Glencross, for her fresh perspective, Sarah Dutton, for keeping us all to schedule, and Polly Lyall Grant for taking on all of my chaos.

Lauren Fortune, thank you for believing so wholeheartedly in Charlie's world.

To everyone at Scholastic, I am so thankful to be part of your family. A special thank you to Hannah Griffiths, Ellen Thomson and my incredible powerhouse publicist, Harriet Dunlea. I am so lucky to have you on my team! Thank you for all that you do. Thank you also to the Sales, Production and Rights teams!

My heartfelt thank you to Andrew Davis for agreeing to create stunning artwork of Charlie and Sam for the cover. A huge thank you to the wonderful Alice Duggan for your incredible design skills. A shout out needs to go to El (@ermreading) for knowing that *Twelve Bones* needed to be burgundy!

A massive thank you needs to go to my superb sensitivity readers Reuben Thomas, Amber Sidbury and Brianna Boehm. Any mistakes and oversights are entirely my own.

To all my fellow Waterstones Booksellers, especially those who have been hand selling and recommending my work, I see you and I appreciate you! To Florentyna, Hazel, Nick and Lucy and everyone at Waterstones head office. Your support and enthusiasm for *Sixteen Souls* and *Twelve Bones* has been incredible! I am so proud to be part of the Waterstones family and incredibly grateful for everything.

Lydia, aren't you relieved you didn't have to read *Twelve Bones* as many times as you did *Sixteen Souls*? Thank you for taking the time to give me much needed support and feedback. I appreciate you!

Palomi, I know this year has been hard. I am proud of you and so grateful to have you in my life. Every story I write is for you and because of you. Thank you for being a wonderful friend.

Charley, I think you love Charlie and Sam the most! Thank you for everything you do at Paper Orange to champion UKYA.

Kat Delacorte, please never forget how incredible you are! I feel so lucky and very privileged to be able to call you my friend.

To my brilliant nephew Noah, thanks for always asking me how my writing is going. Isla, book dragon in training, no you can't read this story yet because it's quite scary, but I love that you'll want to anyway.

Mum, Dad, Helly and Em, Richard and Fiona, thanks for being the best!

My darling Ed, you are the kindest, most patient person and this book simply wouldn't exist without your support. Neither would my mental health, so thank you for believing in me, for the tea and apple turnovers and late-night plot dissections. I'm so glad you told me that weird goat's cheese story that one time.

Finally, and most especially, to everyone who bought, borrowed, read, reviewed, tweeted, TikToked or IG reeled about *Sixteen Souls*, who pre-ordered *Twelve Bones*, took part in the cover reveal, and who supported me on this strange and amazing adventure of being an author – THANK YOU!

About the Author

A lover of dark and tightly woven stories, Rosie is
inspired by creepy things in junk shops, haunted
houses and strange magic. She is a graduate of
Curtis Brown Creative and Write Mentor. By day
she works as a bookseller. By night, she spends time
sewing big skirts with outrageously large pockets
and wondering why her family has a suspiciously
large collection of cauldrons. She currently resides
in a mysterious pocket of the Sussex countryside
with her very patient spouse and two cats called
Tinkerfluff and Captain Haddock. *Twelve Bones* is
her second book, the follow-on to *Sixteen Souls*.

You can connect with Rosie via TikTok
and Instagram (**@merrowchild**) or on her
website **www.rosietalbot.co.uk** where you
can sign up to her scintillating newsletter and
gain access to free stories and artwork.